ASIAN IMPERIAL BANKING HISTORY

Banking, Money and International Finance

ASIAN IMPERIAL BANKING HISTORY

EDITED BY

Hubert Bonin, Nuno Valério and Kazuhiko Yago

LONDON AND NEW YORK

First published 2015 by Pickering & Chatto (Publishers) Limited

2 Park Square, Milton Park, Abingdon, Oxfordshire OX14 4RN
52 Vanderbilt Avenue, New York, NY 10017

Routledge is an imprint of the Taylor & Francis Group, an informa business

First issued in paperback 2020

BRITISH LIBRARY CATALOGUING IN PUBLICATION DATA

Asian imperial banking history. – (Banking, money and international finance)
1. Banks and banking – Europe – Colonies – Asia – History. 2. Banks and banking, Colonial – History.
I. Series II. Bonin, Hubert, editor. III. Valerio, Nuno, editor. IV. Yago, Kazuhiko,
editor.
332.1'095'0917124-dc23

ISBN-13: 978-1-84893-551-8 (hbk)
ISBN-13: 978-0-367-66908-9 (pbk)

Typeset by Pickering & Chatto (Publishers) Limited

CONTENTS

ACKNOWLEDGEMENTS

The publication of this book has been possible:

First, because of the admission of our session, *Imperial Banking History,* at the Congress of the World Economic History Association, held at Stellenbosch in South Africa, in July 2013;

Second, because the *Région Aquitaine* in Bordeaux, France, financed Hubert Bonin's research program about *Investment and Banking History* (2010–13), through the GRETHA research centre at Bordeaux University;

Third, because the School of Economics & Management, University of Lisbon, and the Department of Business Administration, Tokyo Metropolitan University, and the School of Commerce, Waseda University, helped Nuno Valério and Kazuhiko Yago to complete their involvement in the 2013 Congress and the co-edition of the proceedings;

Fourth, because the *Crédit agricole*-CASA historical archives played a key role in the opening of the *Banque de l'Indochine'* archives in Paris;

Fifth, because *Sciences Po Bordeaux* contributed to the technical means necessary to complete the process of pre-editing the typescripts.

LIST OF CONTRIBUTORS

Hubert Bonin is Professor of Modern Economic History at *Sciences Po Bordeaux* and is a member of the GRETHA research centre at Bordeaux University. He specializes in banking and financial history, with particular focus on French banking history, from regional banks to corporate and investment banks, and has published a range of monographs and handbooks on the subject. His research interests also involve the history of businesses, commercial organizations and service companies, such as the Suez Canal Company and colonial and overseas trading houses and their maritime affiliates. He is currently working on a multi-volume history of French *Société générale* (from 1864 to the 1940s), as well as research on both the French global economy of investment banks and the action of French banks in Eastern Asia and in Greece. As a specialist in business history, he has co-guided the research programs *Ford in Europe, 1903–2003* (2003), *American Firms in Europe* (2008), *Old Paternalism, New Paternalism, Post-Paternalism* (2013) and *Investment Banking History* (2014). He is now taking part in research programs on banking and business history from French, European, or Asian perspectives, with focus on investment banking, merchant and trade banking, economic patriotism, entrepreneurship and European business.

Niv Horesh is a Professor (Chair) in the Modern History of China, and Director of the China Policy Institute at the University of Nottingham. He has worked in the past as a Business Development Manager in China, and as a civil servant in Israel and Australia. He is the author of *Chinese Money in Global Context: Historic Junctures Between 600 BCE and 2012* (Stanford, CA: Stanford University Press, 2013).

Ashok Kapoor received his postgraduate degree in Modern Indian History from Delhi University in 1972. For the past 38 years he has worked in a range of archives in India, including the National Archives of India, New Delhi and Reserve Bank of India Archives. In 1988 he received a UNESCO fellowship to study the use of computers in Archives. He is a member of the Indian Historical Records Commission; the National Digital Preservation Committee formed by the Government of India; and the International Council on Archives and

Steering Committee of the Section on Business and Labour Archives. He has contributed articles on Archives and Records Management in various national and international journals, participated in various seminars and conferences and provided technical expertise to Banks, financial institutions and government organizations about the establishment of archives.

Sofya Salomatina is an Associate Professor of History at Moscow Lomonosov State University, Coordinator of the Center for Economic History; a specialist in the history of Russian finance and banking; and a Lecturer on the history of world finance, money and banking. She is also a member of the project "Dynamics of Economic and Social Development of Russia from the 19th–early 20th century", dealing with collection of historical data on Russian Empire. She is the author of a section of this project, entitled "Financial Institutions", which includes summary balances of commercial credit institutions of the Russian Empire in 1861–1917. She has published monographs and articles on the history of commercial banks in the Russian Empire (1864–1917) in various aspects: models of banking, investment banking, banking and stock market development, clients' and foreign correspondents' networks, biographical studies on famous bankers. Her principal publications include: 'Investment banking in Russia, 1890–1917: From Pioneering Finance to Universal Banking', in H. Bonin and C. Brambilla (eds), *Investment Banking History: National and Comparative Issues (19th-21st centuries)* (Brussells, Belgium: Peter Lang, 2014), pp. 347–80; 'Modeli kommercheskikh bankov v Sankt-Peterburge i Moskve, 1864–1917 gg.', in B. V. Anan'ich (ed.), *Kredit i banki v Rossii do nachala XX veka: Sankt-Peterburg i Moskva* (St. Petersburg: Izd-vo SPbGU, 2005), pp. 328–43; *Kommercheskie banki v Rossii: dinamika i struktura operacij, 1864–1917 gg.* (Moskva: Rossiiskaia politicheskaia entsiklopediia (ROSSPEN), 2001.); and 'E. M. Jepshtejn i ego kniga o rossijskih dorevoljucionnyh bankah', in E. M. Jepshtejn, *Rossijskie kommercheskie banki (1864–1914 gg.): Rol' v jekonomicheskom razvitii Rossii i ih nacionalizacija* (Moskva: Rossiiskaia politicheskaia entsiklopediia (ROSSPEN), 2011), pp. 11–33.

Tomoko Shiroyama is a Professor in the Graduate School of Economics at The University of Tokyo. She received her PhD in history from Harvard University in 1999. Her major publications include: 'The Hong Kong–South China Financial Nexus: Ma Xuchao and His Remittance Agency' in S. Cochran (ed.), *The Capitalist Dilemma in China's Communist Revolution: Stay, Leave, or Return?* (Ithaca, NY: Cornell University Press, forthcoming); 'Institutions Governing Long-Distance Trade in Asia During the 18th and 19th Centuries: Example from the Gongguan Archives of Batavia', *Modern Asian Studies Review*, 4 (2013), pp. 15–29; 'The Shanghai Real Estate Market and Capital Investment, 1860–1936' in B. K. L. So and R. H. Myers (eds), *The Treaty Port Economy in Modern China:*

Empirical Studies of Institutional Change and Economic Performance (Berkeley, CA: Institute of East Asian Studies, 2011), pp. 47–74; and *China during the Great Depression: Market, State, and the World Economy, 1929–1937* (Cambridge, MA: Harvard University Asia Center, 2008).

Man-han Siu has been Research Fellow, and Lecturer, in Economic History at Osaka University of Economics, Japan since 2006. She is a historian of modern China and her work examines both the business activities of British international banks in Asia, and China's financial and banking development within an international context. Her main publications include: 'Honkon Syanhai ginkō Rondonten 1875–1889 nen: David McLean Papers no Kentō wo tsujite 香港上海銀行ロンドン店 1875–1889年: David McLean Papers の検討を通じて' [London Office of the Hongkong and Shanghai Banking Corporation, 1875–1889: Through an Examination of David McLean Papers] and 'Honkon Syanhai ginnkō Hanburuku shiten 1890–1913 nen 香港上海銀行ハンブルク支店 1890–1913年' [The Hamburg Branch of the Hongkong and Shanghai Banking Corporation, 1890–1913] in Nishimura Shizuya 西村閑也, Suzuki Toshio 鈴木俊夫 and Akagawa Motoaki 赤川元章 (eds), *Kokusai ginnkō to Ajia 1870–1913* 国際銀行とアジア 1870–1913 [International Banking in Asia, 1870–1913] (Tokyo: Keio University Press, 2014), pp. 617–47 and pp. 649–84; and 'Chūgoku 中国' [China] in Kokusai ginnkōshi kenkyūkai 国際銀行史研究会 [Research Group of International Banking History] (ed.), *Kinyū no seikaishi* 金融の世界史 [World History of Finance] (Tokyo: Yushokan, 2012), pp. 297–332.

Nuno Valério holds a PhD in Economics from the Technical University of Lisbon (1982) and has been Full Professor at the School of Economics and Management, *Universidade de Lisboa* since 1989. He specializes in economic, financial, and banking history, both on a Portuguese level and on a comparative European and Mediterranean scale. His publication history includes his key roles as: co-editor of both *Foreign Financial Institutions and National Financial Systems* (Warsaw: European Association for Banking and Financial History, 2013) and *Growth and Stagnation in the Mediterranean World in the 19th and 20th Centuries* (Leuven: Leuven University Press, 1990); co-author of *The Concise Economic History of Portugal – A Comprehensive Guide* (Lisboa: Almedina, 2011); co-ordinator of both *History of the Portuguese Banking System*, 2 vols (Lisboa: Banco de Portugal, 2006–10) and *Portuguese Historical Statistics*, 2 vols (Lisboa: Instituto Nacional de Estatística, 2001); and author of *The Escudo – The Portuguese Currency Unit, 1911–2001* (Lisboa: Banco de Portugal, 2001).

Kazuhiko Yago is Professor in Economic History at the School of Commerce, Waseda University in Japan. Starting his research in French banking history, he published a monograph, in Japanese, on the French savings and financial institution *Caisse des dépôts et consignations* and *Caisses d'épargne*, titled *Public Financing and Public Savings in France: Caisse des dépôts et consignations and Savings Banks (1816–1944)* (Tokyo: University of Tokyo Press, 1999). Extending his studies on the Franco-Russian financial relations, he has published a series of articles on the Russo-Chinese Bank, one of which has been included in Shizuya Nishimura, Toshio Suzuki and Ranald Michie (eds), *The Origins of International Banking in Asia: The Nineteenth and Twentieth Centuries* (Oxford: Oxford University Press, 2012). A specialist on the history of international financial institutions, he has recently published *Financial History of the Bank for International Settlements* (New York: Routledge, 2012), and is organizing study projects on the history of the IMF and the OECD.

LIST OF FIGURES

INTRODUCTION: ISSUES REGARDING ASIAN IMPERIAL BANKING

Hubert Bonin

This book is the result of a workshop conducted as part of the World Economic History Association (WEHA) Congress held at the University of Stellenbosch, South Africa, in August 2012. Chaired jointly by Professor Hubert Bonin, Sciences Po Bordeaux and GRETHA-Bordeaux University, France; Professor Nuno Valério, *Universidade Técnica de Lisboa*, Portugal; and Professor Kazuhiko Yago, Waseda University, the theme of the workshop was: *Imperial Banking: Imperial Strategies of Exporting Finance Modernisation (19th–20th Centuries)*. The multi-disciplinary programme gathered colleagues specializing in imperial and banking histories. This volume not only contains most of the papers presented at the workshop but also includes other (mostly Asian) contributions, adding to its variety and richness. All in all, the book will add a few stones to the ever extending building of our knowledge about 'global history' and, in this case, global banking history. We admit, of course, that the globalization of banks might be confined to the turn of the 1970s onwards, from the City, with the Euromarket, to Wall Street, the revolution of 'Asian dollars' and 'petro-dollars', and big firms fixing bridgeheads all around 'the capitals of capital'.[1] Yet it can be argued that colonial and imperial times fostered varieties of 'proto-globalised' flows of money, bills of exchange, FOREX markets and trade finance, and, as such, can serve as leverage in the following discussions about imperial banking throughout Asia.

By the time European powers had imposed political control over most of Africa, the Pacific islands and a significant part of Asia, banking systems were already well established and formed a relevant part of the economic life of these colonizing powers.[2] Along with the somewhat raw forms of imperialism and colonialism (army, police, customs, tax collection, mining exploitation and economy of plantation), the imperial banking system was also connected with softer forms of imperialism and colonialism, what may be called 'gentlemanly capitalism'.[3] It was only natural that banks became important instruments of economic exploration in the colonized territories. This volume examines the origins and development of such 'imperial' banking systems, and, where it occurred, their continuation after decolonization. It provides significant insights into seven very different imperial banking systems, based on new research into hitherto not yet accessed primary sources in the French, English, Russian, Chinese, and Japanese languages. It draws lessons from the recent breakthroughs in the knowledge of the imperial economic systems and provides fodder for comparative ways of grappling with issues that contribute to the main theme of the WEHA Congress: *Exploring the Roots of Development*.[4] It is obvious that more research is needed on the 'men on the spot' – both Europeans and Asians – in order to better understand the complex interrelations between political and economic interests and economic penetration into Asia in the 19th and 20th centuries. Overall, there is still an absence of general works as well as case studies of the actors and their organizations in the foreign settlements in China and other parts of Asia; the imperial business history of Asia has clearly been under-worked and under-valued. This monograph thus tries to provide valuable insights into new aspects of these topics, thereby making an important contribution to the closing of a major research gap in this field. Though unique in its specific focus, it is obviously very much in accord with current broader historiographical trends in the study of imperialism, and intends to illuminate how these apply to an area, namely, business banking, which has to date attracted less attention than other more culturally-oriented topics.

Recent developments in methodology, archive retrieval and approaching problems have opened new ways of tackling the history of business banking. This book applies these methods to the specialized field of colonial and overseas territories, draws lessons from the recent breakthroughs in the knowledge of the imperial economic systems and fuels comparative ways of grappling with such issues, as well as the wider issues of 'international banking'.[5] It then draws points of differentiation between them as they both belong, in a fashion, to multinational or transnational firms.[6]

At the same time, the 'varieties' of overseas capitalism demand specific approaches depending on area and territory; the various models of overseas banking differ according to political and economic background and the status of the institutions themselves, for example, the extent to which they are based overseas or in the metropolis, or connected with the State or more independent. Each participant in the WEHA workshop thus produced their own definition and overview of what constituted 'overseas banks'. Some of the key points will be scrutinized in the following sections.

The geographical span of this enquiry covers several continents. The traditional approach deals with the bilateral links between West Europe and Africa (and the Caribbean islands) and the contribution of the banking sector to imperialism in this unequal relationship. But the complexity of 'imperial banking' in Asia has given rise to renewed arguments regarding trans-territorial finance and banking: the balance between British and Indian banking in India; the specificities of the Japanese imperial structures; the role of the 'port cities' in China between 'imperial' dependency (in the concession settlements) and the insertion into global Asian exchanges; the competition between Japanese and Russian financial influence in Manchuria, between imperial and commercial mind-sets; and the deployment of imperial banking in Latin America, amongst others.

Thus, colonial territories as well as imperial areas were involved, that is, the economies of port-cities and trading hubs within independent countries (China, followed by India and South Africa after WWII). 'Colonial' or 'imperial' overseas strategies, practices and skills clubbed all these countries, where port-cities formed key hubs for the deployment of banking institutions, together.

Institutional Business History and Overseas Banking Strategies

Extensive studies on the imperial deployment of European banks have appeared in several collective works, especially *Banks as Multinationals*.[7] The interaction between European and Asian trading hubs goes back to imperial and colonial times,[8] with banking power given as much importance as overseas politics and commerce,[9] to the extent that one talked of 'paradise lost'.[10] Major banking institutions sprang up as part of this imperial deployment, whether in the territories controlled by the Ottoman Empire[11] or within Japan's commercial hegemony.[12] Asia saw the emergence of big imperial banks from Western Europe,[13] Russia and Japan, which positioned themselves at the heart of the information, commercial paper and currency networks.[14] Though Asia had both official and 'informal'[15] empires, the 'imperial' bank was a very real entity, whatever the status of the territory it was active in.

This collection will study the institutional history of central, issuing and rediscounting banks as the cornerstone of the local banking sub-systems overseas, and will asses, with the help of monographs and archives, the founding, maturing and performance of local banking systems overseas. We will outline the strategies adopted by metropolitan private and public institutions or specific colonial bodies. We will also highlight and compare the variety of connections between 'metropolitan' or 'mainland' territories and their overseas outlets. Cases from Japan (with its formal and informal empire all across Asia) and Russia (with its port cities fuelled by continental railway lines but also opened to the Asian maritime areas) are compared to the more classical 'imperial' deployments, such as the British, French and Dutch.

Skills portfolios constitute the centrepiece of the following chapters. The differentiation and convergence between the overseas banking services and the metropolitan banking and financial sectors will be outlined. The specificities of foreign banking practices will be determined: risk management, assessment of creditworthiness, collateralizing and pledges, etc. We will identify the techniques used to preserve the durability of business as well as their corporate culture. Finally, we shall trace the building of human resources from teams of expatriates, the diaspora and local elites.

Corporate banking was the catalyst for enhancing the convergence between metropolitan business forces active abroad and the banking sector, within a 'consolidated' economic system in each imperial area. Banking in colonial 'port cities' is to be seen as an original 'variety of capitalism' – it integrated connections between the colony and the metropolis on one hand and between the colony and the rest of world on the other. The connections between the metropolitan financial market and overseas banking have been analysed regarding investment banking and underwriting. The integration of banking into the development of 'modernised' areas and overseas economic pockets and its contribution to the emergence of local forms of capitalist business and social groups will be outlined. The collapse of the several markets for metropolitan and foreign companies active overseas, along the geo-economic rebuilding of the world frames for production and exchanges, and the evolution of relations with native entrepreneurs and customers could also be a centre-piece of imperial banking: no stability at all predominated, either under the impulse of competition, or because of the changes of the local productive systems – not to speak about the disappearance or the resurgence of market economy in the countries choosing the path of centralized economy (for instance in China or in Vietnam, and somewhat in India).

Colonial Bankers and Imperial Business Communities

There must be a debate regarding these reflections and around the relations between local, international and global. We must deliberate over the imperial banks' 'embeddedness' and their insertion into the life of the business community oriented towards the colonial territories. In the majority of cases, these banks and their branches were 'parachuted' from their Metropolitan headquarters as commercial tools. But there are also those which emerged from the local community itself, especially in the settlements (such as South Africa and Algeria) and those colonies where the number of enterprises and expatriates constituted a significant factor for stimulating the banking industry (like Hong Kong). Still, in the majority of cases, these colonial and imperial banks owed their origin and support to the Mainland, the port-cities, the trading houses, the shipping companies, the banks and the groups of expert civil servants within the Ministries involved in the life of the empire. Such was the case for *Banque de l'Indochine*[16] in 1875 and *Deutsch-Asiatische Bank*.

Imperial Banking and Thalassocracy

It was the growth of capitalism in the mainland, as part of a 'mercantile' mentality, which drove the concerned communities to promote these overseas 'toolboxes' to help develop trade with the colonies. Obviously, economic patriotism played its part in consolidating banking power in support of the economic (industrial) power, not to speak of insurance companies for shipping and warehouse insurance. The fact that every country set up its own overseas bank or endowed its colonies with specific banking institutions (especially Antilles, the Maghreb, Egypt, Sub-Saharan Africa and India) clearly shows that they wanted to have the whole gamut of economic tools which would allow them to have a firm grip on the development of commodity production and prospecting outlets for capital and other goods.

Although they originated from either overseas or mainland port-cities and banking hubs, these banks followed converging paths which, irrespective of their points of origin, led them to serve the immediate interests of mainland companies that were active overseas, the wealthy community and overseas enterprises. In keeping with the overseas mentality and the requirements of each of the colonizing countries, these imperial banks embedded themselves more and more firmly in their territories. Thus, *Banque de l'Indochine* became as much the bank for expatriates and the companies present in French South-East Asia as for those mainland companies with commercial ties with this sub-region. These banking tools served to consolidate overseas and thalassocratic power along the lines set by the United Kingdom, but for the most part with a view to undermine British hegemony.

Several banks came to shake HSBC's monopoly in China, especially the *Yokohama Specie Bank*, *Banque de l'Indochine* and, at the turn of the 20th century, Citibank. Though Hong Kong and the other big Chinese port-cities are exceptional due to the sheer volume of business, competition played a big part in numerous colonies, whether it be Egypt (with banks from every nation, especially France,[17] with *Crédit lyonnais* and *Comptoir national d'escompte de Paris* or CNEP[18]), or Algeria (with at least half a dozen banks). Even India saw some competition when CNEP opened its branches there.[19]

Even at the heart of the community of national interests, implicit or explicit understandings left the field open for these colonial and imperial banks, with the best examples being the HSBC, the City's lever of influence in China, and *Banque de l'Indochine,* which did the same for France. Similarly, Barclays DCO spread all across sub-Saharan and southern Africa and the Antilles – leaving Latin America to Lloyds and its subsidiary BOLSA (Bank of London & South America, founded in the 1920s by a group of banks)[20] – with enough firepower to turn it into the City's main arm in Africa.[21] Meanwhile India and Australia[22] had several big establishments rubbing shoulders with each other such as

Chartered Bank,[23] established in 1853 and *Mercantile Bank of India.*[24] Barclays DCO was tickled by *British Bank of West Africa*, established in 1893 by ship-owners (Elder Dempster), and other establishments here and there.[25]

Meanwhile, the entities that were active in China and India, such as the *Yokohama Specie Bank*, the Chartered, HSBC and *Banque de l'Indochine*, quickly spread over the rest of Asia, as did the American Citibank. One cannot realistically speak of 'hunting preserves' or national monopolies. These were oligopolies, sometimes even from the same country but more often international, which fought against each other even though the competition was not that intense due to the competitors' lack of the required financial, human and relational resources.[26] There is no doubt that economic upswings and the growth in the production of commodities and below-ground resources stimulated this scramble for overseas territories and a loosening of hegemonies.

Diversification or Specialisation

As a result, the strategy adopted was the 'principle of specialisation'. The majority of European banks preferred not to 'internalize' their overseas activities, except in some market segments, especially in the Maghreb (*Société marseillaise de crédit, Crédit lyonnais, Société générale,* CNEP). Each of them carried out a 'strategic diagnosis', weighing the pros and the cons of the growth opportunities presented by the colonial and imperial markets. *Société générale*, especially, was tempted to set up an office in Indochina when Tonkin was colonized. But it abandoned the idea to enter *Banque de l'Indochine* along with other Parisian banks. On the other hand, *Paribas* funded for a while *Banque industrielle de Chine* which shook *Banque de l'Indochine* in the beginning of the 1920s, before collapsing and re-structuring itself into a modest commercial bank (*Banque franco-chinoise*). It was tempting to mobilize the skill and knowledge portfolios and combine the experience in order to draw up a strategy of geographic diversification and establish large 'international financial services firms'.[27] Barclays set its eyes on Africa in the beginning of the 1920s: between 1917 and 1925, its subsidiary DCO gradually grew with the aggregation of Colonial Bank (established in 1836 and active in West Indies, it retained its name till 1952, when it finally became Barclays DCO), National Bank of South Africa (established in Natal in 1888) and Anglo-Egyptian Bank (active in Egypt and Sudan).[28] 'The prospects for increased imports and exports between the overseas areas in which we are represented and Great Britain are most encouraging, and the part which the Bank will take in promoting an increase of trade should prove to be of great public service', said Barclays Chairman Frederick Goodenough at DCO's general assembly on 7 June 1926. 'In these three sentences, the philosophy underlying his 'colonial bank scheme' was concisely set out',[29] which led *The Times* to talk of 'the first Empire bank'! *Ipso facto,* Barclays DCO (on 42 Lombard Street, close to the mother house, on 54 Lombard Street) rose to the level of HSBC and *Chartered* in the field of imperial banking, with activities in West India, Mauritius, Eastern and Southern Africa, and 6,500 employees in 1939 (3,552 in Southern Africa). The number of DCO branch offices grew from 500 in 1945 to 1,400 in 1962, which showcases its Chairman, Goodenough's foresight when he decided to deploy overseas. On the French side, the new protectorate of Morocco quickly attracted the attention of Paribas in the years 1910–50.[30] French deposit banks swarmed all over sub-Saharan Africa in the years 1940–50, when the region saw a spurt in economic development, commercial agriculture and underground resources.[31]

The majority of bankers were aware of the dangers of 'internalizing'[32] their international deployment, the diversification of the field of action in the region and the vertical integration of the colonial or imperial bank's work, especially regarding the risks of information asymmetry which can arise when entering port-cities or markets which need solid local business networks in order to counter business and accounting 'bad practices'. The lure of big profits was balanced by the risk of heavy losses caused by turnarounds in commodity trade or the collapse of so many colonial companies which had become victims of speculation. Leaving the known devil of the mainland market for the unknown one overseas was well and truly an 'adventure'!

Imperial Business Hubs

Meanwhile, overseas banks could not function without their 'home markets' as they worked at the heart of major 'clearing' operations: there was a steady and strong flow of currencies (even bullion), bills of exchange, documentary credits, etc. between the branches of imperial banks and their mainland hubs and commercial outlets. *Banque de l'Indochine*'s branches in China worked in Paris (the cornerstone of their mini banking system), London (the world's compensation hub) and, more and more after the years 1910–20, New York. The core activity was what we call today 'correspondence banking', in close and constant touch with their sister concerns, be they commercial, investment or merchant (London) banks, for bills of exchange, transfer of means of payment or for trade finance. This also explains why the big Japanese bank which was active in South-East Asia and the Far East had satellites in the City.[33] While Barclays naturally became its subsidiary's correspondent, the BBWA was obliged to set up branches in Manchester, Liverpool and London in conjunction with its own birth in 1893 – before forging some relations with Lloyds in 1919.

The flow of commercial paper and bank money resulted in a significant income for the imperial banks: service charges for transferring remittances from abroad to the mainland, charges for sending liquidity in the other direction and the opportunity of using in Europe the stock of unused liquidity – all added to the profitability. To top it all, FOREX operations also garnered much business.

Colonial and Imperial Bankers as a Business Community

We have analysed the sociability, business connections and communities with a special focus on the connections of overseas banks (abroad or in the metropolis) and their insertion into business communities (chambers of commerce, clubs), lobbies and pressure groups. The co-operation between the state, military institutions, public circuits, and colonial banks are to be seen as a leverage force for treasury liquidity, captive markets, and influence. The design of the competitive field was at stake: market share, cartelisation, rules of competition, *hunting preserves*, etc.

Despite their status, colonial territories were rarely 'closed-shop' areas, and still less imperial port-cities. The market's day-to-day life was run by open-minded bankers and businessmen. The communities were a mixture of expatriates with mainly overseas careers, who shared information and enriched the social life of relatively small Europeanized groups which nevertheless were strongly rooted in the land in which they were active. They shuffled between the main hubs and back-end branches which were sometimes lost in the countryside – like it happened in Africa as described by the history of Barclays. Despite the competition, bankers had to maintain the balance of liquidity and trust at their place, which demanded some osmosis among firms – their overall fate depending on each one's resistance.

The most tricky part was reconstituting the 'imperial' or 'colonial' communities of interest in the mainland itself, at the heart of this overseas deployment. We can identify some 'heroes' such as the great Charles Addis, the 'godfather' of British financial and banking deployment in Asia.[34] We also have Frederick Goodenough, chairman of Barclays (1917–34) and Barclays DCO (1925–34), John Caulcutt, director and general manager of Barclays DCO (1925–37) and its deputy chairman in 1935–43, and Julian Crossley, Goodenough's step-son, who was the general manager of Barclays DCO in 1935–44 and its deputy chairman. These individuals epitomized Barclays' role as an imperial bank, just as did Georges Botton for Lloyds-BOLSA before the outbreak of World War II. H. Bonin's chapter analyses the crystallisation of the networks of influence in Paris and how they influenced the authorities by involving certain Ministries (Finance, Foreign Affairs, Colonies) to take decisions favouring colonial development. Here too, within the community of imperial bankers, we saw the rise of eminent personalities such as Stanislas Simon of *Banque de l'Indochine*. He started as early as 1878 to be manager of its Saigon branch (keystone of its presence in Indochina), then, back in Paris, he raised as high officier (1888–1920), and more importantly, general manager-CEO (1920–7), then chairman (1927–31. In Asia he could reliy on Paul Gannay, as the head of the Saigon branch and moreover as the head of the General Inspectorate in Asia in 1926–47, thus a cornerstone of the processes of controls and compliance all over the Asian network of branches, before joining Paris as deputy CEO (1947–52).

The Imperial Bank's Business Portfolio

Though these imperial banks obviously carried on with the usual commercial banking operations such as intermediation, operating costs, cash-flow management, commissions, interest and securities gains, they also specialized in FOREX, documentary credit, stock financing in the port-cities of the mainland or overseas, financing shipping cargo, etc. At the very trough of these commercial territories, these banks financed 'the draft', as it was called in sub-Saharan Africa, that is to say, the collection of commodities and material through various levels of local or expatriate intermediaries and the resale of 'goods' and material and capital goods through these same or other intermediaries.

Money Flows and Documents

The management of money flows was a cornerstone of imperial banking. We can follow the organization of the flows of money (treasury, currencies, national currency, etc.) either through the banks or the central banking institutions. Practicing FOREX business at colonial banks was essential. Clearing operations by colonial banks in the metropolis and international (London, Paris, Berlin, New York, etc.) or quasi-international (Tokyo/Yokohama, Shanghai, Hong Kong,[35] etc.) financial centres was a fundamental competence. Barclays DCO itself disposed of a branch in New York for leveraging its operations in dollars. A review of the refinancing operations in the metropolis (the capital or the main 'port cities' through collateralizing operations) or in international centres would be a fine complement to this inquiry.

We therefore need to assess the emergence of 'local' overseas market-places and determine whether and how the small 'port cities' in the colonies turned into 'regional hubs' for banking and clearing activities and the preferred location for banking headquarters after colonization. In every 'sub-region' of this new movement of globalization, colonial and imperial banks set themselves up as 'masters' of these hubs and underpinned the commercial fabric. They sustained the regional commodity systems within the global web of commerce and commodity networks: in Asia, they financed the inter-Asian flow of rice (from Saigon and Haiphong to Shanton and Guangdong, or Hong Kong), tea, opium, raw cotton or cotton goods (from India to Shanghai to Tianjin) from Shanghai, Hong Kong, Calcutta or Bombay/Mumbai, and mixed trade finance around 'native' and 'internationalised' markets. For instance, in China, imperial bankers, who were later joined by local ones at the turn of the 1930s, fostered the exchange of money and documents (documentary credit, bills of exchange) through the re-export machinery active in Shanghai (to Tianjin or Zhewjan) and Hong Kong (to Guangdong, Qiongzhan and Fuzhou).

Imperial and Correspondent Banking

While local and deposit banks in the mainland toiled through enormous quantities of discount bills, one of the imperial bank's originalities lay in the commerce of large quantities of 'paper' in the form of bills of exchange: the large flow of remittances from one overseas market to another were accompanied by even larger flows of bills towards European clearing centres – partly the national markets, port-cities and capitals, but mainly towards the keystone of the global economy till the 1920s: London.[36] Every bank had a subsidiary or a permanent correspondent in the City as well as a favoured correspondent at its national market – a role played by CNEP and *Banque de l'union parisienne* for many French colonial establishments (*Banque de l'Afrique occidentale*, banks in the Antilles, *Banque de Madagascar*, etc. for the former and *Compagnie algérienne* for the latter).

Imperial Banking and Risk Management

The diversity and richness of the business portfolio and their embeddedness in the overseas business communities had a double effect. One was undeniably positive: the more these imperial banks worked in close conjunction with their partners and fellow-travellers, the denser became their relational networks. At the same time, this intimacy also gave rise to a danger which we come across often in banking history – the relative dependence on client firms: too much intimacy shattered the glass wall required to separate the bank's from its client's interests – the result of a clear and strict risk analysis. Such osmosis is sometimes dangerous because it leads to some confusion because the bank carries in itself a permanent 'operational risk'.

The Dependence on Commodities Cycles

This explains the recurrent crises that litter colonial economic history. A shade too many branch managers, departmental heads, even top managers let themselves be carried away by the rising business opportunities. Raw material and commodity prices (especially textile) along with shipping rates were extremely volatile. Seasonal credit, which characterized the imperial bank's main business, loans guaranteed against stock and the mobilization of liquidity as a lever for upstream (overseas or mainland) and downstream (mainland or overseas) financing inevitably created tensions regarding the recovery of loans in case of fall in prices. This explains the setbacks that afflicted so many branches of colonial banks and their Headquarters in mainland France when the crises accumulated, leading to frozen loans and liquidity crises and sometimes even crises of solvency regarding this or that bank.

The fluctuations in the price of natural commodities and mining products played a central role in the life of the imperial banks which depended heavily on the colony's commercial agriculture and the industrial demand for raw material in an environment of 'uneven development'.[37] Thus, banks active in Egypt, Sudan and Uganda lived in rhythm with the cotton sector, whether it be the leading Anglo-Egyptian Bank, present in Cairo since 1878 and in Alexandria since 1884, or French houses like *Crédit lyonnais* and CNEP. The cotton crisis following the global recession of 1920/1 dealt them a severe blow. Loans were given to farmers, producers and 'export houses'. Anglo-Egyptian Bank, in keeping with its counterparts in Chinese port-cities, maintained its own warehouses in order to use them as levers for loans on goods and warrants.[38] Banks in South Africa lived in rhythm with the market of local products: wool grew in importance (to Europe, especially Hamburg); diamond speculation in the 1880s and the crash of 1889 had dramatic repercussions all across Southern Africa and Europe: 'Financiers transferred a great deal of the region's wealth from investors in the coastal areas to the emerging diamond magnates, and hence subsequently to the mining houses, which so profoundly shaped the development of the entire sub-continent. This was accompanied by concentration on the financial sector itself, as the big imperial banks shook out smaller competitors [...]. The supply of credit ballooned and then burst in 1889'.[39] The discovery of the 'copper belt' in North Rhodesia (Zambia) presented an opportunity as well as a risk – due to the dependence on the demand for copper in the industrialized nations (telephone lines, etc.).

In conjunction with the growth of commercial agriculture (which they linked with the settlers' economy, the establishment of a society of plantation capitalists as it happened in French Algeria, or the development of the indigenous peasantry), colonial banks in South Africa and Algeria were often involved in rural, hypothecated loans, with the resulting exposure to its booms and recessions. Let us not forget the successive crises that these imperial and colonial banks lived through in almost every overseas territory. Even the banks in India faced such troubles in the beginning of the 1890s.

Finally, several of these banks also took part in the urban mortgage credit market to help real estate promoters build 'the modern city' in the British dominions and Chinese concessions. Here too there were some bad loans that resulted from reversals in growth, market and prices. Consequently, as in South Africa in 1920–3, this led to the impounding and liquidation of a large number of hypothecated properties.

FOREX *Risks*

The sheer size of FOREX operations could not but generate risks in keeping with the scope of the involvement in currency markets at a time when imperial banks did not have any real 'covering' techniques, despite resorting to 'reporting' operations. The colonial system attained its peak when currencies turned unstable. The fall of the pound sterling in the early 1930s affected *Barclays DCO* in a big way. It needed all its skills to try to anticipate and navigate the stormy rates of the pound and the dollar. Then, in the 1940–50, fluctuations in the money market and a drastic devaluation of the pound in 1949 created many more risks. Similarly, the French too had to clamp down on their FOREX operations due to the fluctuations in the Franc in 1922–8, 1936–8 and in the 1950s. All this required some astute navigation between the reefs, and the experience thus gained did not fail to serve as protection and lead to the development of preventive tools.

A Strong Culture of Risk Management

We can now understand how important it was to have an efficient General Inspectorate, a system of monthly reporting on the activities, norms and monitoring procedures. These imperial banks presented even greater risks than international or regional corporate banks because all too often their clients lacked sufficient accounting rigor and worked in economies that were still unstructured – excepting South Africa perhaps. One could say that risk management here needed to be even more strict than on the mainland.

One could very well ask whether these imperial banks were 'normal', similar to their sister concerns in the mainland. It is true that *Haute Banque* houses, merchant banks and banks in metropolitan port-cities were also massively involved in overseas and international activities, as the collapse of Hentsch and Baring in the crash of 1889–91 clearly shows. Still, these imperial banks had the lion's share of their business in territories with significantly higher risks: the usual shipping risks, the risks linked to the price cycles of material, commodities and goods, risk of fraud and the risk of various types of 'speculations'. The correspondence between bankers and the monographs on the histories of several colonial banks confirm this perception.

When Barclays bought over National Bank of South Africa, it was also because the latter was in grave difficulties: too strongly embedded within the business community, it gave them too many loans – an all too familiar story in banking history. It was its very own principals – members of its board, business circles and local authorities – who pushed it towards too quick a growth with the result that it had to assume too high a risk of leverage. Thus, when it faced a financial crisis in 1922–3, it had to reduce its capital to erase unhealthy assets and ultimately look for a re-financier and investor – Barclays.[40]

Consequently, imperial bankers' knowledge portfolio needed to include a good dose of 'wisdom' and prudence in risk management. They needed to fight to collect the maximum amount of informal or explicit information from not only the data available at the banking hubs, but also by increasing the number of contacts within the local merchant community, whether foreign or native, based on a multilateral reputation mechanism to facilitate the exchange of data. This explains the creation of the 'specialized' banks which would play this role of intermediation between the markets, the business communities and the communities of interest by assuming the function of an 'agency', if we used the theory of the agency dear to the institutional economy. Though a number of Parisian banks were tempted by an Asian deployment following the model of *Comptoir d'escompte de Paris*, they ended up by contenting themselves with developing *Banque de l'Indochine* into a local community bank. The fact was the risk management in Indochina, China and various Asian port-cities required the pooling of data, of knowledge, a sharing of experience between branch managers, inspectors and experts based at the Headquarters. When *Barclays* acquired its subsidiary DCO (*Dominion, Colonial, Overseas*[41]) in 1925, it chose to isolate the experience gained by its three establishments (*De Nationale Bank der Zuid-Afrikaoasche Republik*, created in 1890, and known by its English name, National Bank of South Africa from 1902, Anglo-Egyptian Bank and Colonial Bank), develop the 'wealth' of knowledge accumulated by the management of these three houses and create a set of methods to better analyse overseas risks. These managers could also use this experience to enrich other managers working in some other sub-regional territory or space.

Issues of 'trust'[42] were central. Despite the establishment of colonial governments and regulations, many of these overseas economies still lacked proper legal, accounting and financial frameworks. There were a shade too many 'bad practices', especially in the form of a lack of accounting transparency. The traditional clues regarding the reliability and accountability of customers were not delivered. Moreover, business in these port-cities was susceptible to fraud regarding the quality and quantity of the goods delivered or stored.[43]

One needed to be well embedded[44] in every trade and banking centre in order to 'be like a fish in water' and to get all the information which could help minimize risks by eliminating information asymmetries.

Debates Regarding the Extent of Autonomy Enjoyed by These Overseas Territories

As in every other economic field, the overseas banking economy was also dualistic in nature with, on one hand, the hegemony of the mainland banks deployed in the colonies and, on the other, the local establishments dedicated to this or that territory or region (the Maghreb, Southern and sub-Saharan Africa, the Far East, the Middle East, the Caribbean, etc.). We need to identify the degree of autonomy, the manoeuvring room enjoyed by these expatriate managers and their capacity for adapting to the specificities of the local business and banking practices.

Decentralization or Centralization?

We have seen here and there the emergence of a local overseas banking system. Some imperial territories had the advantage of having either a developing or even a developed trade and production system either because of a 'settler colonisation'[45] or because the local resources were particularly rich and diversified in the mines or cultures. This led to the formation of a true banking system, with the required density of establishments and the volume of balance sheets in the regions which were to form South Africa: numerous imperial banks set up shop there.[46]

The life of Barclays DCO is very illustrative: 'His aim [Chairman Goodenough] has been to achieve for DCO a decentralized system of control, following the lines by banks in the UK, but subject always to the wide variations in practice necessitated by differing conditions in the various overseas countries'.[47] A representative board of directors sat in Cape Town, a strong management team was set up in Pretoria and managerial responsibilities were conferred on the directors at Cape Town and Rhodesia. The subsequent transition from the imperial system to an autonomous and finally independent economy was based on this imperial heritage. At the same time, Barclays DCO's near federal structure required some flexibility vis-a-vis the local realities and the constraints of distance (in spite of the help provided by telegraph cables which sometimes led to talk of 'cable banking') in adapting to the economies and trade. In the case of Anglo-Egyptian Bank-DCO, a board of directors and a management team were set up in Alexandria, but Nairobi was managed directly from London (Kenya, Tanganyika, Uganda), just like Colonial Bank and its branches in Nigeria, Sierra Leone and Gold Coast, because the top management felt that the business climate was too harsh. 'The variations in the system of control resulted from the character and corruption of the countries themselves, which inevitably influenced the structure of the Bank's organization'.[48]

A key question remains regarding the sociology of these imperial banks' clientele. Obviously, it consisted mainly of expatriates, foreigners (mainly European) residents of the mainland in transit (military personnel, civil servants, corporate executives, intellectuals, etc.), religious groups (including Catholic and Protestant missions). Still, in numerous places, local 'elites' also joined this clientele. For example, CFAT and *Compagnie algérienne* admitted traders and brokers of all sizes and owners of medium sized enterprises from the textile and agri-food industries. Chinese clients too found their way into HSBC's bigger branches (also to a lesser extent, *Banque de l'Indochine*) as and when they developed trading and consumer goods processing companies. The extent of the imperial banks' involvement in the promotion of the local population reflects their contribution to the region's economic take-off.

A Capacity for Autonomy?

The legacy of overseas banking must be seen against the backdrop of the autonomization of these overseas territories and their economies, taking into account the various forms of this process, from colonial hegemony to autonomy and independence. Transfer of skills need to be questioned. This also raises the issue of the training and promotion of local 'elites' within the colonial banks, before the actual move towards independence (and even afterwards, as part of the 'africanization' or 'asianization' processes and well beyond the 'compradors' of China for example). The building of 'pockets' of 'modern business culture' among the local 'middle classes' active as customers of imperial banks has also to be discussed.

This development depended upon the strength of the local elite, entrepreneurs and business community. We know – and Grietjie Verhoef has expounded on this theme in his chapter – that certain territories in South Africa saw the emergence of a regional capitalism, endowed with its own financial institutions.[49] The Canadian Dominion quickly acquired a relative banking autonomy which took the form of establishments that affirmed their own 'imperialism' and sometimes even posed a challenge to imperial banks in the Caribbean.[50] India too began to gradually set up its own 'native banks' which began to compete with the 'chartered banks' as and when the local capitalism grew and gained force from the turn of the 20th century. In fact, National Bank of India (later called National & Grindlays) went all the way to Tanganyika due to the overseas commercial links across the Indian Ocean. Australia too saw the emergence of local banks, even though some 'imperial' tentacles of European banks remained active, including through the subsidiaries of French CNEP.[51]

Over the next several years, every overseas trading centre saw a transfer of the skills portfolio between the management of the colonial or imperial banks and the rising 'elites', whether it be within the banks themselves (accounting, management of commercial accounts) or within their community of interests. This 'spillover' process had been more or less intense depending on the each territory's degree of development. But at the time of independence (for the colonies) or the rejection of imperialism (in communist or socialist countries mainly), this 'hybridisation' really bore fruit when the management of the nationalized banks, or of those handed over to local interests, came directly from the earlier teams, in a sort of modest but real passing of the relay baton.

Imperial Bankers and Imperialism?

Bankers did not fail to participate in the growth of imperialism,[52] in what a book called 'the official mind of imperialism'.[53] With close ties to colonial administrations, whether in Paris, Lisbon or London, and working intimately with the expansionist business communities in these two capitals, Japan and New York, they participated indirectly in developing strategies of economic conquest for the Mainland (including Japan, after the conquest of Korea and Taiwan) and the United States, like the entire community of Powers in China. The overseas 'growth block' based itself on a 'block of interests' and a 'block of social networks', with the whole underpinned by an imperialist or imperial 'block of ideas'. This overseas push did not fail to result in the usual hegemonic relations, and the banks were very much part of it.

This explains the balance between anti-imperialism and heritage when the time came for the move towards independence. The process of the transfer of power from overseas banks and financial institutions to local authorities provides an insight into the permanence or its lack. The redeployment of companies, of their equity, treasury, availabilities and management needs to be evaluated, and their future as eventual autonomous institutions as opposed to an integration into metropolitan groups debated. Were they able to join the strategic poles of influence and development in their country, or were they deprived of entrepreneurship, human resources and financial means?

Several chapters dwell on the anti-imperialist sentiments which prevailed in the former colonies after independence or the institution of socialist regimes. For example, Niv Horesh talks about the 'boycott' of Japanese interests in China, especially the branches of the Japanese Yokohama Specie Bank, just after World War I. A little later, in 1923, it was the whole gamut of 'imperialist' interests that were denounced by nationalist movements in Hong Kong and Canton, which also led to a generalized 'boycott'. Then, in the 1930s, the young and frail Guomingdang government in Nanjing set as a priority the creation and promotion of 'national' banks: whether it be a central bank with a commercial bent or banks issued from Chinese capitalism. Later still, the nationalization of foreign and colonial banks served as the first blow in loosening the foreign hegemony: this was obviously the case in communist China between 1945 and 1952, but also in socialist India of the Congress Party, as shown by Ashok Kapoor's study in this book. Later still, this anti-imperialist movement also swept through a number of African countries such as Algeria in the mid-1960s, and Barclays DCO lost its entities in Tanganyika (1967) and Sudan (1970).

The process of nationalization took shape in a number of African countries that retained a market economy. In many others, it meant the creation of subsidiaries of entities which were active in the territory, for the benefit of mixed banks, with foreign and national shareholding, private and public. This happened in Nigeria[54] and Côte d'Ivoire among others. The BBWA, which had become *Bank of West Africa* (BWA) in 1957, tried to rid itself of its 'colonial' aspect. But Ghana replaced it with its Bank of Gold Coast in 1953 as its issuing and commercial bank. Finally reality sunk in: the BWA integrated itself into the South African Standard Bank in 1965 and turned into its subsidiary under the name of Standard Bank of West Africa, which was retained after the constitution of Standard Chartered Bank in 1969. The process of creating subsidiaries in Africa intensified, with Standard Bank of Ghana (with the Barclays Bank of Ghana in 1971), Standard Bank Nigeria and Standard Bank of Sierra Leone, which lived semi-independent lives by being open to both local capitalist groups and multinational opportunities. The Africanization went to the extent of a complete loss of control of Standard Bank Nigeria (which had become First Bank of Nigeria in 1979) in 1996, before the establishment of a new direct subsidiary, Standard Chartered Bank Nigeria in 1999. This showed that after independence, these outgrowths of imperial banks needed to use all their dexterity to meet the political, nationalist, capitalist and financial expectations.

The case of India, which has been dealt with in numerous books as well as here, is emblematic of the post-colonial dilemma: at first, there was an intertwining and symbiosis between imperial and local banks at the turn of the twentieth century. But the young country's nationalism and the influence of socialist theories on the Congress Party were so strong that the imperial bank, identified with imperialism, found itself condemned. This led to the progressive nationalization and Indianization of these establishments and the victory of the State and (more modestly) private bank which the majority thought were more suited to some real, internal development, more oriented towards the national production system, with a better redistribution of the income derived from international trade. In China, the abrupt nationalization of banks and enterprises put an end to imperial banking, forcing HSBC to return to Hong Kong, while the subsidiaries of European, Japanese and American banks had either to redeploy towards the rest of Asia or close down.

Whatever might have been their fate, these 'imperial banks' have left a lasting legacy. In fact, some institutions have even managed to withstand the shocks and setbacks of History by reinventing their strategy, rebuilding on multiple occasions their portfolio of strategic activities and developing their skills and knowledge portfolio. HSBC is by far the best example as it benefited from the continued existence of the colony of Hong Kong. It could prepare for an eventual withdrawal by spreading out across Asia (later even into continental China) and by establishing itself as a great commercial bank in Europe and the United States. The old Chartered[55] too managed to turn itself into a major transnational bank in Asia and Africa by becoming Standard Chartered. 'To change so that nothing changes' seems to have been the motto of these two banks, which managed to replicate the strategy used by several business houses which had been active in the colonial empires and which subsequently completely changed their methods and lifestyle in order to continue well into the 21st century. The examples of Vlasto[56] and CFAO[57] in Africa come to mind, before Unilever's advent in the ex-empires, but by adopting an operational mode suited to the emerging or under-developed countries, far from the imperial methods used earlier by its subsidiary UAC.[58] But the same thing had also been done by the flexible British business houses in Asia (hong) such as Swire and Jardine & Matheson.[59]

Barclays DCO too felt the 'the winds of change'[60] as the British Empire began to disintegrate (independence of Ghana in July 1957, Nigeria in October 1960, Caribbean in 1962, etc.): 'Inevitably, with the paring of the colonial era, we, at the DCO, have become more and more an international bank and it seems plain to us that our future role must be seen in the context'.[61] This explains the subsidiarization of its activities in South Africa (Barclays National Bank in October 1971) and its own metamorphosis: the subsidiary became the *Barclays Bank International*, with 1,584 branches of its mother company *Barclays* outside the United Kingdom, for what is called the 'retail bank', oriented towards individuals and local enterprises and leaving 'wholesale banking' to its mother company (*Barclays Capital*).

Let us note here that almost all the 'colonial' or 'imperial' banks have been eliminated by History. The famous *Banque de l'Indochine* transformed itself into a major commercial bank in France in the years 1940–70. It was then absorbed by the *Compagnie financière de Suez* to become *Indosuez*. Then, when this financial group conducted a strategic redeployment in the 1990s, it was taken over by the *Crédit agricole* group and integrated into its division of corporate & investment banking. *Compagnie algérienne* and *Crédit foncier d'Algérie et de Tunisie* turned into retail banks in France before various mergers culminated into their disappearance via an integration into *Société générale*. BOLSA returned to its parent company's fold (Lloyds), which refocused its strategic activities towards the British commercial bank. By chance, two British-origin houses kept the imperial bank's flag flying high: HSBC, which will celebrate its 150th anniversary in 2015, and Chartered, which merged with Standard to become Standard Chartered – both straddling Europe and Asia. The former got itself a foothold in the United States and the latter in Eastern and Southern Africa. In 2000, 'StanChart' accounted for 59 per cent of its turnover, with 29 percent from Hong Kong. It also made inroads into India and Pakistan. As the first foreign bank in Bangladesh, it strengthened itself with the purchase of *Anz Grindlays'* Asia-Pacific and Middle East activities in 2000 – in fact, it inherited from the imperial bank, *Grindlays*. After all, History seems to have bequeathed at least some imperial banking legacies to the present banking economy!

About a Few Foibles

A few pieces of criticism might be expressed anyway. The rich variety of case-studies is also a handicap since it does not allow to draw a comprehensive and rounded-up picture of the history of foreign banking in Asia. However, in light of the actual state of research on the history of imperial banking systems, such obvious weakness could hardly be overcome for the moment by any serious academic research. There is, of course, always something to wish, e. g. chapters on the colonial banking system of Germany in her leasehold-colony in China, or of other Western countries (Belgium, Italy, etc.) in the so-called 'treaty ports' in China but also in major trading hubs in the Asiatic-Pacific region, or on Chinese and Southeast Asian local and overseas banks and their links to the foreign banking systems in Asia. I admit that we do not compare here American, British, Japanese and Russian banks in terms of their historical development, impact made, strength and weakness. However, since the proposed book builds on research already done there would always be gaps in the coverage: it lies in the nature of a book based mainly on conference papers that it can only offer a variety of approaches to the general topic of the book. But the perception of variety can be balanced by the efforts which I developed when I tried in the previous sections to define some 'conceptual' approaches of our topics; but the team of this book had not intents at all to supply some kind of an 'encyclopaedia' of imperial and colonial banking in Asia: our objectives remained modest, and we remain well aware of the gaps to be filled... My major challenge was to provide an altogether broad and deep introduction to the book which strongly binds together the different approaches and offers a comprehensive and rounded-up overall picture, to clearly work out certain patterns in strategies of market accesses and also in geographical and transnational interactions with similar and different partners in the imperial banking systems, and to present the complexity of the entire story in a readable and comprehensible language.

Further essays could insert the results of this book and of its chapters into the broader scope of arguing about imperialism itself. We must recognize that we might have more consistently connected these research results with the overall history of economic imperialism in Asia at the time to demonstrate its relevance for our understanding of this process. Strengths and weaknesses of the existing literature on the topic ought to be discussed in order to explain which new insights the book is going to offer to further enhance knowledge on imperialism 'on the spot', soft forms of imperialism, or 'gentlemanly capitalism' in imperialist/colonialist contexts. But our book will stay on the level of 'empiricism', without dreaming of asserting itself as some kind of a 'treaty' of business imperialism.

1 FRENCH OVERSEAS BANKING AS AN IMPERIAL SYSTEM: A BACKGROUND FOR ASIAN DEVELOPMENTS

Hubert Bonin

This chapter presents the background of the expansion of French banks in the 'imperial' Far East, that is, to set it back in the context of economic and financial imperial moves from the Metropole to the various colonial areas overseas. The deployment of French banks, particularly *Banque de l'Indochine*, both in the European concessions in China but also in Indochina itself and other territories such as Singapore, cannot be understood without such a retrospective and broad reconstitution.

Strong vestiges of the British Empire are still very much active within the international banking community, mainly HSBC[1] and Standard Chartered Bank.[2] Paradoxically, *Banco Santander* and BBVA have completed a strategy of development in the ancient Spanish empire all around Latin America, renewing souvenirs of the glorious past... Conversely, not a single French bank today is entertaining the flame of imperial history: *Banque de l'Indochine* has been amalgamated into the present *Crédit agricole*-CASA; *Crédit foncier d'Algérie & de Tunis* was swallowed by *Société générale*; and the *Banque internationale de l'Afrique occidentale* almost collapsed and its assets joined a Euro-African body. The sole vestiges of the empire might be the offshoots of big banks overseas, inherited from the outlets set up during the colonial years, within the groups of *Société générale* or the BNP Paribas (with the legacy of *Comptoir national d'escompte de Paris*-CNEP). Only archival bodies, pictures, and academic or institutional books bolster knowledge and, perhaps, nostalgia about the extension of Parisian banking deep into the colonial empire.

This latter also benefited from 'imperial banking',[3] with different stages of growth: banks to prop up the establishment of the colonial rule (until the end of the 19th century); banks to accompany the move of investment and modernisation (*'mise en valeur'*) from the 1900 to World War II; then banks as stake-holders of the apex of the ultimate imperial economic system, till the independence move. The City had long been equipped with such leverage forces as to extend its grip over the British Empire's economy, with, from London, Barclays

DCO (Dominions, Colonies, Overseas),[4] set up in 1925 by the amalgamation of the Colonial Bank, the National Bank of South Africa and the Anglo-Egyptian Bank. Brussels could rely on the group of Société *générale de Belgique*[5] and its *Banque belge d'outre-mer.*

Thus, this chapter intends to provide a new perspective through which to understand how the banking industry took part to the structuring of a French economic empire, along the concepts defined by David-Kenneth Fieldhouse,[6] balancing between 'the economics of Empire' and arguments about imperialism. 'Imperial banking' could be perceived as mere 'economics of empire' and parts of the 'colonial economic system' as a whole; or it could be a component of economic 'imperialism',[7] all the more than several French academics debated about the reality and extent of French 'imperialism'[8]. We'll ponder which functions it assumed, which trades it dispatched and reinforced abroad, and how such developments contributed to the internal evolution of the organization of the firms involved. We shall also determine the process of 'differentiation' among the 'imperial banks', that is, assessing the variety of business models which took shape at each bank: the different paths taken in the bid to fuel their portfolio of strategic activities; their different geographical basis; and their different connections with the French business community. One key issue will be that of competition within the colonial territories: were there *chasses gardées* – monopolistic strongholds kept by some banks in their area of expansion – or did competitive challenges benefited from a 'free market' policy, opening doors to the whole Paris community of banking? The last point lies with the argument about 'open door' policy; on the one side, were foreign banks allowed or able to take part to the economic life of the French empire? On the other side, did French banks become actors on the stage of other imperial systems, particularly the British?

We shall therefore examine the outline and structure of the French imperial banking system, its cohesiveness and its efficiency, up to the point where it even reached some degree of 'completion', if not 'harmony', at the turn of the 1950s. The synthesis of ideas and arguments drawn from across the chapters will facilitate the scrutiny of the ways in which the banking industry contributed to the structuring of a French economic empire[9], from the Metropole itself (either in Paris, in the merchant cities inland or in the port-cities involved) or from the port-cities abroad. The imperial connections wove a brokered world[10] of trade and finance. Such an investigation provides our inquiry with an overall background about the French empire as a whole, which, as a result, furthers our understanding of the Asian deployment of the French banks and their various offshoots.

Managing Means of Payment

A discreet yet commonplace function of imperial banks was to manage, with efficiency, reliability, and relative speed, the transfers of the means of payment from the Metropole to the empire, and vice versa. This was done in favour of the public bodies: the more the French colonial empire extended, the more financial flows gathered momentum, first of all to sustain the life of the administration and the army themselves, and then to support the emergence of the 'modern economy'.

The first issue of the imperial banking system was therefore to manage the transfers of payments needed by the Administration and the Army, tackling both the process of extension and the deepening of colonization. This involved paying the civil servants and the troops; financing the day to day facilities and amenities; supporting those trade houses that acted as suppliers of the Army (that is discounting their bills on the State bodies); and providing treasury advances to the public system emerging abroad. These were altogether very important tasks because of the growing amount of cash required not only to maintain the basic functioning of the public colonial system, but also to pursue the penetration, pacification and, sometimes, repression of rebellious areas and populations, either through military initiatives or the establishment of a strong police. Money was the key to keeping the balance of power tilted in favour of the colonial authorities, and banks were intimately committed to managing the flows of treasury. *Banque de l'Indochine* was thus entrusted with tackling the circulation of the treasury throughout the administrative and military bodies, whether in the Indochina colony or in the Chinese concessions.

In the meanwhile, banks also moved the means of payment between the various territories in each area, such as North Africa, Sub-Saharan Africa and Indochina; the islands abroad; and the other territories, particularly the Metropole. They also managed the amounts remitted to the Metropole by the expatriates, in favour of their family, their banking accounts or for their real estate investments there. More and more, in special segments of the market, they tackled the amount sent by the emigrants of the empire, in the Metropole, to their family, but such a 'modern' transfer method actually only really took shape at the very end of the colonial period, and notes were transported in cash more often in that case.

Indeed, an ultimate tool was set up during World War II when the Gaullist authorities of the *France libre* had to equip themselves with some kind of central bank, the *Caisse centrale de la France libre*, to manage the treasury of the territories that had already joined the Allied forces, mainly in Sub-Saharan Africa, between 2 December 1941–February 1944, pending the *Libération*.

Duplicating Structures of a Financial and Banking System

The second and far bigger issue was of course the building of a modern monetary system that was able to fuel the development of the modern colonial companies and to prop up the insertion of agriculture and local commodities trading into a market economy that mixed agriculture for subsistence with agriculture for export. The process of monetarization thus gathered momentum, which explains the growth of local central banks. Colonization and central banking followed a parallel and intimate path, epitomised by the creation of the *Banque d'État du Maroc*. The grip of France over Morocco, first to be managed as a somehow internationalised protectorate, was actually asserted thanks to the management of this institution by the French business community, with the guidance of the investment bank Paribas, under the tutelage of the French authorities.[11] Such a body was able to introduce a 'modern' monetary system to the Protectorate and create a stable frame in favour of the economic penetration of French business[12].

Similar processes took shape in Algeria, where the foundation and the mission of the *Banque de l'Algérie*[13] appear as fundamental to the colonial system that was being built, by the Second Empire regime in North Africa, after the first wave of colonization, and then was consolidated by the Third Republic.[14]

In parallel, as soon as the *Afrique occidentale française* (AOF) was set up, the *Banque du Sénégal*,[15] which grappled with the monetary business of the ancient colony, was transformed into the *Banque de l'Afrique occidentale* (BAO),[16] to supervise the progression of the whole French Sub-Saharan area into a modernised monetary system that was far from the traditional signs of exchanges (*cauris*); old-type coins (*thalers*); or clearing habits among native merchants. In a final example, the establishment and extension of *Banque de l'Indochine*[17] can be seen as landmarks of the intimacy between colonization and central banking, first from Cochinchina, to Tonkin and then to the whole of French 'Indochina'. The renewal and extension of the concession of the central banking mission in 1883 consecrated the importance altogether of its function of bolstering the colonization move of Tonkin and the prospects of economic influence there, to relay military penetration.

The imperial central banks thus assumed the responsibility for ordering coins and notes to French manufacturers: the *Monnaie de Paris*, the printing unit of the *Banque de France*, or private notes printers, then putting them in circulation in the various territories, with a relay of banks to dispatch them throughout the colonies and protectorates. For a short while, the *Caisse centale de la France libre* became the *Caisse centrale de la France d'outre-mer*,[18] in charge with the monetary functions in the French colonies until 1955, the step to independence, which reduced its tasks to the Caribbean islands, assumed afterwards by the IEDOM.[19]

But these central banks brought another key basis of colonial power: trust. The confidence of investors; local bourgeoisies (native or, mainly, expatriates); the whole European society in Algeria (with various social layers); and the foreign partners of business meant that they relied on the stability of the currency, the quality of its management, and the liquidity of each local economy, thanks to the internal clearing operations from merchant to merchant places. Classically, such immaterial capital could not but ease the flows of investments useful to the '*mise en valeur*' (development) of the empire. As 'modernity' was at stake, such 'trust' favoured the perception of French colonies as promising offshoots for European companies and emigrants.

Banks and Imperial Commodities Trading

The modern concept of 'trade finance' or 'banking' has roots in the colonial banking system that was set up to accompany the development of the modern economy of exports of commodities by the empire. 'Commercial agriculture', as opposed to 'agriculture for subsistence', could not have gathered momentum without an efficient contribution by banks to the seasonal financing of wholesale houses. Each one had to collect the goods, thus paying the suppliers, to pile them up in the warehouses along rivers (such as Sénégal and Mekong), railways or roads, thus immobilising assets, to export and transport them, before selling them in the European (or other) harbours, along a well-known chain.

An obvious and basic chain of credit had taken shape, but banks had to complement efficiency with reliability, whilst they also had to assess the solvability, liquidity and perspectives of each stake-holder within the chain of the exchanges of commodities, bills of exchange, advances against pledges and warrants guaranteed by deposits of goods in harbour warehouses. At the headquarters themselves, robust teams of specialists in overseas business joined those grappling with international banking and finance, generally in relation with London, Brussels, Geneva or a few other places involved in support of worldwide trade and European imports of commodities and raw materials. In each of the big banks, there were thus layers of hyper-specialists in a range of fields of business. They were hubs for 'correspondent banking', either with the places and port-cities all over Europe (such as London,[20] Hamburg, Brussels, Marseille and Anvers), or with the imperial off-shoots. They built a strong portfolio of skills in risks assessment; the knowledge of 'speculation' on goods; the access to the data piled up by the insurance companies about international trade or shipping (reflecting the degree of risks); and in the positions reached by bankers about collaterals, FOREX coverage, and counterparts.

Their main branches in the port-cities or in the main regional places committed to international and imperial trade (Lyon, Lille, Bordeaux, Le Havre,[21]

Marseille,[22] Mulhouse, Nantes, and Dunkerque, for instance) increasingly became kinds of medium-sized banks, where poles of expertise grew up. Numerous archives and, in more recent periods, testimonies tell about the high degree of empirical know-how entertained there by experimented middle managers and head managers – those latter turning around the network of commercial bankers through a process of promotion to bigger outlets. This capital of knowledge comprised an acute art in FOREX, documentary credit management, and the relationships with shipping companies and, moreover, with the wholesale trade houses. They were the main actors in the 'warrantage system' articulated around the warehouses, that is, credit against pledged inventories and, of course, within a French system of banking deprived of the merchant banks *à l'anglaise*, they practiced high degrees of discount and seasonal credits (*crédits de campagne*) to the purchasers and importers of colonial goods.

In the meanwhile, the metropolitan banks were also committed to 'refinance' the banks active in the imperial port-cities themselves. Originally the 'correspondent' in Paris of the very first 'colonial banks' set up in the French Caribbean, after the abolition of slavery, to refinance their commonplace credit activities[23], CNEP increasingly became the actual 'correspondent' of the *Banque de l'Afrique occidentale* (hereafter BAO) for its commercial banking portfolio. But the CIC group became a partner of imperial trade too, through its sister banks active in the metropolitan port-cities. One relevant case-study can be found in the *Société bordelaise de CIC,* which was in charge of covering the needs of the trade houses oriented towards Sub-Saharan Africa[24]overseas. These trade houses issued a huge amount of seasonal commercial paper and needed short or middle-term refinancing. The houses disposed of twin bodies abroad and in Bordeaux, emitting paper between themselves, to be discounted in Bordeaux, often with a collateral from BAO in Sénégal, or elsewhere in western Africa, for exports to Europe; conversely, the Bordeaux bank supplied its collaterals as paper to be re-discounted by BAO in the other way of trading. Documentary credit also reigned either between Africa and France, or often between French Africa and other merchant port-cities elsewhere in Europe (such as Liverpool or Hamburg). The same micro-system was active in Nantes for the subsidiary of CIC there, *Crédit nantais* then *Crédit industriel de l'Ouest,* and in Rouen and Le Havre, for *Crédit industriel de Normandie.*

Independently, the case of the *Société marseillaise de crédit* has ever been promoted as a beacon for such an imperial banking system, as it directly financed and refinanced (discount, signature as a pledge of collateral, seasonal loans, warrant credits, documentary credits) the trade houses of this big port-city. An imperial micro-banking system functioned there too, on a large scale, oriented towards North Africa; Madagascar and La Réunion; Indochina; the French empire; and Egypt, about the British empire. But the case was even more complex as, in Marseille, SMC, or the branches of the Paris banks (CNEP, mainly) refinanced Greek banks to allow them to fuel their own import–export trade between Athens and Egypt, or the Levant.[25]

In the field of 'trade banking/finance', CNEP[26] and the *Crédit lyonnais*[27] became more and more involved in financing the commodities trade; they established outlets in Egypt (for the cotton trade) and in Australia (for the wool trade) to get chunks of this huge trade where their British rivals were predominant. To finance the ultimate stage of sales in Europe, both banks thus intervened afterwards either in the UK through their branch in London, or in France (Dunkerque, Lille or Le Havre/Rouen) through their local branches, along the whole chain of imperial banking. *Banque de l'Indochine*[28] asserted itself as the key banker of the chain connecting silk exports from Indochina and, mostly in the interwar period, Guangdong to Marseille and then Lyon, or from Asia to Europe and the US, despite the efforts of HSBC to maintain its stronghold in this segment of the banking market, either abroad or in Europe (and even in Lyon, thanks to its own branch there).

The more the natural (and mining) resources of the empire were exploited (along the project of '*mise en valeur*' explicited by minister Albert Sarraut in the 1920s) within the economic colonial system, the more the flows of commodities, and ore materials, from the empire to the Metropole or towards foreign countries caused flows of credit in both overseas and 'developed' areas. This assertion, while not revolutionary, further portrays the array of connections that contributed to build, densify, and entertain the structure of imperial banking in Asia.

Financing Imperial Trade

A similar path was followed by 'commercial banking'. The new/second colonial empire opened doors to huge outlets for banks: the more the empire conquered parts of French trade, the more it was dedicated to a function of '*chasse gardée*' (except in Morrocco from the Algeciras agreement, and in the low Niger area in 1898–1936), and the more it became a key market for so many big firms or SMEs (for instance, textile, cloth, daily household equipment, and spirits). This bolstered 'imperial' commercial banking;[29] the basis of which consisted of the financing of exporters of manufactured goods destined to the empire, whether purchased in France itself or exported from other countries, through direct trade or re-exports from French ports.

Specialized Imperial Banking

A few banks were first mostly active abroad, with only headquarters in Paris, acting as a key platform or 'hub' for credits, refinancing, risk management and controls, and the main network in the empire itself. They were the core of 'colo-

nial banks', with a high degree of specialization due to the constraints of original
risk management or simply because of the scramble for empire among investors
and bankers, who tended to duplicate overseas the commercial system of the
mainland. The issue boiled down to the matter of competition between banks.

On the one side, the community of banking and business, and the State,
had agreed that French economic and colonial interests would be far more pro-
tected and promoted through a single monopolistic institution. The BAO was
altogether the issuing and central bank in French Sub-Saharan Africa, and the
sole commercial bank there[30] – even if British and Belgian banks dared to cut
into its monopoly in French central and equatorial Africa. A similar process was
followed in Indochina and then also in China: *Banque de l'Indochine*[31] kept its
monopoly in the Tonkin, and obtained it in the Chinese concessions, due to
the sale of branches there by CNEP. The whole banking community ended up
joining the capital and the business of *Banque de l'Indochine* when its concession
was renewed and extended in 1897, thus transforming it into the arm of the co-
operation of French business to try and alleviate the hegemony of British banks
there and to resist the US and Japanese offensive.

Conversely, in the other colonial territories, competition prevailed. North
Africa, mainly Algeria, were somewhat rich colonies (or protectorates), with
plentiful commercial agriculture, day to day trade, and a European population
enlivening the same banking needs as found in the Metropole. A 'scramble for
banking' ocurred; financial and commercial interests coalised to set up various
types of commercial banks (*Crédit foncier d'Algérie et de Tunisie*[32] and the *Compagnie algérienne*[33]); and some of the Paris bigwigs joined the fray, opening branches
in Algeria (*Société générale* and the *Crédit lyonnais*) or in Tunisia (CNEP). The
imperial 'cake' was so big that competitors could make profits even by having just a
slice of it, along some kind of a Trans-Mediterranean banking system.

Whatever the competitive background, all these banks worked intimately
with the French business communities, locally (for internal exchanges) or at the
service of imports/exports – and they also supported the native business, when
it gathered momentum for some art-crafts, cloth or commodities such as oil,
as will be indicated in our analysis of CFAT in Tunisia, for instance. The connections between *Banque de l'Indochine* and the *Denis frères* from Bordeaux
epitomized such osmosis between banking and business, as this firm was the
leading multi-purpose trade house in Indochina. As will be explored later, the
permanent co-operation of big trade houses in Subsaharan Africa and bankers
abroad (BAO),[34] evolved as a result of their dependence upon them for seasonal
credits and a variety of documentary credits.

Overall Imperial Banking

Meanwhile, as regards the commodities trade, metropolitan banks were more active to intervene into the financing of the wholesale trade in the imperial overseas. From upstream, they supplied credits to allow the trading houses to purchase the manufactured goods they exported afterwards to the empire. In Paris or in the exporting merchant cities, bankers, individually or through syndicates, granted permanent lines of credit to the merchant houses; the manufacturing areas themselves were involved in such supplies (cloth, equipment goods, etc.), with chains of credit set up to fuel the discount or overdraft processes. Even still upward, the *Banque de France* itself, from its headquarters or through its provincial branches, re-discounted bulks of bills of exchange (*papier de commerce*), as the final 'pump' of the machinery of imperial banking. This was somewhat specific to France; in the UK, the merchant banks often tackled 'bills of acceptance' with their signature and pledge as collaterals, whereas, in France, discount prevailed in a direct form, thus fostering rediscount at the central bank[35]. Banks' archives frequently reveal the extent to which the European, the commonplace overseas and the imperial trades were intertwined, as goods crossed borders to be re-exported from France towards the colonial port-cities, causing flows and layers of bank loans.

Economic Patriotism at Stake

Despite this embedded nature of French banks as active, whether directly or indirectly, in the service of the French colonial empire within the various business communities, another commonplace issue to be found is that of the argument regarding 'open door' policy versus the pressure of protectionism, as 'economic patriotism' demanded that French banks supported French business in its bastions overseas and along the whole process of trade. However, the realities imposed themselves upon this process. Firstly, for commodities, numerous goods, cloth, and pieces of equipment and machinery had to be bought in foreign countries – Caterpillar or Ford vehicles or engines from the UK, Germany or the US. Banks thus had to insert themselves into the channel of credit starting in foreign places, for instance London, as the clearing platform for remittances of bills created by such orders. The CFAO disposed of purchase offices in Liverpool and Manchester in order to secure good quality consuming goods (fabric), which stirred a move of exchange bills from London to Paris and overseas, and back. French banks couldn't but intervene along these flows, thanks to their branch or affiliate in London.[36]

Secondly, because so many French trade houses were also active in empires other than that of the French, banks had to accompany these breakthroughs. The CFAO and SCOA had established a strong basis in the Sub-Saharan British empire – Nigeria, Ghana[37] – and they either used the French banks present in the

UK, or they altogether relied upon British banks overseas and in the UK. The same practice occurred in Asia: French trade houses often resorted to HSBC offshoots to broaden their lines of credit or merely to benefit from the excellent and deep connections of the Hong Kong bank throughout the Chinese concessions and merchant areas. Indeed, *Banque de l'Indochine* complained that several of their good customers were also clients to its rival in the Chinese concessions. Traders weighed different bankers against one another so as to get better interest charges or larger loans; in fact, *Banque de l'Indochine* was satisfied to alleviate its burden of credits in the name of the diversification of its portfolio of risks.

Thirdly, because several parts of the empire did not earmark their whole production to the Metropole and diversified their commercial outlets, French banks had to commit themselves to the financing of these flows between the empire and foreign countries. The 'colonial pact' was therefore often short-circuited, for the sake of developing the added value of French imperial productions. Morocco exported its phosphates to the US and Indochina exported its rice to Hong Kong, while silk traders bought raw silk for their Lyon basis and for other countries (Italy, the UK and the US, for instance). As such, the British Indian empire opened windows of opportunities for some trade, with CNEP as French tool there.[38] The predominance of the principles of economic reality thus prevailed, fueled by some pathways of open economy. In exchange for the cash earned as a result of these exports, banks had to manage the transfers of means of payment between international places, purchasing bills to be swapped against other ones back in Europe or in Shanghai or Hong Kong.

Imperial banking thus couldn't avoid being transformed into international banking, as 'multinational traders'[39] were partners and French harbours connected, at the same time, to foreign port-cities and imperial ones.[40] *Banque de l'Indochine* tackled large amounts of bills from China to Europe, and back, but also used the French–American Banking Corporation (set up in 1919), its co-affiliate CNEP, to manage its business of bills remittances, documentary credit and FOREX with New York, for the account of its French (or other) customers in the Chinese concessions. From Paris, bodies involved in imperial banking entertained large wheels of correspondent banking all over Europe (London, Anvers, Brussels, etc.), Asia (Japan, Eastern Russia) and America. Imperial banking could not have lived long without such nodes of correspondent banking – even with banks at 'rival' companies and capitalism (in Hamburg, or elsewhere). In the Far East, French and British banks were at the same time competitors and co-operators, as they had to share means of payment, exchange and refinancing, along complementary bodies.[41] In Table 1.1, the simplified scheme of goods, commodities, and money flows involving the *Banque de l'Indochine* Hong Kong branch[42] confirms such a perception of reality:

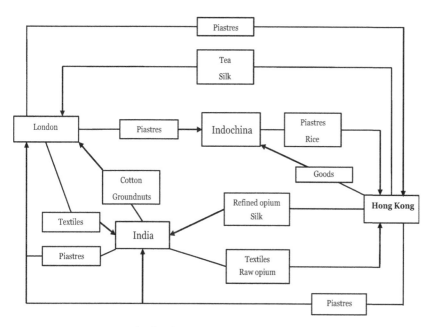

Figure 1.1: The Circuit of Bills of Exchange and Piastres within *Banque De Indochine* Offshoots

Imperial Investment Banking

The last section of this chapter will evoke the financial flows themselves, organized and managed by the metropolitan banks as leverage for the creation and modernization of the economic infrastructures overseas. In parallel with the exports of capital abroad, the art of 'project financing' in the colonial empire took shape, following the programmes of investment conceived by the State, and the Governorships, or, sometimes, by industrialists. Several investments were financed thanks to tax collection or, after World War II, State bodies and funds. But banks were involved in the issuing of bonds by the State or the Colonies: after the creation of the *Afrique occidentale française* (hereafter AOF), where the Government of the Federation issued bonds, FRF 100million, as in 1907, which commercial banks brokered in their metropolitan networks – CNEP, the *Crédit lyonnais*, *Société générale*, and the *Crédit algérien*.

Layers of successive bonds were designed by the syndicate of bankers to mobilize European savings in favour of electrification[43] and dams, railways[44] and harbours, whilst they also pledged the issuing of equities of durable, or, sometimes, speculative, companies oriented towards the valuation (officially named '*mise en valeur*') of the empire, with a few industries,[45] several wholesale trade firms and banks. Specialized imperial banks, like *Banque de l'Indochine, Banque industrielle de Chine* (for a very few projects in the Far East), the *Crédit algérien*, or, after World War II, *Banque industrielle d'Afrique du Nord*, were thus seriously involved in 'industrial banking' – granting middle term loans to friendly companies – or organizing issuances. But they were joined by the French investment banks, with a few merchant banks (from the Haute banque), Mirabaud and Rothschild, Worms (after World War II) and, of course, the big *banques d'affaires* Paribas and *Banque de l'union parisienne*.[46] Each one entertained its own circle of companionship, although their whole community often shared operations, because such overseas projects could appear as adventurous. In each territory and/or activity, there were 'confederations' of business interests dedicated to the colonial empire. And, because of the crisis of the 1930s, banks ended holding stakes in clouds of failing firms; *Banque de l'Indochine* evolved therefore as an investment bank in addition to its traditional activities in money and commercial banking; *Banque de l'union parisienne* emerged from the 1930s–1940s as a nod to imperial interests; and Rothschild was deeply involved in colonial mining and, in the 1950s, in oil.[47]

Imperial Bankers

The portfolio of activities of the 'imperial bankers' was somewhat classical: their intervention was displayed in favour of several customers and partners, whether state institutions, private companies or individual customers (migrants, expatriates and native elites).

Table 1.2: The Various Basic Functions of the French Imperial Banking System

	Commercial Banks and, also, Banks of Issue	Central Banks	Commercial Banks	Banks of Issue and Commercial Banks	Investment Banks and Departments of Investment Banking at Commercial Banks
For the State, Public Bodies and the Army	Management of means of payment	Management of the monetary system	–	–	Issuing securities
For Industrial and Commercial Companies	Management of means of payment	Management of the monetary system	Granting loans	Management of foreign exchange	Issuing securities
For Commodities Trading Houses	Management of means of payment	Management of the monetary system	Granting loans, delivering collaterals, managing warranting and documentary credits	Management of foreign exchange	–

	Commercial Banks and, also, Banks of Issue	Central Banks	Commercial Banks	Banks of Issue and Commercial Banks	Investment Banks and Departments of Investment Banking at Commercial Banks
For the Development of Infrastructures	Transfers of payments	–	–	–	Issuing securities
For Individuals	Transfer of the remittances by expatriates towards the Metropole; transfer of remittances in favour of emigrants in the Metropole	Management of the monetary system	Granting loans	Management of foreign exchange	–

All in all, imperial bankers were to be found on three levels. First, they constituted a community of specialists who managed the colonial banks (central banks, commercial banks, even investment banks) overseas, in direct contact with the field of imperial business. *Banque de l'Indochine*, *Crédit foncier d'Algérie et de Tunisie,* and the *Compagnie algérienne* exemplify such institutions. These developments offered opportunities for interesting careers, fuelled a relevant portfolio of skills, inserted managers within the business communities of each port-city where they were embedded for a few years. Some of these bankers became bigwigs within their banks, evolving to higher responsibilities, even as General Inspectors or in top jobs at the Paris headquarters – as revealed in the studies by H. Bonin into *Crédit foncier d'Algérie et de Tunisie* and the *Compagnie algérienne* and by M. Meuleau into *Banque de l'Indochine*.

A second layer of bankers was constituted by commercial bankers active in the branches of the big metropolitan banks and their affiliates or offshoots in the UK, Brussels or Geneva and, later on, in the US. They were highly specialized in documentary credits, refinancing or bringing collaterals, warrantage, and FOREX. They also built up an intimate knowledge of the business communities all along the chain of trade with the empire, from or to its port-cities, because they had to foresee the evolution of the firms, their risks, and the value of their inventories or cargoes. All these bankers remained low-key managers, as unknown key forces of imperial banking.

A third group was comprised of the top managers of the commercial, investment or merchant banks, who were committed to overseas and colonial business, generally in connection with big business. They were part of the 'colonial community', mixing politics, business, finance, and information, and were connected to the informal 'colonial party' and with the '*Bureaux*' which, within the ministries, held the tool-box to orient the programmes of modernization and investment. Some kind of a lobby of imperial bankers[48] did take shape, easily denounced by anticapitalists and anticolonialists. But the successive forms of this group did also contribute to provide refinancing to commercial and colonial banks, credit to commercial firms, trust in the operations overseas. They were not ever focused on 'economic patriotism' or on the defence of the *chasses gardées* of the Colonial Pact; their connections all over Europe, in New York and in Japan, helped in structuring correspondant banking at the service of imperial business and colonial exports and imports. They were indeed key leverage forces of 'the business of empire',[49] as influential as industrialist groups, shipping and transit firms,[50] or business lobbies.

'Imperial banking' might at first seem a far-fetched concept, as the skills and activities of bankers had always been similar across the various places and markets, and they had traditionally entertained broad arrays of connections. Despite this, taking an active role in the colonial empires necessitated the defining of new types of portfolios of skills, mainly surrounding the risks to face, the difficulties to mobilize economic intelligence, the speculative moods of the commodities traders, the intense variations of the values of goods to be sent overseas, and the issue of the value of inventories as pledges to loans. All of these were issues that had often be a far more worrying concern for bankers than their ordinary business in developed and industrialized countries. Archives, correspondence between the Paris headquarters and the branches abroad, the cases of bad loans and the crisis all prove that working as an imperial banker demanded a specific art of banking.

Within the 'economic colonial system', being that of France or another colonialist country, imperial banking therefore played its role as a bridge between pockets of purchase power in the colonies – of the expatriates, It can clearly be concluded that French imperial banking could not have been conceived without the other imperial banking systems, due to the fact that French bankers tackling the overseas business worked intimately with their counterparts, correspondents, and refinancers in other places, often (for the Far East) New York, as they were in the midst of large networks of correspondent banking, collaterals, FOREX, and refinancing services. Imperial banking had thus ever been a Europeanized system imperial banking, extended to US and Japanese offshoots.

2 CORRESPONDENT BANKING NETWORKS AND BRANCH ACTIVITIES IN 'IMPERIAL BANKING': THE RUSSO-CHINESE BANK IN SHANGHAI IN 1902

Kazuhiko Yago

In the theory and practice of international banking, the conventional view is that establishing a correspondent network by a bank on the one hand and establishing its own branches abroad on the other are two contradictory strategies. Geoffrey Jones, for example, in referring to the strategy of the nineteenth-century private banks, explains that 'correspondent or independent agent-type relationships provided a profitable means of engaging in international banking without the risks often associated with owning branches abroad'.[1] This conventional view is also consistent with the 'internalisation theory' of multinational enterprises.[2] Of course, the views of Jones in his book and the aims of contributors that followed were to cast doubt on this explanation, 'Why, then, did banks set up branches abroad?'

This conventional view, however, can be criticized based on the historical evidence of international banking in Asia. In fact, the international banks of the great powers in Asia, especially in China, were competing with each other over branch activities, but *at the same time* cooperating through correspondent networks. Correspondent networks spread not only within the branches of Western banks, but also among indigenous networks of local financial institutions. Thus it is possible to revise the above question posed by Jones as to 'why banks set up branches abroad *and also* maintained their correspondent networks?'

This chapter aims to present an alternative historical view based on the case of the Shanghai branch activities of the Russo-Chinese Bank (*Banque russo-chinoise, Русско-Китайский Банк*).[3] Founded in 1896 through French and Russian initiatives, it was one of the largest banks in the world at the time, in terms of its total balance sheet. Headquartered in Saint-Petersburg, it constructed a huge network of branches and offices in Russia and overseas: to begin with Shanghai, various ports and cities in China and Japan, but also in Calcutta, Paris and San

Francisco. It was involved in French and Russian lending to the Qing dynasty, offered financial facilities to Western enterprises in China and, above all, contributed to trade financing. The bank was dissolved in 1909 after a management crisis and then reorganized into the Russo-Asiatic Bank (*Banque russo-asiatique, Русско-Азиатский Банк*), but provides a wealth of experience in branch activities through its archival records. Shanghai was, and still is today, the most outstanding port city and business centre of China. Opened as a treaty port following the Nanjing Treaty of 1842, Shanghai grew as a global city where the head offices and branches of international banks were located, including that of HSBC, Chartered Bank and *Comptoir national d'escompte de Paris* (hereafter, CNEP). Thus active in a foreign concession imposed by the Treaty Ports rule, the Russo-Chinese Bank is a relevant case study of imperial banking, mobilizing international banking in favour of its development in the port-city of Shanghai, at times when the Powers imposed their imperial rule over China.

In this chapter, the first section gives an overview of the Russo-Chinese Bank, followed by a section which presents an analysis of the Shanghai branch balance sheet of the bank. The third section discusses historical documents concerning the local financial agents of the Russo-Chinese Bank Shanghai branch. Since the whereabouts of the full archival records of the Shanghai branch balance sheet is still unknown, this chapter focuses on the records for the fiscal year 1902, which are available in a complete form.

The Russo-Chinese Bank: A General View

This section deals with the origins, the governance structure and the management scale of the Bank. The origin of the Russo-Chinese Bank dates back to the Sino-Japanese War (1894–95).[4] After defeat in this war, the Chinese Qing dynasty debited a huge amount of indemnity. To help with the payment of this sum, the French and Russian banks organized a syndicate for the acceptance of the Chinese loans.[5] The Russian Finance Minister Sergei Witte proposed the setting up of a bank to handle the loans promoted by this Franco-Russian syndicate. In response to Witte's plan, the Petersburg International Bank, on the part of the Russians, and the *Banque de Paris et des Pays-Bas*, on the part of the French, concluded the raising of the funds to establish the Russo-Chinese Bank. It opened for business in St Petersburg on 21 January 1896.[6]

Besides the loan syndicate operations, other motives prompted the opening of the Bank: first of all, to help in the construction of the Trans-Siberian Railway, which had been under way since 1891. The intention of establishing the Russo-Chinese Bank was to handle the loans and provide financial services, as well as to undertake the management of the railway. The second motive was to finance trade between Russia and China. In those days, Russia exported hemp products such as sacks, twine and linen, petroleum, as well as pig iron to China, and in return imported tea from China via Hankow. Russian merchants, however, had to rely on foreign banks, mainly the Hong Kong & Shanghai Banking Corporation (hereafter HSBC), for payments due in these exchanges. It was this situation that led to the establishment of an international bank representing Russian commercial interests in China.[7] In fact, China was the third largest exporter to Russia from 1898 to 1912. The major export goods from China to Russia consisted of tea, whose value amounted to 41.3 million rubles (85.5% of the total tea imports of Russia) in 1903, 51.4 million rubles (76%) in 1908, and 39.9 million rubles (67.3%) in 1912.[8]

Of the founding capital, which amounted to 6 million rubles, the Franco-Belgian Bank syndicate took a majority share of 5/8.[9] At the beginning, the French influence was thus dominant. In August 1896, the Chinese Government paid up 5 million *kouping taels* of 'entrusted capital' as a resource for the construction of the Eastern Chinese Railway, following the Sino-Russian agreement. This huge sum was the only 'capital' that the Qing dynasty paid for a foreign company in its more than 300-year reign, but yet the Chinese government had no say in the management of the Bank. In 1898, on the occasion of a capital increase of up to 9 million roubles, the Russian National Bank took over a whole series of an additional 12,000 shares and thus took up the majority of the issued stock. From this year on, the Russian stakeholders held a leading position in the governance of the Bank. At least from 1898 on, the governance of the Russo-Chinese Bank was dominated by Russian interests, and it came to be a Russian international bank instead of a French one.

Figure 2.1 shows the development of its operations from 1897 (the year following its foundation) to 1909 (the year before its restructuring) by the balance sheet total. This figure also indicates the considerable contribution of branch activities to the balance sheet total. In 1897, for instance, deposits collected by the branches accounted for 80 percent of the total deposits of the bank. In 1909, when the contribution of the branches to deposits marked the lowest in the history of the bank, the rate still stayed over 50 percent. What is noteworthy from the viewpoint of this chapter is that the most successful branches in terms of deposit collection and profit gain were also those that had been Chinese branches headed by the Shanghai branch. Moreover, the Shanghai branch was the only branch to issue banknotes in the Russo-Chinese Bank: the rouble banknote issued by the branch circulated not only around the city of Shanghai, but also in North-East China and Korea.[10] Eventually, after the heavy debt caused by the cotton crises in Russia, the Russo-Chinese Bank merged with the Northern Bank (*Severnii Bank*) in 1909 to become the Russo-Asiatic Bank. The Shanghai branch of the Russo-Chinese Bank was also closed after the restructuring of the bank.

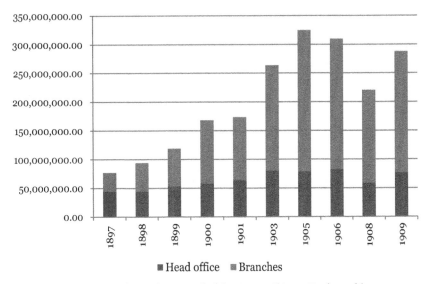

Figure 2.1: Balance Sheet Total of the Russo-Chinese Bank, roubles

Source: Отчет по операциям Русско-Китайского банка за 1897–1909 гг. СПб., 1898–1910

The Activities of the Shanghai Branch in 1902: Balance Sheet Analysis

An analysis of the branch balance sheet is indispensable in order to examine the branch activities in detail. The 1902 balance sheet is utilized here since it was thoroughly recorded compared to other years.

Assets and Liabilities Overview

Table 2.1 is a breakdown of the assets account of the Shanghai branch balance sheet as of 13 December 1902.

Table 2.1: Shanghai Branch Assets Account in December 1902

Assets	in Shanghai taels	%
Cash	1,626,656.64	5.62
Head Office General a/c	1,178,206.10	4.07
Inward Bills	2,418,654.54	8.36
Outward Bills	6,709,020.96	23.19
Bills for collection	2,472,322.07	8.55
Correspondents 'Nostro'	1,769,914.82	6.12
Correspondents 'Loro'	609,346.19	2.11
a/c with branches	2,035,819.61	7.04

Assets	in Shanghai taels	%
a/c with Shanghai branches	4,246,223.88	14.68
Current a/c	2,543,369.28	8.79
Loan a/c against native orders	2,028,472.37	7.01
Others	1,291,909.31	4.47
Total	28,929,915.77	100.00

Source: RGIA St. Petersburg, F632-O1-D578

The largest share is accounted for by 'Outward bills', which expresses the importance of trade settlements in the branch activities. The composition of these outward bills is shown on Table 2.2, which indicates the receivers of the bills sent from the Shanghai branch. The bills that had been expressed in several currencies were converted into Shanghai taels by the branch itself. It is thus possible to examine the share of each institution in the chart. After the 'Outward bills' two accounts follow, the 'a/c with Shanghai branches' and 'Current Accounts'. The sum of the three largest accounts adds up to more than half the amount of the total assets account. As for the 'Current Accounts', 89 percent of which are overdrawn accounts, 7 percent is the Shanghai taels account and 4 percent the dollar account. The 'Loan a/c against native orders' includes loan operations against compradors, the details of which are examined in the third section.

Table 2.2: Shanghai Branch Liabilities Account in December 1902

Liabilities	in Shanghai taels	%
Dotation a/c	10,583,603.60	36.58
Banknotes Dept. a/c	949,803.55	3.28
Head Office a/c	908,914.71	3.14
Acceptance a/c	671,192.51	2.32
Correspondents 'Nostro'	5,951,931.98	20.57
Correspondents 'Loro'	158,342.26	0.55
Fixed Deposits a/c	1,003,758.22	3.47
Current a/c	5,328,369.07	18.42
Collection a/c	2,472,322.07	8.55
Interest a/c	140,517.24	0.49
Others	3,373,999.87	11.66
Total	28,929,915.77	100.00

Source: RGIA St. Petersburg, F632-O1-D578

The largest item is the 'Dotation a/c', which is the sum distributed to the branch from the head office. The original dotation at the head office, as mentioned in the first section above, consists of 'entrusted capital' paid by the Qing dynasty as well as paid up capital. The second largest item in the liabilities account of the branch is the Correspondents 'Nostro' account, which indicates the net liabilities of the Bank to correspondents converted from rubles. Of the 'Current a/c', which is the third account, 93 percent is accounted for by the Shanghai taels account, 3 percent by the dollar account and the rest by the ruble account. The 'Banknotes Department a/c' consists of dollar banknotes, copper cash notes in circulation and Kouping taels notes.

The above overview of the Shanghai branch balance sheet explains the level of active management by the branch: depending upon the capital distribution from the head office, the branch developed local loan activities as well as trade finances. The branch was also active in collecting local deposits in Shanghai taels. The following charts demonstrate the branch activities in more detail.

Outward Bills and Correspondent Accounts

Table 2.3 shows the outward bills drawn by the branch, in debit and credit figures and their net balance in taels. The net balance of 6,709,020.96 rubles corresponds to the 'Outward Bills' account in the assets account (Table 2.1). The 'Foreign Values' expressed in various currencies are converted into Shanghai taels in the original document, although the exchange rates are not indicated. In this chart, the head office received the bills either in pounds sterling or in Russian rubles and other currencies. These currencies were added together in taels, the head office held more than a 50 percent share of all the outward bills account. The second largest share is taken up by 'CNEP Lyon', which is the Lyon branch of CNEP, the third French major deposit bank. It should be noted that the above figures are net ones, after subtraction between the 'debit' and 'credit' columns. From this 'movement' point of view, the head office outward bills in pounds sterling has a particular feature with a high record either on the 'debit' or 'credit' side, while the 'CNEP Lyon' account has much higher 'debit' figure than the 'credit' one. This contrast between the head office account and the CNEP account would possibly explain the content of the outward bills, the former including the remittances of the branch profits to the head office, while the latter representing exclusively the trade balance between China and France.

Table 2.3: Outward Bills of the Shanghai branch, 13 December 1902

Portfolio		Debit Balance			Movement in taels	
		Foreign Values	In taels	%	Debit	Credit
Head office	£	380056-7-0	3,079,109.21	45.90	8,806,657.01	5,727,547.80
Ladenberg, Thalmann & C°, New York	£	1257-12-2	10,776.86	0.16	10,952.20	175.34
Paris Agency	Frs	847,578.63	269,564.17	4.02	1,010,380.08	740,815.91
CNEP Lyon Clean Bills	Frs	1,007,616.03	336,798.34	5.02	437,194.77	100,396.43
CNEP Lyon Documentary bills	Frs	4,480,491.11	1,476,530.50	22.01	2,303,027.00	826,496.50
Chablières, Morel & C°, Marseille	Frs	325,180.44	110,019.86	1.64	209,200.17	99,180.31

Portfolio		Debit Balance			Movement in taels	
		Foreign Values	In taels	%	Debit	Credit
Société de crédit suisse, Zurich	Frs	–	–	–	–	–
Deutsche Bank, Tsingtau	$	–	–	–	–	–
Head office	Rbls	1,002,657.27	903,899.80	*13.47*	1,276,697.73	372,797.93
Vladivostok Agency	Rbls	61,431.99	53,032.55	*0.79*	128,938.73	75,906.18
Head office	Mks	551,231.09	221,954.89	*3.31*	670,462.85	448,507.96
Ladenberg, Thalmann & Cº, New York	G.$	121,006.67	208,450.90	*3.11*	220,123.28	11,672.38
Banque impériale otto-mane, Amsterdam	£	1244-1-7	10,726.88	*0.16*	13,312.95	2,586.07
Liebmann Rosenthal	£	462-14-8	4,204.70	*0.06*	5,934.43	1,729.73
Liebmann Rosenthal	FLS	62,843.50	23,952.30	*0.36*	26,719.79	2,767.49
Total			6,709,020.96	*100.00*		

Source: RGIA St. Petersburg, F632-O1-D578

Table 2.4 indicates the structure of another important account, the Correspondents 'Nostro' account. This account has a relatively small proportion of the accounts in Table 2.1, however, it is only the net figure after summing up the 'debits' and 'credits' of the correspondents. The largest debtor among the 'nostro' correspondents is the CNEP Calcutta branch, which accounts for about 41 percent of the net debtor balance. Together with the CNEP Bombay branch, the Indian offices of this French deposit bank played an outstanding role as a correspondent of the Shanghai branch of the Russo-Chinese Bank. It was in 1908 that the Russo-Chinese bank opened a branch in Bombay, so that in 1902 the bank needed a correspondent relationship with CNEP branches in India. On the creditor side, the largest share is taken up by Glyn, Mills, Currie & Co. London,[11] one of the major British clearing banks, with a sum equivalent to more than 4,740,959 taels, accounting for approximately 87 percent of the total creditor balance.

This net figure, a product of subtraction between the debit of more than 23,331,749 taels and the credit of 28,072,709 taels, is larger than the debit balance of the outward bills for the head office account (see Table 2.3 above). Behind the net figure of the 'nostro' account, it is thus possible to observe the considerable effect of the correspondents, as both debtors and creditors, on the Shanghai branch. Another point of our findings was that these important correspondents were either French or British Banks: this fact suggests the strong trade relationship inward and outward from China with these banks operating in areas of imperial influence.

Table 2.4: Correspondents 'Nostro' accounts of the Shanghai branch, 13 December 1902

		Balances in foreign values	Balances in taels				Movement in taels	
			Debtors	%	Creditors	%	Debit	Credit
Banque de l'Indochine, Hongkong	HK$	93.43	70.38	0.00			1,705.32	1,634.94
Banque de l'Indochine, Saigon	S$	12,769.86	9,370.30	0.58			14,530.47	5,160.17
Borneo & Co., Singapore	S$	6,418.02			4,812.03	0.09	5,479.64	10,291.67
Butterfield & Swire, Foochow	F$	3,305.12	2,460.67	0.15			2,913.23	452.56
Butterfield & Swire, Swatou	Shanghai taels							
Chabrières, Morel & Cº, Marseille	Frs	29,097.04	8,109.38	0.50			184,826.55	176,717.17
CNEP London	£	1309-2-8			10,327.29	0.19	3,465.58	13,792.87
CNEP Manchester	£	4456-8-1	39,276.84	2.43			39,276.84	849,145.56
CNEP Lyon	Frs	317,996.38	124,763.34	7.72			973,908.90	8,322,009.23
CNEP Bombay	Rps	636304-9-11	458,585.12	28.39			8,780,594.35	2,093,103.59
CNEP Calcutta	Rps	1069314-9-6	665,036.83	41.18			2,758,140.42	
CNEP San Francisco	G$	2,538.14	549.29	0.03			233,260.94	232,711.65
Deutsche Bank (Berlin) London Agency	£	236-12-2	2,041.11	0.13			2,041.11	
Glyn, Mills, Currie & Co., London	£	529958-10-1			4,740,959.98	87.37	23,331,749.49	28,072,709.47
Heidelbach Ickelmeier & Co., NY	G$	192.76	339.66	0.02			339.66	
Holme Ringer & C, Chemulpo	yen	33,826.12	29,733.69	1.84			33,118.03	3,384.34
National City Bank of NY Joint A/c	G$	3,029.26			6,539.00	0.12	157,920.51	164,459.51
Netherland Trading Cº, Singapore	S$							
J.M.Robertson & Cº, Columbo	Rps							
Lippmann, Rosenthal & Cº, Amsterdam	FLS	25,323.45	17,590.62	1.09			18,521.12	930.50
Samuel Montagu, London	£	17745-14-11	152,367.16	9.43			383,290.76	230,923.60
I. Henry Schroeder, London	£	4693-8-11			35,861.75	0.66	520,965.04	556,826.79
Société de crédit suisse, Zurich	frs	46.50	15.84	0.00			15.84	
Ladenburg Thalmann, NY	G$	6,554.87			9,513.78	0.18	374,929.69	384,443.47
Guarantee Trust NY, Hongkong	A$	248,640.46	71,568.16	4.43			7,360,640.75	7,289,072.59
Inchbald, London	£	10-5-5			26.07	0.00	1,708.82	1,734.89
Stcherbatchoff Schechoff, Columb	£	11-0-0	95.83	0.01			601.54	505.71
Glyn Mills & Currie, Deposit a/c	£	5047-2-7	33,155.83	2.05			551,920.76	518,764.93
National City Bank nº2 A/c	G$	347,628.18			617,961.17	11.39	142,188.19	760,149.36
Total			1,615.130.05	100.00	5.426.00.01	100.00	45,878,053.55	49,688,924.57

Source: RGIA St. Petersburg, F632-O1-D578

How about the Correspondents 'loro' accounts? The features that are slightly different from the 'nostro' account are shown in Table 2.5 below. The largest account in terms of debtor balances is the 'Guaranty Trust Company of New York, Hong Kong', followed by the 'Shansi Railway Preliminary Expenses a/c'. Those two accounts together represent over 78 percent of the debtor balances. The former Guaranty Trust account shows active transactions in terms of 'movement', on both the debit and credit sides, while the latter Shansi Railway account appears only in the creditors balance. As for the creditors balance, the largest item is the *'Fonds d'emprunt Société d'études'*, of which the details are unknown, but related to the plan to set up a project financing structure for the railway. The 'Glyn, Mills & Currie C° n°2 a/c' comes next, then the 'Chinese Eastern Railway' and 'Guaranty Trust C° of New York, Manila' follow. It is noteworthy that Glyn, Mills & Currie has only a 20 percent share of the net balance, though in terms of 'movement', it represents a large sum in both the debit and credit accounts. The above three charts incarnate the active management by the Shanghai Branch in terms of trade finance, not only through its proper bills drawing, but also through its correspondent relationships, especially with international banks of the imperial powers.

Table 2.5: Correspondents 'Loro' Accounts of the Shanghai Branch, 13 December 1902

		Balances in foreign values	Balances in taels				Movement in taels	
			Debtors	%	Creditors	%	Debit	Credit
American Trading Co.	G.$							
Bank of China and Japan, Hongkong	Tls							
Banque de l'Indo-Chine, Hongkong	Tls				1,100.16	0.69	28.00	1,128.16
L.R.Burkhardt	Frs	164,377.75	55,898.22	9.17			69,789.96	13,891.74
Chancellerie de Credit	$							
Chancellerie de Credit, Silver a/c Poods	Tls							
Chinese Imperial Railway Administration	£							
Chinese Eastern Railway	Rbls	32,439.98			29,225.20	18.46		29,225.20
Chinese Imperial Railway Administration	Tls				4,343.77	2.74		4,343.77
A.Ebrahim and Co	Rps							
Fonds Emprunt Société d'études	Tls				35,641.32	22.51		35,641.32
Netherlands Trading Society, Singapore	Tls				3,732.06	2.36		3,732.06
E.Pabaney	Rps							
Russian Post Office Administration	Rbls	263.27			245.37	0.15	3,568.14	3,813.51
E.Sacharoff	G.$	10,084.24			17,769.58	11.22		17,769.58
Shansi Railway	Tls				8,250.08	5.21	82,237.29	90,487.37
P.E.Lintilhec (Unpaid bills)	£	7494-15-1	64,055.62	10.51			69,349.57	5,293.95
P.E.Lintilhec (Unpaid bills)	FLS	9,784.70			3,333.80	2.11		3,333.80
L.R.Burkhardt	G.$							
R.S.N.Talati and Co.Cr 427	Rps							
Shing Lai Co, Yoko.Cr.209	Rps	186-12-9			105.59	0.07		106.59
Shansi Railway Preliminary Expenses a/c	Tls		207,427.50	34.04			207,427.50	
Guaranty Trust Co. of NY, Hongkong	Tls		269,025.12	44.15			954,703.98	685,678.86
The National Bank of China Hongkong	Tls							

	Balances in foreign values	Balances in taels				Movement in taels	
		Debtors	%	Creditors	%	Debit	Credit
Chancelier du crédit du ministère des Finances St Petersburg	$ 2,989.28	1,840.67	0.30			5,055.28	3,214.61
Guaranty Trust Co. of NY, Manila	Tls			24,125.03	15.24	300,063.58	324,188.61
Shansi Railway n°2 a/c	Tls	7,652.45	1.26			7,652.45	
H. Loptin	£ 39-11-3	45.02	0.01				1,168.67
Maurice Cuvelier	Y.$						
Glyn Mills Currie n°2 a/c	£ 5046-12-7			30,469.30	19.24	2,383,803.03	2,414,272.33
Choisy Simson	£ 128-18-3	1,028.09	0.17			7,901.23	6,873.14
National Bank of China	Tls	2,373.50	0.39			70,838.80	68,465.30
Total		609,346.19	100.0	158,342.26	100.0	4,163,632.50	3,712,628.57

Source: RGIA St. Petersburg, F632-O1-D578

Accounts with the Branches

The accounts with the branches, both inside and outside Shanghai, are of particular interest since they represent the intra bank relations among the branches of the Russo-Chinese Bank. However, the data shown in Tables 2.6 and 2.7, which are monthly figures, do not correspond with any branches accounts on the general balance sheet in annual terms. Due to the lack of all the monthly figures, only a fragmented image of intra bank relations can be ascertained.

Table 2.6: Shanghai Account with the Branches, Original Accounts, Creditors, 13 November 1902

		Balance		Movement in Taels		Total balance of each group
		Foreign values	in Taels	Debit	Credit	
in China						
Chefoo	$	41,715.82	33,470.29	701,968.48	735,438.77	
Newchang	N.Taels	23,844.09	22,134.07	3,258,526.28	3,280,660.35	
Peking	P.Taels	2,548,049.21	2,720,965.12	1,397,398.79	4,118,363.91	2,776,569.48
in Japan						
Kobe	\	214,116.21	141,725.24	227,248.55	368,973.79	
Yokohama, Loro	Taels		75,853.29	4,821,782.29	4,897,635.58	217,578.53
in Mandchourie						
Harbin, Loro	Taels		942,096.17	1,587,841.62	2,529,937.79	
Ourga, Loro	Rbles	13,893.13	12,800.78	1,977.45	14,778.23	954,896.95
in Siberia						
Irkoutsk, Loro	Rbles	51,845.98	46,254.24	122,798.59	169,052.83	
Vladivostok, Loro	$	18,772.05	14,174.14	12,335.46	26,509.60	
Vladivostok, Loro	Taels		211,135.12	2,366,620.36	2,577,755.48	271,563.50
Vladivostok, Provisional	Rbles	345,170.17	311,021.41	3,549.16	314,570.57	311,021.41
Total				14,502,047.03	19,033,676.90	4,531,629.87

Table 2.7: Shanghai Accounts with the Branches, 13 December 1902

		Balance		Movement in taels		Total balance of each group
		Foreign values	in taels	Debit	Credit	
in China						
Chefoo	$	34,216.83	28,805.39	909,889.50	938,694.89	
Hankow	H.Taels	164,697.82	176,954.36	4,251,252.43	4,428,206.79	
Newchang	N.Taels	174,231.13	176,461.21	3,834,111.03	4,010,572.24	
Peking	P.Taels	2,734,509.01	2,914,189.92	1,875,581.89	4,789,771.81	
Dalny	Rbles		40,494.95	1,485,310.07	1,525,805.02	3,336,905.83
in Japan						
Yokohama, Loro	Taels		130,281.12	4,892,206.58	5,022,487.70	130,281.12
in Mandchourie						
Harbin, Loro	Taels		475,678.63	2,900,290.26	3,375,968.89	
Ourga, Loro	Rbles	15,763.46	14,607.86	1,977.45	16,585.31	490,286.49
in Siberia						

		Balance		Movement in taels		Total balance of each group
		Foreign values	in taels	Debit	Credit	
Irkoutsk, Loro	Rbles	30,672.71	26,942.98	145,344.46	172,287.44	
Vladivostok, Loro	$	23,528.22	17,672.31	16,210.10	33,882.41	
Vladivostok, Loro	Taels		215,801.84	3,201,033.98	3,416,835.82	
Vladivostok, Provisional	Rbles		311,070.14			260,417.13
Total				25,313,207.75	27,731,098.32	4,217,890.57

Source: RGIA St. Petersburg, F632-O1-D578

Tables 2.6 and 2.7 show the close relations between the Shanghai branch and the Peking (Beijing) branch in net figures. In gross figures, however, the other Chinese branches like Hankow and Newchang, as well as the Japanese branch of Yokohama and the Russian branch in Vladivostok also have high records. The Peking branch as well as the Harbin branch demonstrates a large imbalance between the credit and debit movement accounts. Imbalances in the accounts at these two branches influence the imbalance of the accounts between the Chinese branches as a whole and the Shanghai branch.

The Russo-Chinese Bank's Relations with Local Financial Agents: The Role of the Shanghai Branch

Depending upon the above analysis of the accounting records of the branches, the relations between the Russo-Chinese Bank and the local financial agents will be investigated through the archival records of the Shanghai branch. Local financial agents in China, compradors and other native banks, played important roles in relation to international banks: negotiating loans, issuing chop loans, and even drawing and discounting bills. These agents were often small and worked in a close network unknown to outsiders. The Russo-Chinese Bank, to cope with this variety of local financial agents, asked each branch to send their information to the head office, especially as regards the bad debts of the agents. This section examines their information through letters sent from the Chinese branches to the head office, which were found in the BNP Paribas Historical Archives in Paris.

Through the archival documents of the branches, originally written in French, it is possible to observe the important roles played by the Shanghai branch. One typical example is referred to in the auditing report on the Beijing branch of the Russo-Chinese Bank dated January 1908:

> 50,000 taels loan to Han Loz Dza Pu has been guaranteed with the permission of the head office and the intervention of the Russian Ministry of Finance. Whether any reserve fund would be necessary, and whether we should ask for instructions from the head office, are up to the decision of the Shanghai office.

The Shanghai branch was the 'head branch' in China governing the loan policies of other Chinese branches. Another example: '50,000 taels loan to Marquis Li has been covered by his time deposit in the Shanghai branch, which is superior to this sum',

> 2,000 taels loan to Comte Po-Yun-Chuk, 19,460 taels loan to Comte Su. These loans fall due in a few days. The Shanghai branch is to supervise the above process, and cover the loan with the reserve on the balance sheet of the Peking branch in case of failure.[12]

The above document clearly demonstrates the role played by the Shanghai branch as a supervisor and a reserve manager of the loans to the local agents.

Another example is that of the Tientsin branch in 1908, which shows a similar picture of the role of the Shanghai branch. The documents complain that the Tientsin branch Manager Murray-Campbell had given a loan to two doubtful lenders, Dallas & C° and Leykauff, despite a previous refusal of the loan by the Shanghai branch. As a result, the report says, the two loans have never been repaid and turned into bad debts.[13] This episode tells us the superiority of the information that the Shanghai branch had over that of the Tientsin branch.

Table 2.8: Hankow Branch Bad Debts, in taels (December 1907–January 1908)

Lenders	12 December 1907	3 January 1908
Bavier & C°	51,534.00	34,177.00
Carlowitz & Co	24,208.00	36,103.00
A. Grosjean & Co	9,702.00	8,648.00
Max Mittag & Co	10,829.00	5,409.00
Melchanoff, Pechatnoff	134,275.00	44,820.00
Racine Ackermann & Co	24,581.00	7,195.00
L. Vrard & Co.	89,952.00	89,952.00
Consul Ostreverkhoff	251.00	442.00
Total	345,332.00	226,746.00

Source: Archives of BNP Paribas, «Correspondance, Succursale de Hankow à la Banque russo-chinoise, St. Petersburg», s.d.

What are the final results of these bad debts? A report by the Hankow branch demonstrates the special role played by the Shanghai branch in dealing with bad debts. At the beginning of 1908, the Hankow branch listed the names and amounts of bad debt lenders as shown in Table 2.8. All of them were Russian and European dealers and agents, including a Russian Minister (vice-ambassador). What is important here is that the sum of the bad debts decreased between 12 December 1907 and 3 January 1908. The Hankow branch report says that 'these loans have been compensated for by bills drawn on the Shanghai branch. This operation was quite profitable for the Hankow branch'.[14] The intra-branch account, a part of which is shown in Table 2.8 above, was a route to settle the above Hankow-Shanghai operation.

How did these bad debts occur? The above Hankow branch report discloses the story.[15] The report was a reply to the Russo-Chinese Bank head office inquiry to the branch over the bad debts issue. The branch report states the reasons why the local agent's bankruptcy resides in the system of 'trade finance', one key activity of 'imperial banking':

- Exporters of Chinese tea, for example, before they purchase the goods for export, conclude an exchange contract with an international bank in China like the Russo-Chinese Bank.
- Once the contract is concluded, the exporter lends the current sum in local money to an international bank at the exchange rate fixed by the contract, against the payment for the goods delivered by local merchants and producers.
- Most of the goods, after delivery, go through production processes (drying and packaging of the tea, for example), which takes several days or even several months.
- The finished goods are dispatched to numerous destinations in Europe, and several Chinese agents deal with the process. These goods are shipped from riverside Hankow to Shanghai, waiting for a cargo ship to be filled with various goods.
- After the shipment, the exporter presents the bill of exchange with the bill of lading to the international bank. However, due to the upper limit on the total amount of a bill set by the exchange contract, the bills are often divided into smaller amounts.
- The problem is that the coincidence of the smaller amounts of the bill with the correct shipped goods is only certified by a monthly receipt called 'godown-orders'. The process of production being too complicated, no person in the branch of an international bank is able to check the 'godown-orders'.

In order to cover the risk from discrepancies in the 'godown-orders', the bank could ask for a premium of about 20 percent on the loan interest, but the premium makes the bank's position harder in terms of concurrence with the operations of other international banks. If the branch should strictly audit 'godown-orders', as the head office requires, 'we would have to close our offices'.

This document reveals the problems that the Hankow branch faced in trade finance business dealing with tea exports. Also important are the risk aversion of local agents and the weakness of international banks that could not manage their local business: the international banks were competing with each other in front of local merchants under unfavorable conditions. The role of the Shanghai branch was to cover the loss of the Hankow and other branches due to this competition.

The Shanghai branch itself faced the problem of improper transactions by local merchants and financial agents. In November 1908, a comprador Ni Pao Tien opened a deposit account in the Shanghai branch through the good offices of Murray-Campbell, the Tientsin branch manager of the Russo-Chinese Bank. This comprador then obtained a loan from the Tientsin branch for a fictitious salt trade on the security of the above deposit account in Shanghai, which was in fact empty. The final loss to the Russo-Chinese Bank amounted to 930,592 taels and the head office severely criticized the branch managers who could not avoid this case.[16]

Another case occurred in 1910, this time around Davidoff, the director of the Russo-Chinese Bank itself. According to the accusation presented to the Russian parliament Duma, the Russo-Chinese Bank, during the Russo-Japanese War, adopted a fictitious exchange rate in the remittance services of the Russian public fund. The exchange rate was in favor of the Russo-Chinese Bank at over 2–4 percent the normal rate, and Davidoff was responsible for these transactions. The Shanghai branch was the pivotal element of this fraud and the Russian government owed 5,038,389 roubles in debts to the Shanghai branch in 1906. Davidoff was also a suspect in dealings with other forms of swindling, and the affair developed into a political scandal.[17] And each case symbolizes a particular position of the Shanghai branch in supervising the branches in China and covering the losses due to bad debts. This position finally led to the unfair operations by Davidoff, which in turn brought improper profits to the branch.

Conclusion

The Russo-Chinese Bank was founded to perform multiple functions: investment, management of Russian interests abroad and trade finance. At the outset, the Bank was a genuine 'international bank', but later on it became a 'regional bank'. One of the factors that brought about this change was that the most profitable field of operations changed from international trade finance and settlements to domestic loan operations. The branch operations clearly reflected this change.[18] The Chinese branches headed by Shanghai were the most promising in terms of deposit collection and profits throughout the period of activity of the Bank, but the most profitable service was that of the provision of local credit via compradors, involving a high level of risk-taking. The Shanghai branch represented these Chinese branches of the Bank, which were profitable but with a risky lending policy.

Regarding Jones's thesis presented at the introduction of this chapter, it can be noted that branching was not the only strategy chosen by international banks: the Russo-Chinese Bank operated a strategy with two fronts, branching at the profitable centre on the one hand, but building a dense corresponding network with competing international banks on the other. In fact, the Shanghai branch established a close and active relationship with large British and French banks through discounting and correspondent operations. It should be highlighted that the balance sheet figures are net ones, while the branch documents often present far higher gross figures, inward or outward. The bills account of the head office seems to have represented the remittances of profits gained by the branches through their operations, expressed by these high gross figures. In this sense, the Shanghai branch of the Russo-Chinese Bank functioned as a commercial and financial intermediary between China and the rest of the world.

The branch archives show us another picture: the international banks not only had relations with each other through correspondent networks, but they also competed against each other in front of local merchants and financial agents. The competition was harsh and, as the Russo-Chinese Bank Hankow branch manager lamented, they even thought of withdrawing the branch. The Shanghai branch itself faced several cases of fraud, which means that the 'internalization' of information, in the case of international banking with Russian and French capital, could not overcome the information asymmetry. Neither branching, nor correspondent networks, could fully manage this asymmetry. Imperial banking, as in the case of the Russo-Chinese Bank's Shanghai branch, was particularly weak in dealing with local agents. To answer the question 'Why, then, did banks set up branches abroad *and also* maintained their correspondent networks?', it could be stated that the dual management of branching and correspondent networking was a negative strategy chosen by international banking under such circumstances.

3 COMPETING IMPERIAL BANKING: THE YOKOHAMA SPECIE BANK AND HSBC IN CHINA – 1919 AS A WATERSHED?

Niv Horesh

Over the last three decades, a considerable body of English-language academic work has shed much light on Japan's empire-building project in Greater China during the first half of the twentieth century. At the same time, Japanese-language studies of the country's pre-war financial history have also grown in leaps and bounds. Yet, to date, neither body of literature seems to have fully examined what might appear to the naked eye as one of the critical pre-war junctures: where Japanese financial history converged on imperial policy and Chinese nationalist responses thereto.[1] This chapter will therefore aim to fill *part* of the gap by examining how the Yokohama Specie Bank (hereafter YSB), arguably the backbone of Japanese finance in China Proper,[2] modelled itself on the British privately-run Hongkong & Shanghai Banking Corporation (hereafter HSBC, established in 1865), insofar as monetary emissions were concerned, and how both banks were affected by Chinese anti-foreign boycotts throughout the pre-war era (1842–1937).

It is crucial to stress right at the outset that the following passages will pursue the interplay between finance and empire through the prism of overseas bank-note circulation figures – a non-metropolitan prism not commonly employed in the pertinent literature. If anything, scholars have so far tended to focus on the impact of Chinese boycotts on Japanese manufacturing firms in the mid-1920s or later. Much *less* has been published on the fate of Japanese banks in China during that period. Moreover, to my knowledge no study in English, Japanese or Chinese specifically examined how Japanese banks fared in the Chinese market through the famous anti-Japanese boycott that broke out on 4 May 1919, commonly known nowadays as the May Fourth (*Wusi*) Movement. It is therefore hoped that this chapter – particularly when read in conjunction with recent ground-breaking studies by Richard Smethurst, Mark Metzler, Tomoyuki Taira and Michael Schiltz[3] – might lead to a more complete understanding of the monetary mind-set behind Japan's colonial policy.

This chapter argues that the *Wusi* boycott dealt a severe blow to the Yokohama Specie Bank's note issue in Shanghai in 1919. However, the longer-term effects of that boycott underscore demand-side pressures that could valuably tell us much more about the rising tide of nationalist sentiments in China than they suggest a 'mortal' threat to the bank's overall operations in pre-war East Asia. This is primarily because YSB banknote issuance in China Proper was limited both in terms of its share of total YSB liabilities and in terms of its volume compared with Japanese colonial bank circulation volumes elsewhere. In short, YSB banknotes in China were a means to an end: a 'managed currency' initially designed to support more important objectives like the amassing of local silver deposits and the facilitation of trade between Manchuria and China Proper.4

The five chapter sections that follow are organized thus: the first section will explore the circumstances which led to the establishment of the Yokohama Specie Bank and trace its China operations until 1919, with particular emphasis on banknote issuance; the second section will contextualize banknote issuance within more important YSB business ends. It will place particular emphasis on the bank's deposit-base as compared with other foreign and local banks operating in China; the third section will examine in detail the impact of the *Wusi* upheaval on the bank's overall operations, and compare its performance during this period with other phases of anti-foreign agitation in China during the 1920s and 1930s; and the last section will aim to isolate the net effect of the *Wusi* boycott from non-political factors that may also have impinged on circulation volumes that year. Finally, the conclusion will set out the historic significance of the YSB's banknote issuance in China Proper against the larger backdrop of Japanese colonial policy, and in the light of what is known about the performance of other foreign banks operating in pre-war China.

The Yokohama Specie Bank Before 1919

First envisioned by the renowned Meiji intellectual, Fukuzawa Yukichi, and modelled on the HSBC charter, the YSB was set up in 1880, two years *before* the establishment of Japan's lender of last resort, the Bank of Japan. In the 1870s, a large number of Japanese joint-stock banks had been authorized to issue notes domestically, but the Japanese government rejected the YSB's preliminary request to be allowed to issue paper money within Japan itself. Instead, Finance Minister Masayoshi Matsukata worked to create a central bank, the Bank of Japan, modelled on that of Belgium, a European economic latecomer whose specialized bank of issue (*Banque nationale de Belgique*, established in 1850) was strictly state-run.[5] At the same time, the YSB was tasked with banknote issuance in China, which was then one of a few nominally-sovereign countries where new foreign privately-run banks like HSBC could exercise extra-territorial privileges and issue notes with the approval of their home governments.[6]

To fully appreciate the circumstances in which the YSB was conceived it should be recalled that foreign banknote issuance in China Proper had only taken off in the early twentieth century because of a deep-seated, popular suspicion of fiduciary money there hitherto. Back in the 1870s, when a Japanese overseas bank along the lines of HSBC was first broached, Japan itself was still forced to abide by extra-territoriality which allowed for foreign banknote issuance on its very own soil. Yet, unlike imperial China's bureaucrats – who were subjected to similar 'unequal treaties' with the West but began opposing foreign banknote issuance *only* at the turn of the twentieth century – Japan's Meiji reformers sought to curtail foreign banks as early as the 1870s, when foreign (mostly British) note circulation volumes were still negligible.[7]

The British banks, on their part, were not encouraged at first by the low circulation volumes of their fiduciary notes in China and Japan. Because of the sunken printing costs of these notes, and a one-third bullion reserve requirement imposed by the British Treasury against notes outstanding, the future viability of note issuance looked uncertain compared with more profitable business such as issuing exchange bills. On 21 October 1875, HSBC's Shanghai branch manager, David McLean, suggested to senior colleague James Greig, for example, that reserve requirements would have to be made malleable if the note issue were to sustain itself:

> I should say it is hardly worthwhile continuing the issue of notes at Shanghai-the amount outstanding there is so small it won't pay if you have to keep 33% of the value [as reserve] in your treasury. [It is] a question whether it will pay to continue the issue in Yokohama. If you keep a third of the value then there is no necessity for your keeping so large an amount of your current accounts idle. Suppose Japan and yourself have 25 lacs of notes out, $833,000 would be ⅓ and if you kept 3 or 4 lacs more for current accounts this would be sufficient idle cash, the day has now arrived when you can work more closely being in daily communication by wire with us all and in a position to raise a lac or two when hard pressed. Of course when you happen to be so low in cash you would take care to advise the Branches not to draw large amounts upon you. In addition to drawing by wire I suppose you have always a lot of bills receivable falling due so that I think you run very little risk in working as closely as I suggest.[8]

McLean's prognosis should also be read against the backdrop of early-Meiji Japan's efforts to curb foreign note circulation domestically, whilst envisioning the very same property as part of its own future exchange bank operations.

We know this because of concerns publicly raised within the British expatriate community in China and Japan's treaty-ports. For example, on 1 July 1876, the British-run Shanghai daily, the *North-China Herald*, reported apprehensively from Yokohama that

> the Japanese government still pursue their short-sighted policy with respect to foreign bank-notes. In the Imperial Government Telegraph Office an announcement, dated 10th ult., is posted up [to] the effect that from and after that date no foreign

bank-notes would be received in payment of telegrams. The Custom House Authorities also refuse to receive foreign notes in payment of duties.[9]

As these measures were put in place, and as foreign note issuance on Japanese soil was diminishing, Japan's own exchange bank was being fleshed out. The YSB was first endowed with a paid-up capital of ¥3million, of which ¥1million was in the form of specie forwarded by the Japanese Treasury, and the other ¥2million represented private equity. Thus, it was not a state-run colonial bank in the full sense of the word but, rather, a semi-official bank, much like HSBC, with a unique stated mission of facilitating Japan's overseas trade. Implicitly, it was expected to play a pivotal role in Japan's longer-term mercantilist exercise: the accumulation of foreign-currency reserves, which eventually allowed Japan to move off the silver standard in 1897 and re-base the yen on gold. The ability to maintain the yen's convertibility to gold was ultimately achieved in no small measure thanks to the colossal war indemnities Japan had been able to extract from China in 1896, and the flotation of Japanese government bonds at the London stock exchange.[10]

The first China branch of the YSB was opened in Shanghai as early as 1893 but it was not until 1902 that the bank started issuing notes on the Mainland, first in Shanghai, Niuzhuang (Yingkou), and then Tianjin. The reason behind this time-lag has to do with the fact that Japan greatly depended on London finance for the purchase of Western machinery at the turn of the century, and was therefore cautious not be seen as a competitor of Western financial institutions in China.[11] It was only later that the YSB also started issuing silver-denominated notes in Beijing (1910), Qingdao (1915), Hankou (1917), Jinan (1920) and Harbin (1921). Overall, the bank issued more than 88 different types of note on Chinese soil, primarily in tael and silver-dollar denominations, as well as smaller volumes of gold-yen notes in Dairen, Liaodong peninsula (as of 1913).[12]

As Table 3.1 clearly shows, it was the Qing dynasty's downfall in 1912, and the attendant financial meltdown in the Chinese-run banking sector, that elevated the YSB's note circulation in China Proper throughout the early 1910s, translated into lower circulation volumes in the Japanese sphere of influence across north-east China. This was partly because the YSB total fiduciary issue at the time was capped by the bank's charter, which was similar to the one that the British Colonial Office had imposed on HSBC.[13]

Table 3.1: YSB Note Circulation in China Proper (Excluding Manchuria) vs YSB Total
Note Circulation, 1906–1912 year end, in Silver $10,000

	YSB Note Circulation in Shanghai	YSB Note Circulation in Tianjin	YSB Note Circulation in Beijing	YSB Total Note Circulation *	Circulation in China Proper as % of Total circulation
1906	144	41.2	-	752.8	24.6
1907	133.8	42.2	-	619.5	28.4
1908	108.3	49.2	-	417.2	37.7
1909	81	47.1	-	292.8	43.7
1910	75.8	33.6	14	367.4	33.5
1911	66.7	63.9	12	673.7	21.1
1912	152.6	89.1	97.5	657.6	51.5

In 1909, the Shanghai branch balance-sheet switched from taels totals to local silver $
totals. Yen and local tael figures have been converted to silver dollar terms based on
the exchange-rate data in Hsiao Liang-lin, *China's Foreign Trade Statistics, 1864–1949*
(Cambridge, MA: Harvard University Press, 1974), pp. 190–2 and Hosea Ballu Morse,
The Trade and Administration of China (New York: Russel & Russell, 1921), pp. 156–73.
Sources: Guo Yuqing, *Jindai Riben yinhang zai Hua jinrong huodong: Hengbin zhengjin yinhang, 1894–1919* [Pre-War Japanese Banks' Operations in China: The Yokohama Specie
Bank, 1894–1919], (Beijing: Renmin Chubanshe, 2007), p. 195, Tables 3–18.
    * figures derived from Tōkyō Ginkō and Shinji Arai (eds), *Yokohama shōkin ginkō zenshi*
横濱正金銀行全史 / [A Comprehensive History of the Yokohama Specie Bank], 6
vols (Tokyo: The Bank of Tokyo, 1980–4), vol. 6, pp. 399–401.

In 1908 the YSB's total circulation volume in China Proper amounted to just
1.57 million silver dollars, and notes were yet to be issued in the imperial capital
of Beijing. That the YSB note issuance was still a phenomenon confined mainly
to the treaty-ports of Shanghai and Tianjin, and relatively distant from China's
seat of government, might explain why it had not yet incurred much imperial
wrath. As late as 23 May 1908 the *North-China Herald* reported that the enfee-
bled Qing dynasty's Treasury (*duzhibu*) 'has now come to the conclusion that, as
foreign bank-notes are not circulated widely in the interior of the various Provinces, [it] will not interfere with them at the present moment'.[14]

The malaise that struck the Chinese financial market on the eve of the Qing
dynasty's downfall was in part due to the fact that it had by then become reliant
in no small measure on foreign endorsement. Yet the spike in the YSB Mainland
China circulation volumes for 1911–12 should be placed in a wider context. As
late as 21 October 1911, the *North-China Herald* opined in an editorial that,
even at that stage, too many Shanghainese refrained from accepting foreign
banknotes in lieu of drafts issued by near-insolvent Chinese banks:

Steps [by foreign banks] are in contemplation to stop this mad rush, and save the native banks from impending bankruptcy. It need not be told that if the Chinese even had confidence in the foreign banknotes there would be a good deal of relief and the market would have time for readjustment. As it happens, there is a heavy load of short loans and native orders for the native banks to pay, and in spite of the extension of time granted by the foreign banks they do not see their way to meet obligations if the rush continues ... It is surprising that the Chinese authorities should have done comparatively little to relieve the ignorant people of their anxiety. We understand that at the instance of the Banker's guild the [Governor] is contemplating a proc-lamation urging upon the people the value of sobriety at this moment, and making them understand that the notes of the foreign banks and principal Chinese banks are absolutely safe and the rush would not be permitted.[15]

Parallel developments are critical to understanding the spread of YSB notes across Manchuria. After Russia's defeat in its war with Japan in 1905, the YSB was asked to convert Japanese military coupons, disbursed by the Japanese Kanto Army and nominally worth ¥15million, into its own banknotes. In that way, the Japanese government sought to stamp out the use of gold-based roubles along the South Manchuria Railway. Then, in 1916, when the government of Yuan Shikai suspended the convertibility of Chinese banknotes, the YSB increased its note issue (of both silver and gold denominations) over and above the previous cap, so as to take advantage of the collapse of popular trust in Chinese govern-ment-backed banks. Thus, the YSB's *total* circulation volume, as measured in Japanese gold yen, more than doubled between 1915 and 1916 from ¥7million to ¥18million. Partly in order to allow the YSB to meet the robust demand for its notes through this period, its paid-up capital – as stipulated in the charter – was consistently lifted from ¥30million in 1916 to ¥100million in 1920.[16]

However, in 1917 the YSB's stature as a regional bank of issue suffered a setback by the Terauchi government's decision to nominate the Bank of Cho-sen as its primary bank of issue in Manchuria, with a view towards narrowing Korea's trade deficit with that region, and towards a future monetary unifica-tion of Manchuria and Korea. Established in 1907, the Andong [present-day Dandong] branch of the YSB, near the Korean, border was closed down at the end of 1917, and its operations were taken over by the Bank of Chosen, which had been present in the city only since 1909. Several other Japanese banks that were 'mostly commercial' continued to transact business in Andong too. The YSB's old silver-yen and gold-yen notes subsequently lost legal-tender status in Manchuria, and were progressively 'redeemed' in favour of the Bank of Chosen's new gold-yen notes.[17] Conversely, demand for its silver-denominated notes in China Proper continued to rise, to the extent that the overall circulation volume remained at around ¥20million until mid-1919.[18]

In the Chinese port city of Dalian [Dairen, occupied by Japan since 1905], 500 km southwest of Andong, it was reported in 1919 that Chinese traditional copper coinage 'disappeared from circulation entirely' in favour of modern Chi-nese and Japanese-issued subsidiary coinage and gold-yen notes. The volume of

YSB silver-denominated yen notes circulating there at the time was estimated to be only ¥100,000. Like elsewhere in the Northeast, the YSB had been authorized to issue gold-yen notes in Dalian since 1913 and, for that reason, was described by the British-run Maritime Customs service of China as 'instrumental in the pursuance of the financial policy of the Japanese Government'.[19] However, as indicated above, a special Japanese government ordinance was issued on 1 December 1917, whereby YSB gold-yen notes lost their compulsory circulative power in the Kwantung [Kanto] Leased Territory and Railway Zone in South Manchuria, enveloping Dalian, as well as places like Andong.[20]

The Bank of Chosen's note issue cannot be meaningfully treated here, not least because it was conceptually different to that of the YSB. Not only did the Bank of Chosen *not* issue convertible silver-denominated notes (be they in dollar or yen units), but the great bulk of its note circulation remained in Korea too. What is more, since Japan suspended the yen's convertibility to gold in the wake of World War I, and temporarily returned to the international gold standard only in January 1930, the Bank of Chosen's gold-yen notes were effectively rendered inconvertible during that period, whereas the YSB needed to maintain the convertibility of its silver dollar notes in China Proper because the latter remained on the silver standard until 1935.[21] Primarily an exchange bank rather than a bank of issue, the YSB was by contrast more concerned with the stability of its notes, rather than its market share. In that sense, YSB notes were fundamentally different to those of the Bank of Chosen or the Bank of Taiwan because of a different perception of their role within the Chinese economy. Internal documents published by the YSB make it clear that its notes were in fact a 'managed currency' designed to smooth over seasonal trade flows between Manchuria and China Proper, and that the value of those notes was to be regulated by selling or buying drafts using an exchange fund held in Shanghai.[22]

Imperial Banking Beyond Banknote Issuance

In order to further understand YSB note circulation patterns, the bank's monetary properties should also be placed in the context of more important business ends. After all, as M. Schiltz has recently shown, the crux of the bank's activity in China Proper, like that of its British competitors, revolved around the finance of intra treaty-port trade and Sino-Japanese trade through the provision of short-term exchange bills and around the granting of 'political loans' to successive Chinese governments.[23] The bank did attract deposits from Chinese clientele in Tianjin (mainly Qing officials prior to 1912) but – according to T. Taira's important study – the proceeds of these deposits were mostly allocated to *foreign* merchants residing in Shanghai. In T. Taira's view, YSB China branches as a whole ran a net surplus with the Tokyo head-office in those years; in other words, the head-office did not seek to employ all China resources locally but to 'sacrifice' the surplus there to fund Japan's substantial imports of machinery from Europe and America.[24] Ishii

Kanji similarly has shown that during the 1910s the YSB relied heavily on deposits by ethnic Chinese and Indians in Shanghai and Bombay, respectively.[25]

Guo Yuqing complements Taira and Ishii Kanji's incisive analyses by showing how the YSB China deposit-base had evolved from the ground up. Guo suggests that, whilst the Shanghai and Tianjin branches accounted for the great bulk of YSB deposits in China Proper (60 percent on average between 1901 and 1913), well under a fourth of its Shanghai deposit-base had been attributable to ethnic Chinese clients *before* 1900. Notably, in its pre-1900 phase, the YSB had not yet set up deposit branches in Manchuria. Since the YSB was unable to accept deposits within Japan, the vast majority of its deposits at the time were therefore attributable to European (60.4 percent), American (27.3 percent) and Indian (6.4 percent) branches. Yet, by 1913, over a third of the bank's worldwide deposits were attributable to Greater China (Manchuria alone made up about 9 percent, and China Proper, 15 percent), whilst previously significant American deposits were declining sharply. In other words, by the 1910s, China, and in all probability the Chinese clientele, had become much more vital to the bank's worldwide operations, just when popular resentment over Japanese expansionism was building up there.[26] Table 3.2 shows the findings of previous studies on the regional make-up of YSB deposits.

Table 3.2: YSB Deposits and Loans vs Other Banks, in 10,000 Silver $

Year	Shanghai Deposits	YSB Shanghai Standard Loans (excluding 'Chop Loans')	YSB Shanghai 'Chop Loans'	China Proper Total Deposits	YSB Deposit Total *	YSB Total Net Profit *	Bank of Taiwan China Proper Deposits †	The 'Ta Ching' Imperial Bank Deposits (re-named 'Bank of China' in 1912) †	HSBC Deposit Total †
1906	421.4	395.4	761.8	1,752.7	12,431.4	506.6	44.9	1,466.7	19,920
1907	364.0	313.8	406.1	1,482.3	12,350.7	416.4	74	3,066.7	22,410
1908	463.2	137.5	7.2	1,617.0	9,885.3	395.8	127.3	4,897.2	29,860
1909	517.1	129.3	700.2	1,340.6	11,882.1	377.8	111	6,779.2	27,240
1910	650.1	193.6	2.9	1,467.3	10,225.8	361.7	96	7,501.4	26,410
1911	842.4	317.6	220.0	1,775.9	11,972.2	396.5	304.3	8,201.4	29,830
1912	891.7	468.4	0.0	2,117.9	15,992.6	446.8	532.9	313.1	38,840
1913	1,237.1	606.7	0.0	2,627.7	17,834.3	412.8	637.6	2,620.6	29,820

Sources: Taira Tomoyuki, 'Nihon teikoku shugi seiritsuki, chūgoku ni okeru Yokohama shōkin gijkō', pp. 69–71, Tables 2–3.

*   *Yokohama shōkin ginkō zenshi*, volume 6, p. 398, Table I.

†   Guo Yuqing, *Jindai Riben yinhang zai Hua jinrong huodong: Hengbin zhengjin yinhang, 1894–1919*, p. 190, Tables 3–14.

Silver $-Yen exchange rate from Hsiao Liang-lin, *China's Foreign Trade Statistics, 1864–1949*, pp. 190–2 and Hosea Ballu Morse, *The Trade and Administration of China*, pp. 156–73.

Table 3.2 clearly shows that the YSB's Shanghai deposit-base considerably exceeded standard loans between 1906 and 1913. However, until 1910 the YSB, like many of the foreign banks in Shanghai, also advanced a substantial amount in unsecured 'chop loans' to local money-shops (then known to the Chinese as *qianzhuang* 錢莊, and to Westerners as 'native banks'). For the most part, the combined value of 'chop' and standard loans exceeded the value of deposits in the Shanghai branch prior to 1910, the year in which many of the city's money-shops became insolvent.[27] The gap between such liabilities and assets was narrowed down – perhaps strategically – by the issue of notes in Shanghai. Note-bearers could, for example, be depositors who had pledged specie over the counter, occasionally withdrawing 'cash' from their current accounts in the form of notes. The fiduciary portion of the specie corresponding with the note value, could then be on-lent by the bank at a higher interest (the notes themselves did not bear any interest).

Equally important, Table 3.2 shows that in terms of its ability to attract deposits worldwide, the YSB did not fall much behind HSBC in the early twentieth century, even though the latter had been established earlier and was formally endorsed by the British colonial establishment in East Asia. Conversely, the Bank of Taiwan, which also attracted deposits in Mainland China (mainly in Xiamen), was no match for the YSB there. But one of the first Chinese-run modern financial institutions, Ta Ching Imperial Bank (*Daqing yinhang* 大清銀行, re-named 'Bank of China' after 1912) could, by 1907, outpace the YSB in terms of deposit mobilization in China. Ta Ching seems to have scraped through the turmoil in Shanghai's domestic financial sector in 1910. However, the result was that much of its deposit-base was later withdrawn as a consequence of its association with the moribund Qing dynasty.[28]

Imperial Banking Facing Anti-Foreign Boycotts

Quite apart from the financial crisis that befell Japan in early 1919, the May Fourth Movement augured trouble for the YSB's note issue in China Proper later that year. Although not the first popular boycott directed against Japanese imports to China, the *Wusi* boycott of 1919 was certainly the first whereby Japanese banknotes were poignantly targeted, ushering in similar waves of effective agitation throughout the 1920s and 1930s. Even though, nominally, the YSB's China note issue prevailed a few years beyond 1935 – the historic juncture at which the Kuomintang [KMT] government proclaimed its *fabi* currency as China's sole legal tender – its circulation volumes would never again reach the late-1918 peak. Yet, despite its formative role in shaping Chinese socio-political consciousness, economic research into the May Fourth Movement primarily deals with its effects on Sino-Foreign trade, neglecting the boycott's effects on the local operations of foreign-run banks and multinationals.

Western financial institutions operating in China were beset by numerous crises through much of the same period. Upon the outbreak of World War I, the

Allies forced *Deutsch-Asiatische Bank* branches in China to shut down. These branches were barely able to resume operation in 1918. Crises in the foreign banking sector persisted after the war. The Russo-Asiatic Bank was arguably the first foreign financial institution to be targeted by boycotts. It was nominally a Sino-Russian joint venture, but effectively a French-owned firm that had to be reconstituted in the wake of the Bolshevik Revolution, and which ultimately failed in 1925.[29]

The Asiatic Banking Corporation, a Sino-American joint venture, had come to the brink of failure in 1924, and was eventually sold off to the International Banking Corporation. The Chinese-American Bank of Commerce, another joint venture, suspended business in 1928. Based in Tianjin, the Sino-Scandi-navian Bank (established 1921) suffered a severe run on its notes in 1928 and closed its business shortly thereafter. But, arguably, the failure most inimical to the reputation of foreign financial institutions in China occurred in 1921. This was when *Banque industrielle de Chine* had to suspend the convertibility of its Shanghai notes into silver due to overprinting. At the last moment, Chinese banks came to its rescue and redeemed the notes.[30]

Anti-foreign boycotts proved equally if not *more* inimical to the interests of British firms operating in China in the mid-1920s, and is probably the reason why the performance of these firms is covered more widely than Japanese firms in pertinent academic literature.[31] Yet almost all the Chinese popular ire came to bear on Japan in 1919. It is therefore critical to unearth the Japanese perspective on the events unfolding at the time. Hirofumi Takatsuna's recent comprehensive study highlights the extent to which Chinese labourers' agitation in the Nagai Wata cotton filatures disquieted the Japanese expatriate community in pre-war Shanghai, but it does not address the activities of the YSB at all. Neither does Guo Yuqing's aforementioned study of the YSB go beyond 1919, thereby eliding the implications of the May Fourth Movement.[32] Similarly, Kikuchi Takaharu briefly mentions in his classic study of Chinese nationalism that Chinese clients had withdrawn deposits from Japanese banks in 1919, but is otherwise much more preoccupied with the May Fourth Movement's effects on the sale of Japanese imported goods.[33]

Japanese intelligence reports from Shanghai do nonetheless attest at length to the sheer anxiety with which expatriate Japanese financiers and bankers – not just industrialists – viewed the mounting agitation against Japan as of 1919. As part of this agitation, not only were Japanese-imported goods boycotted in the 1920s, but often Chinese-run money-shops and modern banks refused to honour IOUs or notes presented by Japanese firms for encashment.[34] Although there are numerous intelligence reports detailing such events in the mid-1920s, there are also similar primary materials attesting to the incipient alarm that seeped through the Japanese expatriate community during the formative 1919 boycott.

For example, the commercial gazette (*Tsūshō kōhō* 通商公報), which was pub-lished by the Japanese Foreign Ministry (*Gaimushō*), frequently alluded in its 1919 issues not only to a downturn in the sales of Japanese goods like toothpaste or tyres in the Chinese market, but also to runs on the YSB and the Bank of Chosen branches in places as far-away from Shanghai as Changchun or Zhifu (Yantai).[35] Likewise, consular reports now held at the Japan Centre for Asian Historical Records suggest that Japanese colonial policy-makers were concerned about the implications of the 1919 boycott of Japanese banks in places like Qingdao, close to their sphere of influence in the Northeast.[36]

Edmund S. K. Fung has insightfully described the wave of Chinese popu-lar agitation directed against the British during the mid-1920s as the driving force behind the most effective boycott ever carried out by the Chinese against foreigners; this agitation sparked a reaction in comparison with which 'the anti-Japanese boycott of 1919–1921 pales into insignificance'.[37] E. Fung's observation is of value precisely because the May Fourth Movement, unleashed on the heels of the Versailles Peace Conference and Japanese territorial encroachments in Shandong, has commanded far greater attention from cultural and social histo-rians than it has from economic historians.[38] Certainly, insofar as the circulation of Japanese banknotes in China is concerned, both periods remain critically under-studied. A closer look at the YSB indices for 1919 might suggest, how-ever, that the impact of the *Wusi* boycott on Japanese banks was far from trivial.

On 17 May 1919, Shanghai's money-shop guild announced that its mem-bers were to halt the clearing of quasi-foreign notes issued by Japanese banks, even though alternative reliable Chinese paper money was hard to find at the time.[98] At that moment, however, the epicentre of anti-Japanese agitation had largely been confined to North China. Japanese reports recount that Chinese student activists had campaigned there for the boycott of Japanese goods, par-ticularly in Beijing and Tianjin. However, silver dollar notes issued in Shanghai by the YSB and, to a much lesser extent, the Bank of Taiwan, were a highly vis-ible manifestation of Japanese penetration, and subsequently became one of the most pronounced targets for agitation by mid-May 1919.[40]

The overall impact of the 1919 boycott of Japanese-issued notes in China Proper can be inferred from YSB balance-sheet totals, as shown in Table 3.3 in pounds-sterling terms. The unit of account is of importance here because, as indi-cated above, YSB notes were actually denominated in a raft of fairly arcane local Chinese tael and silver-dollar denominations, as well as in gold-yen denomina-tions. The YSB was conveying this information in English to an international readership beyond East Asia. In other words, this information was purposefully converted into a familiar unit of account and would have been widely available to political and financial analysts, even though none seem to have publicly acknowl-edged nationalist sentiments with banknote circulation volumes at the time.

Table 3.3: Yokohama Specie Bank Select Midyear Balance-Sheet Entries, 1915–23, GBP £million

Year	1915	1916	1917	1918	1919	1920	1921	1922	1923
Notes in Circulation	0.6	1.0	2.3	2.1	1.6	0.7	0.8	0.6	0.3
Cash Reserves	2.2	2.4	3.3	4.2	4.1	4.5	3.5	3.6	2.7
Deposits	16.3	25.0	33.7	66.0	53.5	56.4	50.1	50.6	47.9
Balance Sheet Total	32.4	42.5	64.3	115.9	124.9	139.0	101.9	99.7	109.3

Source: *Bankers' Magazine*, 1916–1924

Unlike the Bank of Taiwan or the Bank of Chosen, the YSB was an overseas bank whose note issue at the time was predicated on demand in areas beyond formal Japanese domination: China's Northeast, Tianjin and Shanghai. It is therefore particularly instructive to note that its total circulation volume in pounds-sterling terms had peaked in 1917; dropped by no less than 66.6 percent by mid-1920; and waned further in 1922–3. The 1919 setback was much less pronounced when confined to YSB total deposits – those fell by just 28 percent between the 1918 peak and 1923. The anti-Japanese climate in China is still less traceable in balance-sheet totals, which ultimately reflected Japan's trade volume with the rest of the world. Here, an increase of 11 percent was recorded in fact in 1919–20. The stark variance between these different balance-sheet entries suggests World War I and the onset of Japan's own financial crisis in early 1919 were not the only factors at play in explaining the YSB's performance.

Crucially, China-based British bank figures are indicative of similar dynamics. As the first foreign financial institutions to set up shop in China in the mid nineteenth century, British banks were also the first to issue banknotes. The comparative reliability of British banks in Shanghai turned them, from the 1870s, into one of the lynchpins of the expatriate community in this increasingly vital treaty-port. British financial institutions in Shanghai were preponderant in the local stock exchange, and stalwarts like the Oriental Bank Corporation, HSBC and Chartered Bank not only funneled a large share of the total foreign investment in the country, but also issued a considerable share of the city's fiduciary-money supply. Ultimately, these banks were a cornerstone to Britain's informal empire in East Asia, and to catalyzing the monetary reform of imperial China.[41]

Yet anti-British sentiments infused Chinese student agitation in 1925–6, as a result of grievances against the brutality of the British-run Shanghai Municipal Police. These sentiments adversely affected note circulation volumes more than any other balance-sheet entry; British bank fixed-deposit receipts were only temporarily affected by student activists' calls on all Chinese to withdraw funds from British banks. It would appear that, in at least one sense, the anti-Japanese student agitation of 1919 produced a longer-term result in the YSB case than in the 1925 British case. After 1919, several contemporary observers noted that the

YSB issue in Shanghai had in effect been wiped out by nationalist campaigns.[42] In contrast, British-run Chartered Bank's *total* note circulation volumes in China recovered swiftly after the 1925 setback, whilst HSBC decided to scale down its China note issue despite a resurgent demand in fear of future boycotts.[43]

The difference in the durability of the boycott in either case may have stemmed from the turnaround in British policy after 1927 – from confronting to appeasing Chinese nationalists – as opposed to intensifying Japanese aggression and concomitant Chinese mobilization against Japanese banks in Shanghai.[44] Chinese boycotts proved particularly thorny when directed at one power at a time. Since the early twentieth century, Chinese campaigners had improved their ability to identify cracks in each power's China policies. At the height of the 1919 anti-Japanese wave, the Western expatriate community largely distanced itself from the fray. But, in 1925 the campaigners so adroitly manoeuvred Britain into the dock that British expatriates in Shanghai came to believe a Bolshevist conspiracy was afoot to single them out from the French and Japanese.[45] At the same time, student-led anti-foreign campaigns in 1919 and 1925–6 made the Chinese press turn its attention to foreign banknote issuance as an internationally anomalous monetary phenomenon that must be redressed if China were to rehabilitate the flagging reputation of its financial institutions and achieve respect amongst the nations of the world. Calls on successive Republican Chinese governments to suspend foreign bank privileges began to be heard from 1919, and articles lamenting the considerable discount which Chinese banknotes incurred in the marketplace were not uncommon.[46]

Because of its macro-level and rather apolitical approach, there is hardly any mention of the effects of these anti-Japanese boycotts on the YSB's China operations in its six-volume official history, released in 1980–4. Rather, this official history laconically refers to note forgeries as a factor adversely affecting circulation in inland commercial hubs like Hankou in 1922, as well as to local incidents that are deprived of a nationwide political context.[47] Be that as it may, one of these laconic references cites in passing an internal YSB memorandum of 1 March 1936, written shortly after the promulgation of the *fabi* legal tender and the rollback of foreign banknotes in China. This retrospective memorandum confirmed that the YSB Shanghai issue was valued at 2 million silver dollars at its height, or just under 0.5 million higher than the figure available for mid-1912 (see Table 3.1).[48]

Total YSB note circulation for mid-1917 peaked in pounds-sterling terms at £2.3million (see Table 3.3), arguably as a result of a growing demand in Shanghai. By 1912, over half of the YSB's note circulation could be attributed to demand in China Proper – quite plausibly related to the 9 percent drop in the mid-1918 bullion price fluctuations. We must recall that YSB notes were disbursed in both gold and silver-denominated units of account whilst the pounds-sterling was purely on gold at the time. On the other hand, the much bigger mid-year drop recorded in

1920 (24 percent) was, in view of the qualitative evidence presented above, almost certainly related to the surge in anti-Japanese sentiments in China Proper.

In yen terms, broader trends can be observed based on a different *year-end* data set that was compiled *ex post*. Overall, YSB banknote volumes clearly took off on the eve of the Qing dynasty's downfall in 1912. This take-off, however, dramatically accelerated through the ensuing political instability of the early warlord era in China. At play during this period, perhaps, was not only popular mistrust of Yuan Shikai's interventionist bank reforms (1916), but also concerns about the solvency of Western banks of issue during World War I.[49] Circulation volumes had started dropping around 1917–18, at first as a result of the YSB's loss of note-issue exclusivity in Manchuria. Thereafter, successive waves of anti-Japanese boycotts in China (1919, 1923, 1925 and 1932) seem to have taken their toll on total circulation volumes with partial recovery in the interim.[50]

Notably, there is one difference between the data sets: in terms of the yen, no dip was recorded in December 1917. Rather, circulation peaked in December 1918 (¥22,603,000). Whether this mismatch between the yen and the pounds-sterling data sets is purely a result of exchange-rate vagaries or perhaps a time lag, the long term impact of anti-Japanese boycotts on circulation volumes force-fully emerges from both data-sets. The yen circulation figure for December 1919 (¥15,154,000) is no less than 33 percent lower on the previous year; the December 1920 figure (¥7,543,000) is more precipitously lower (67 percent) compared with December 1918.

Can the Boycott Effect be Isolated? Imperial Banking Still Active

Unless additional in-house correspondence is discovered, it would be almost impossible to seamlessly disentangle the boycott effect from other factors at play.[51] Quoted on the Tokyo Stock Exchange, the YSB share price during 1919 can nevertheless serve as a rough guide to the problems at stake. The 12-month share price average during 1916 was ¥231, climbing fairly stably to ¥268 by December 1918. By September 1919, however, the share price peaked at ¥360. Prior to 1919 there had been no dramatic price swings recorded between September and October, yet in October 1919 the share price plummeted by 32 percent, reaching as low as ¥220 by November and then curiously bouncing back up to ¥304 in December. However, the share was to trade at an average below ¥200 until the mid-1920s.[52] At face value, the drop of nearly 40 percent in the share price between September and December 1919 would dovetail fairly well with the known progression of the May Fourth Movement, but it would be absolutely wrong to jump to conclusions, as the subsequent protracted trough suggests other recessionary factors were at play.

The world price of silver, which was in decline after 1919, may have conceivably affected the YSB's Tokyo share price to some extent, as the bank had substantial operations in silver-standard China. But, more fundamentally, the post-World War I slump in East Asia is likely to have engendered the share price trough thereafter.[53] So how big an impact did the 1919 anti-Japanese boycott have in the larger scheme of things? If there was not much impact on YSB deposits, can the May Fourth boycott alone account for the drop in banknote circulation volumes? In the absence of in-house YSB correspondence, part of the answer might rise from the pages of the *North-China Herald*. Twenty days after the May Fourth Movement was unleashed in Beijing, the *North-China Herald* reported from Shanghai that the boycott had been 'increasing in efficiency' and that 'the refusal to accept Japanese notes is now being multiplied in many ways', with many calling on Japanese bank branches with the purpose of converting notes into silver. Another article in the same issue divulged that 'in quite a number of shops there now appear notices that Japanese banknotes will not be taken, while even where these notices are not supplied there is an almost unanimous reluctance to accept the notes'.[54]

Anti-Japanese sentiments did not dissipate soon enough, which is illustrated by the fact that on 31 January 1920 an expatriate *North-China Herald* reader named Zadoc sent the newspaper a complaint to that effect. Published on 7 February 1920, Zadoc's Shanghai observations read:

> The Chinese are using the banknotes of the Hongkong & Shanghai Bank to promote their anti-Japanese propaganda by stamping them on both sides in English and Chinese 'Boycott Japanese Goods'. If such stamped notes were refused, or only taken at a discount, it would soon put a stop to so impertinent and illegal a proceeding.[55]

Yet these reports should be read with the onset of Japan's 1919–20 financial crisis and the protracted recession thereafter in mind. In fact, runs on Japanese banks began well before May Fourth. As early as 4 January 1919, the *North-China Herald* reported on the rumoured imminent failures of Japanese banks milling about in Osaka, precipitating a 'mild run' on Japanese banks in Shanghai:

> Local Japanese banks experienced runs on Monday, Chinese holders of their notes having become distrustful because of reports of bankruptcy and failure of various firms in Osaka. In the afternoon there was a steady stream of callers at the Bank of Taiwan, [with] holders of small amounts in notes demanding silver. After three o'clock, the usual closing hour, a line was formed on the pavement and the bank continued to pay out until four o'clock. The crowd was not in the least excited and apparently the bank experienced no difficulty in meeting the sudden call for silver, the manager [suggesting] to a representative of this paper that his vaults contained sufficient coin to meet the notes in local circulation. The Yokohama Specie Bank also found an unusual number of notes being handed in for silver coin, and although the amounts exchanged at this bank were individually larger, there were fewer applicants.

> Appreciating that the nervousness of the Chinese public might well be extended over
> to the next morning, and that the run might assume large proportions, the Yokohama
> Specie on Monday evening decided, if the step seemed necessary in order to restore
> confidence, next morning to place in the hands of all Chinese banks that are members
> of the bankers' guild sums of hard coin with instructions to pay out immediately on
> any Yokohama Specie notes that might be presented.[56]

As indicated above, from 1920 right up to the formal banning of foreign banknotes
in China Proper by the KMT government in 1936, a series of less pronounced
note circulation troughs and peaks can be observed in Shanghai. Total YSB note
circulation partially rebounded around 1928 and 1931 but never caught up with
the 1918 peak. Although lateral evidence in the YSB records has not been found
to prove this beyond doubt, it is reasonable to assume that the 1928 and 1931 partial rebound might also be linked to the concurrent withdrawal of HSBC's China
issue, or to the failure of smaller foreign banks during that period, rather than
purely as a result of any putative downward demand pressures in the Northeast,
where the bank's standing had by then greatly diminished.[57]

It is instructive, at any rate, to use the YSB circulation figures as a bellwether
for the geo-politics of the Sino-Foreign encounter and for the variation in economic conditions across Greater China. But the vitality of this note issue to the
YSB's worldwide operations in the 1920s should not be grossly overstated. This
is because, even at its peak in 1918, the total note issue did not make up more
than 4.2 percent of the bank's total deposits, and embodied a smaller fraction
of the balance-sheet bottom line. Rather, the diminution in note circulation
should be seen as compounding the effects of Japan's domestic recession on its
colonial banks in the 1920s. Additionally, smaller circulation volumes overseas
probably meant less ability to offset Japan's current-account deficit with a surplus of silver specie holdings in China.

Conclusion

This chapter aimed to provide a detailed analysis of the YSB's banknote issuance,
while stressing that it was moulded in the image of HSBC, not least regarding the
provisions of metallic reserve in its charter. Like HSBC, it was a publicly-listed
exchange bank, in the first instance, rather than a dedicated colonial bank of issue.
Within this framework, three critical developments can be traced over the course
of the pre-war era: demand for the bank's notes in China Proper first shot up as
a result of the breakdown of the Qing dynastic reign in 1912 and the attendant
financial crisis in Shanghai; by 1917, YSB banknotes lost their legal-tender status
in Manchuria due to important shifts in Japanese colonial policy, but was offset by
higher circulation volumes in China Proper until late 1918; the YSB circulation
volumes had started to fall from the absolute late-1918 peak with the onset of

Japan's post-war recession in early 1919, but more dramatically (and irreversibly) dropped later that year as a result of the *Wusi* anti-Japanese agitation.

YSB banknotes in China were designed from their inception to support more important business objectives like the amassing of local deposits and the facilitation of trade between Manchuria and China Proper. There is no evidence to suggest that the notes were ever conceived as the future currency of a Japanese-dominated China amongst Tokyo's 'empire-builders'. Ultimately, therefore, the YSB banknote issuance in China Proper proved to be limited, both in terms of its share of total YSB liabilities and of its volume, compared to Chinese, foreign and other Japanese banks that disbursed notes in Greater China. Yet, the available data would suggest that, beginning in mid-1919, the YSB notes came under more sustained pressure on the part of Chinese nationalists than British banks were to experience six years later.

The historic significance of the YSB's banknote issuance in China Proper therefore lies in its amplification of important and concrete permutations in Japanese colonial policy; in its parsing of the degree of Sino-Japanese resistance to Western imperialism in the economic sphere; and in its foregrounding of regulatory commonalities, as well as competitive thrusts within the broader sweep of the Sino-Foreign encounter, from the era of High Imperialism right through to the Pacific War. In essence, what the YSB was doing in Shanghai until the Japanese invasion of China in 1937 does not look significantly different -- at least in terms of banknote issuance – to the way in which recent studies have portrayed the Shanghai operations of the British-run HSBC or Chartered Bank. Put otherwise, this chapter underlines an important point for students of modern Japan: we should not let Japan's post-1937 unbridled militarism entirely over-script the nuanced patterns of international monetary rivalry and co-adaptation before the war. By the same token, it remains the job of historians to help elucidate the complex patterns of contemporary Sino-Japanese rivalry with a more meaningful pre-war context.

4 NATIVE BANKING VS IMPERIAL BANKING IN EARLY TWENTIETH-CENTURY CHINA: THE FORMATION OF THE JOINT RESERVE BOARD IN SHANGHAI TO FOSTER CREDIT AND CREDIBILITY

Tomoko Shiroyama

In many modern nation states, a central bank serves as the pillar of the monetary and financial system. The Bank of Japan, for example, refers to its role as ensuring 'smooth settlement of funds among banks and other financial institutions, thereby contributing to the maintenance of stability of the financial system'.[1] To realize those goals, the Bank of Japan secures the liquidity of the market by issuing money, managing payment and settlement systems, stabilizing the financial system by serving as a lender of last resort, and controlling the currency by influencing interest rates through operational instruments such as money-market operations. China, by contrast, did not have a central bank until the final decades of the last century. The People's Bank of China (hereafter the PBC) was established on 1 December 1948, based on the consolidation of the Huabei Bank, the Beihai Bank, and the Xibei Farmer Bank. However, under the socialist economic system of the People's Republic of China (hereafter the PRC), the role taken by the PBC was obviously different from the role of central banks in a market economy. As late as September 1983, the State Council of the PRC decided to have the PBC function as a central bank and play an important role in China's macroeconomic management of 'the socialist market economic system'. The PBC not only issued the renminbi (RMB) currency, but also regulated financial markets and prevented or mitigated systemic financial risks to safeguard financial stability.[2]

Even before the establishment of the PRC regime in 1949, central banking did not have a long history in China. In 1928, the Nationalist government founded the Central Bank as 'the state bank of the Republic of China'. Its capital was fixed at 20 million yuan, an amount contributed entirely by the government, and provisions were made for the public distribution of shares. It had the right to issue notes and was the fiscal agent of the Nationalist government and of all state enterprises, as well as the treasury's agent in floating domestic and foreign loans and in servicing such loans. However, it did not occupy the special position that central banks did in other countries; it shared the right to issue notes with other banks, but domestic banks were not required to deposit legal reserves with the Central Bank.[3] Thus, the government had no way of guiding the financial market, for example, by controlling discount rates or rediscounting bills.

The absence of central banking in China marked it as dissimilar to its neighbours in Asia, where the colonial banks did play the role of central banks; examples include *Banque de l'Indochine* in French Indochina and *De Javasche Bank* in the Dutch East Indies. The key question about the Chinese financial system in the early twentieth century is how it worked without an organization like a central bank to lessen the systemic risks and guard against crises by supplying credit to the market. The problems facing the Chinese financial system were especially challenging because three different groups of financial institutions coexisted in the financial centres, namely, native banks, modern Chinese banks, and foreign banks. How did those banking groups of different origins and scale run the financial system collectively?

This chapter investigates this issue by focusing on Shanghai, the most important financial centre during this period; in particular, focus is on the formation and the functions of the Joint Reserve Board. As the following section of this chapter shows, prior to the establishment of the Board in 1932, the Shanghai financial market had already developed the means for clearing, settling, and loaning. During the political and economic turbulence of the early 1930s these functions, shared by both foreign and Chinese financial enterprises, had to be formally institutionalized. The foundation of the Joint Reserve Board and its adjacent institutions, the Shanghai Clearing House and the Shanghai Acceptance House, was a case of such institutionalization occurring. Thus, the dynamics of the Joint Reserve Board shed light on how the banking institutions coped with the challenges in sustaining the liquidity of the market during the sequence of crises, including the 1929 Great Depression and the Japanese aggression in 1932.

This chapter is divided into three sections. After introducing the three different banking groups, native banks, modern Chinese banks, and foreign banks, the first section examines the procedures involved in intergroup clearings. It also points out the lack of negotiable instruments shared by the banking groups and the underdevelopment of the market for bill discounting. With these features of the financial system as the background, the second section investigates how bank loans were extended, which, to some extent, complemented the lack of the market for commercial bills. It also points out the critical role played by the foreign banks in the banking system. The third section first turns to the crisis of 1932, which led to the establishment of the Joint Reserve Board, and then focuses on the subsequent development of the Shanghai Clearing House and the Shanghai Acceptance House as an endeavour to sustain the liquidity of the market during the Shanghai financial crisis in 1934–5. Finally, the conclusion summarizes the empirical findings and considers their theoretical implications in terms of the development of a credit market in developing economies.

Imperial Banking and Native Banking: The Three Groups of Banking Institutions in the Shanghai Financial Market

In early twentieth-century Shanghai, banks of different origins and scales coexisted in three banking groups. The first group was the native banks; dealings in remittances and exchange may have been the beginning of native banking activity in China. It is very difficult to determine when those shops engaging in remittances and exchanges between silver dollars and copper coins turned into institutions involving more complicated banking transactions, such as handling deposits and advancing loans. The merchants from Shanxi Province had taken charge of the imperial treasury's funds from the eighteenth century and operated deposits, loans, remittances and domestic exchanges at their chain of branches located in all of the important trade centres in the country. In the early nineteenth century, Fujian came into prominence as a money market, with the inflow of silver brought by the trade in tea, and the Shanghai market was set up by Ningbo and Shaoxing merchants from Zhejiang Province before it was opened to the West as a treaty port.

While the significance of the Shanxi merchants from the north declined toward the end of the Qing dynasty in 1911, banking firms of the central-southern type, called native banks, developed under the impulse of foreign trade. At first, they mostly resided in the southern part of Shanghai, that is, in the native city and along the South Bund. After the Taiping Rebellion in 1864, the native bank centre shifted from the southern part of the city to the international settlement.[4]

The clearing of the native orders and the checks of native banks were done through the Native Bank's Clearing Association, adjacent to the Native Banker's Association.[5] The native banks were classified as clearing banks and non-clearing banks. Only the clearing banks, of which there were fifty-five in 1935 (out of a total of 120 native banks), were members of this clearing organisation. The non-clearing banks had to clear through the clearing members.[6]

The second group was the modern Chinese banks. Modern Chinese banks were different from the native banks in terms of their organization and business methods, which were based upon Western models. In 1897, the famous entrepreneur Shen Xuanhui established the first private bank, the Chinese Bank of Commerce in Shanghai. The establishment of two semi-government banks then followed: Hububank in 1904 (reorganized as Bank of China in 1913) and Bank of Communications in 1907. After that, the number of modern Chinese banks continuously increased, with eighty or ninety such banks existing in the early 1930s. Although the modern Chinese banks set up a Bankers' Association, it did not have a clearing association, unlike its counterpart, the Native Bankers' Association. Thus, even clearings among the modern Chinese banks themselves were conducted through the agency of the native banks at the Native Bank's Clearing Association. As early as 1921, plans were repeatedly drafted by several leading Chinese banks for the establishment of a centralized clearing organization. However, none of the plans materialized, owing to the divergent opinions regarding the custody of settlement funds.[7]

The third banking group was that of the foreign banks. Chartered Bank of India, Australia, and China (hereafter Chartered Bank) was the first, established in 1857, followed by the Hong Kong and Shanghai Banking Corporation (hereafter HSBC) in 1867. As of 1935, thirty foreign banks operated in Shanghai, of which twenty-two were members of the Foreign Exchange Banks Association. Although their status was not backed by a political authority such as that of the colonial government, these banks played a key role in the Chinese financial market by handling most of the foreign exchange business.[8]

With these different organizations of banking groups, intergroup clearings were complicated.[9] Payment and collection between Chinese modern banks and native banks were done through the of Native Bank's Clearing Association. For the purpose of clearing, the modern banks had to carry accounts with member native banks. Before the establishment of the Joint Reserve Board of the Shanghai Bankers Clearing Association in 1932, the foreign banks also used the member native banks as their agencies. As for clearing between foreign banks and modern Chinese banks, the members of the Foreign Exchange Banks Association, together with seven Chinese banking institutions, including the Central Bank of China, Bank of China, Bank of Communications, the Commercial Bank of China, the Jiangsu Bank, and the Joint Savings Society Bank, formed a clearing group. Strictly speaking, there was no formal clearing system among the clearing group, the so-called 'Bund Banks', the Foreign Exchange Banks and the Chinese banking institutions. Each bank cleared independently, while Bank of China rendered the service of checking and took care of the odd amounts in balances in Chinese dollars; before the abolition of the tael in 1933 HSBC rendered a similar service with regard to tael settlements. The banks were not requested to keep any deposits with Bank of China or HSBC, as the difference would be settled with cash payments or with call loans.[10]

The intrabank and interbank clearing systems highlighted the fact that the loose linkages connecting the three independent banking groups were not necessarily managed by any single organization. With this decentralized financial system, the lack of a market for commercial bills was a potential risk for liquidity crises. In the first place, the issuing of commercial bills was not popular in the Shanghai financial market. Nevertheless, in order to carry on transactions, native banks issued checks, bill of exchanges and native orders, which potentially could be negotiable instruments. The native order, in particular, was the most important document issued by a native bank at the request of its clients and represented an unconditional promise of the bank to pay. It was payable to the bearer upon presentation on or after a fixed date. The merchants widely used the native order as a way of deferring payment of goods. However, the native order was rarely discounted by either the native banks or modern Chinese banks. The 1906 regulation of the Shanghai Native Bankers' Association stated that, except in the case of clients who had accounts and sound records of transactions, the member banks should not meet requests for discounting bills. Modern Chinese banks were also conservative about discounting bills. In 1916, Bank of China, for example, discounted bills of 112,900 yuan, which was only 0.1 percent of the amount loaned by the bank, 99,377,800 yuan. In the same year, Bank of Communication discounted bills of 3,600,300 yuan, which was 8.8 percent of its total loans of 40,992,000 yuan. Overall, in 1927, only six of the fifty-nine modern Chinese banks in Shanghai offered discounting services, which amounted to 1,631,000 yuan, or 1 percent of the total amount of loans.[11]

The Mechanism of Bank Loans: Cooperation Between Native and Imperial Banking

Against these institutional features of the financial system – the decentralized, loose structure; the scarcity of negotiable instruments; and the lack of a market for them – the expansion of credits based upon assets and commodities, both among banking institutions and toward industrial and commercial enterprises, is worthy of special attention. In Shanghai, although the underdevelopment of the bill market limited the possible credit expansion, bank loans at least partially compensated for it.

When lending money to the industrial enterprises, banks requested collateral. For long-term loans, the mortgaging of factory sites and equipment was very common, especially among factories in Shanghai.[12] Under the loan contract, the most important item of security was real estate, not only because the value of other securities such as machines and buildings generally depreciated, but also because the title deeds to land were the most trusted securities among both Chinese and foreign financial institutions in Shanghai. For example, the records of the four native banks in Shanghai show that mortgages were increasing, particularly from the 1920s (see Appendices 4.1–4.4). In the prewar Shanghai financial market, title deeds for land in the settlements were the most highly esteemed collateral.[13] Because of the people's trust in real estate values in Shanghai's foreign settlements, real estate and financial markets in Shanghai were closely connected. Richard Feetham, who was commissioned to study the administration of settlements by the Shanghai municipal council, first pointed out this relationship:

> The great piles of banks, offices and warehouses along the Bund, as seen from the deck of an ocean liner steaming up the river, are at once recognized by the newcomer as evidence of the wealth and enterprise of Shanghai, and of the belief which its merchants and citizens have in its future. But they have a deeper economic significance than this; [...] that is, the fact that land is held on titles of unquestioned validity and is immune from the risk of illegal exaction - has not only given faith and courage to local investors, but has also had beneficial results in a much wider sphere. It has been one of the factors in enabling Shanghai to function as the financial center for a great part of China, which, while it attracts large sums of money for investment from outside, also mobilizes credit by providing, in the shape of assets safely held within its borders, a basis of trading operations not only in Shanghai itself, and in adjacent areas, but also in distant parts of the country, where legal rights are often uncertain or held of small account, and conditions are often so disturbed as to admit of little or no security for either person or property.[14]

Feetham's insights were echoed by Yang Yinpu, a professor at Guanghua University who specialized in banking and monetary systems. Yang noted that land in Shanghai's foreign settlements had two significantly desirable features: legal security and liquidity. As to security, the accurate measurement of property and the legal protection provided by this system were highly regarded by both foreigners and the Chinese. At the same time, the perpetual rise in land values made investment in land attractive. Because the title deeds of settlement properties were widely accepted by financial organizations in Shanghai, these organizations readily exchanged title deeds of properties in any settlements for cash. Yang stressed that the real estate market was integrated with the Shanghai financial market.[15]

Foreign banks, in particular, favoured land in the settlements as collateral. Business people considered that title deeds were equivalent to securities in other countries because they could be rediscounted easily at foreign banks. Although foreign banks hesitated to lend money directly to individual Chinese customers, foreign real estate agents would handle mortgage business for foreign banks. Real estate agents applied to banks for mortgages with the collateral that they had been offered by their Chinese customers, and re-lent with commission the money that they had borrowed from the banks. In 1930, fourteen foreign and Chinese banks owned real estate valued at 121,283,631 taels, which formed half of their collateral holdings. Real estate credits were important for Chinese banks, which depended on foreign banks for working capital. Chinese banks also accepted real estate mortgages, which constituted half of their collateral-backed loans.[16] By convention, in the Shanghai financial market, around 80 percent of the market value of real estate was offered to a borrower on the condition that the borrower would pay the annual interest rate of 7–9 percent.[17] The value of the Shanghai International Settlement real estate rose steadily from 1903 to 1930 (see Figure 4.1). Here, the potential redemption of these items served as a safeguard against default, but a drop in the value of any of these forms of collateral could shake the stability of the loan system.

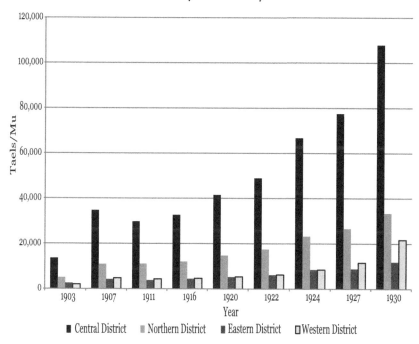

Figure 4.1: The Value of Shanghai Real Estate, 1903–30

Source: Luo Zhiru, *Tongji biaozhong de Shanghai* [Shanghai as Seen in its Statistics], (Nanjing: Guolizhong yangyan jiuyuan, Shehuikexueyanjiusuo, 1932), p. 20

For short-term loans, collateral, such as agricultural products and textiles, was integral to credit expansion among financial institutions. On the one hand, although foreign banks had enough funds to lend, they did not loan them directly to local Chinese enterprises. On the other hand, native banks lacked ample funds, which made loans from foreign and modern banks indispensable to them.[18] Native banks used the raw materials or end products offered as collateral by industrial enterprises to negotiate loans from foreign banks, using certificates designating the warehouses that stored these items. The four native banks in Shanghai all engaged in loans backed with commodities including silk, cocoons, raw cotton, cotton, yarn, and rice (see Appendices 4.1–4.4). The records of short-term loans by HSBC, the leading foreign exchange bank in Shanghai, also illuminate the importance of collateral items. Until 1911, it lent call money to native banks without securities (chop loans). However, after many native banks defaulted on their loans during the confusion of the 1911 Revolution, HSBC limited chop loans and began requiring collateral. During the six years from 1923 to 1929, it had 1,182 outstanding loans to native banks, worth 72.2 million taels. For most of these loans, security items were mandatory. The most important items used for collateral were agricultural crops (cocoons, raw cotton, and wheat) and the products of light industries (silk, cotton yarn, and flour). At an average length of six years, the loans secured with these products made up 54.6 percent of the total number of loans and 52.6 percent of the total amount lent. The foremost collateral item was cocoons; cocoons used as collateral amounted to 64.8 percent of the total number of cocoons and accounted for 56.6 percent of the total amount loaned. In addition to offering HSBC certificates from the warehouses storing those items, native banks paid the insurance for storage.[19]

In this way, both agricultural products and manufacturers were treated as negotiable instruments among Shanghai's financial institutions as they attempted to reduce the risks involved in making loans. At the same time, these items constituted key links between foreign banks and Chinese native banks, between Chinese native banks and manufacturers, and between the urban industrial and the rural agricultural sectors. Against this background, the value of the items accepted as secure collateral came to play a crucial role in maintaining liquidity in both urban and rural financial markets.

The key point is that, under the loan contracts, the confidence of financial institutions in these enterprises was grounded in the value of their collateral. This type of loan contract, involving collateral and careful monitoring, does not fit the conventional conclusion that most loans in China were based on personal credit.[20] The rapid growth of the Shanghai financial market in the early twentieth century meant that more business was done between 'strangers', for whom conventional forms of loan were inappropriate. The foreign banks in particular, with ample funds to lend to local native banks, preferred loans with tangible collateral and they therefore initiated the change in the method of extending credit. The economic situation in China was crucial to the financing of loans with collateral. In the first few decades of the twentieth century, the value of silver was declining, which led to a mild inflation in China (see Figure 4.2).[21] Rising prices led to an expansion of credit backed by collateral.

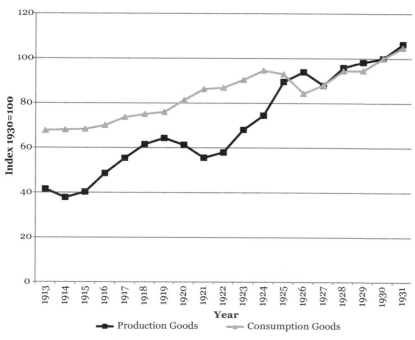

Figure 4.2: The Urban Wholesale Price Index, 1913–31

Source: Wang Yuru, 'Kindai Chūgoku no toshinio keruoro shiuribuk kahendō' [Wholesale Price Fluctuations and Urban Economic Development in Modern China], *Kagoshima kokusaidaigakuchiikisōgōkenkyū*, 31: 2 (March 2004), p. 25

The Crisis of 1932 and the Formation of the Joint Reserve Board: The Solidarity Between Chinese and Imperial Banks

The end of the silver depreciation in 1931 and the Japanese attack on Shanghai in 1932 critically undermined the economic conditions that made possible those credit expansions. While much of the world was suffering from a severe deflation from 1929 to 1931, the Chinese silver standard economy did not experience the vast drop in prices that occurred elsewhere. Because silver was heavily depreciated in terms of the gold standard currencies, China avoided deleterious effects during the first two years of the Great Depression.

From September 1931 on, however, many governments abandoned the Gold Standard and devalued their currencies in an attempt to inflate their economies. Great Britain was the first country to do so and other countries soon followed suit, such as Japan in December 1931 and the United States in March 1933. The move away from the gold standard international monetary system had a serious impact on the Chinese silver standard economy. As the devaluations raised commodity prices, the international price of silver rose, as did the exchange rate for the Chinese currency. Handicapped by a higher exchange rate, Chinese goods experienced intensified competition from foreign products both inside and outside China. The trade deficit increased and, at the same time, inflows of both remittances from overseas Chinese and investments by foreign companies decreased. China saw a net outflow of silver and a drop in commodity prices. In the middle of this economic difficulty, the Japanese military aggression hit Shanghai. In autumn 1931, to protest the Japanese aggression in Manchuria, the Chinese boycotted Japanese products by cutting sales of Japanese products in China by two-thirds. The Japanese military declared that the boycott was an act of aggression and, on 28 January 1932, attacked the Zhabei area, damaging the north-eastern side of Shanghai.

In the unprecedented emergency, the Shanghai Bankers' Association and the Shanghai Native Bankers' Association decided to close the financial institutions in the city for three days. The bankers were most concerned that public requests for deposit withdrawals would lead to financial panic. To avoid such confusion, the modern Chinese banks met requests for cash from 1 February 1932, but the financial market remained very nervous. When all the financial institutions restarted their operations on 4 February, the Shanghai Bankers' Association discussed organizing the Joint Reserve Board in order to ease the public fear of the total stagnation of the financial market. On 8 February, only ten days after the Japanese attack on the city, the Joint Reserve Board held its first meeting. The Joint Reserve Board of the Shanghai Bankers' Association was officially founded on 15 March 1932. All Shanghai banks, whether members of the Shanghai Bankers' Association or not, were admitted to the Board. Once they joined, they were required to deposit the following kinds of properties, which were to serve as the reserve properties of the Board: any real estate situated within the limits of the International Settlement and of the French Concession in Shanghai; readily marketable commodities; bonds and stocks quoted in Shanghai, London, or New York, as well as deposits with banks abroad; gold coins and gold currencies redeemable in gold or gold bullion; and, with the approval of the board's committee, securities other than those mentioned above. Once member banks had deposited these reserve properties, the board issued custody receipts and delivered Joint Reserve notes, Joint Treasury certificates, and security certificates up to 70 percent of the total value of properties, as estimated by an appraisal committee appointed by the Board. Security certificates were accepted by member banks as security for loans.

Although the Shanghai Bankers' Association initiated the establishment of the Joint Reserve Board, the Board consisted of members broadly encompassing the Shanghai financial market. While Li Ming, General Manager of the Zhejiang Industrial Bank, served as Chairman of the executive committee of the board, the following members served on the committee: Tsu-Yee Pei (Manager of Bank of China); T. D. Woo (Managing Director of Bank of Communications); Y. M. Chien (Assistant General Manager of the Joint Savings Society Bank); S. M. Tong (General Manager of the China State Bank Ltd.); K. P. Chen (General Manager of the Shanghai Commercial Savings Bank); Y. Hou (General Manager of the China & South Sea Bank); C. C. Woo (Manager of the Jincheng Banking Corporation); C. M. Shu (Managing Director of the National Commercial Bank); Chen Chieh (Manager of the Yanye Commercial Bank); and F. S. Yeh (Assistant General Manager of the Continental Bank). Under the executive committee, the appraisement committee was formed, with three sections on which leading specialists, both Chinese and foreign, were requested to serve. The real estate section consisted of N. L. Sparke (Manager of the Shanghai Land Investment Co.), F. W. Sutterle (Vice-President and Treasurer of the China Realty Co.) and Yen-Fong Kwei (Manager of the Realty Trust department of the National Commercial Bank). The stocks and bonds sections consisted of J. E. Swan (Partner of Messrs. Swan, Culbertson & Fritz), Ellis Hayim (Partner of Messrs. Benjamin and Potts), and S. Y. Woo (Member of the China Merchants stock exchange). Finally, the commodity section consisted of J. Madier (a French silk merchant), S. P. Woo (Proprietor of the Soy Lun Silk Filature), S. M. Wong (General Manager of the Poh Yei Cotton Spinning Co.) and Russell Y. Sun (Manager of the Fou Foong Flour Mills Co.). The board was ready to liquidate the not-readily-cashable assets in bank portfolios. According to the appraisement records, the securities deposited were as follows (see Table 4.1). The most important security was the real estate in the foreign settlement, which accounted for 85.5 percent of deposits with the Board; the securities came next, at 14.44 percent, with 'others' accounting for 0.06 percent.[22] Possibly in order to avoid competition among the modern Chinese banks and to enhance the credibility of the organization, the title deeds, securities and commodities were deposited with HSBC, Chartered Bank and the National City Bank of New York. Although the foreign banks were not officially members of the Board, the composition of the appraisement committee members, the deposited securities, and their role as a depository indicated that securing the foreign banks' trust was essential to maintaining the liquidity of the Shanghai financial market.

The first adjacent institution to the Joint Reserve Board was the Shanghai Bankers' Clearing House. In establishing the Shanghai Bankers' Clearing House, the Chinese bankers utilised the US system of organization as a model. Zhu Bochuan, the Manager of the Joint Reserve Board, who had studied at New York and Columbia Universities, wrote to his friend, R. R. Reeder at the Central Trust Company of Illinois, on 20 March 1932: 'My further task will lie in the perfecting of the existing institution and the establishment of a banking clearing house which has been sadly lacking in China in spite of its great necessity'.[23]

Table 4.1: Securities Deposited at the Joint Reserve Board of the Shanghai Bankers' Association

Types of Bonds
Chinese Government 5% Reorganization Gold Loan of 1913
    British Issue, Stamped
    French Issue, Stamped & Unstamped
    German Issue, Stamped & Unstamped
    Belgian Issue, Stamped & Unstamped
    Russian Issue, Stamped & Unstamped
Chinese Government 5% Gold Dollar Bonds of 1925
Chinese Government 6% Gold Dollar Bonds of 1928
17 Year Short-Term Currency Bonds

Types of Debentures and Stocks
Asia Realty 6% Debentures
Cathay Land Co. Debentures
International Investment Trust Co. 1930 Debentures
Shanghai French Municipal Council 6.5% 1925 Debentures
Shanghai Land Investment Co. 5% 1930 Debentures
Shanghai Municipal Council 6% 1925 Debentures
Shanghai Municipal Council 6% 1927 Debentures
Shanghai Water Works 7% Debentures 1922
Shanghai Dock & Engineering Co. Shares
Shanghai Land Investment Co. Shares
Shanghai Power Co. Preferred Shares

Title Deeds

Registrations	Number
British Council Lot	139
French Council Lot	52
US Council Lot	14
Belgian Council Lot	9
Japanese Council Lot	4
Shanghai Municipal Council Lot	1
Other Lot (Chinese Lot 143)	1

Types of Commodities

Commodities	Number of Go-down Warrants
Hongay Coal	1
Honan Anthracite	1
San Yang Brand Cotton Yarn	1
Paper	1
Broadcloth	1
Crêpe de Chine	2
Gold Bars (Ten ounces each)	NA

He asked Reeder to forward him as much information as possible, including the Central Trust Company of Illinois's organization chart, its regulations, and its functions and practices, as well as to send him the layout of the Chicago Clearing House. He asked for the same items from the Clearing House of New York City.

Twenty-five banks joined the Shanghai Bankers' Clearing House when it was opened on 10 January 1933. The member banks were requested to deposit the amount specified in the charter of the Clearing House at the Joint Reserve Board, and the Board transferred 70 percent to Bank of China and 30 percent to Bank of Communications. The Clearing House facilitated clearings among the modern Chinese banks, but also between the modern Chinese banks and the native banks. Previously, the banks had opened their accounts at native banks for the purpose of clearing; after the establishment of the Shanghai Clearing House, the native banks in turn opened accounts at member banks to take advantage of the swift and simple procedure. As of 1936, thirty-eight banks had joined the Shanghai Clearing House. The Shanghai Bankers' Acceptance House, another subsidiary of the Joint Reserve Board, was established on 16 March 1936. In the 1920s, economists and bankers had pointed out the need for an acceptance house for all of the Shanghai banking institutions. When the Shanghai financial crisis occurred in June 1934, the member banks of the Joint Reserve Board sought to set up the acceptance house to introduce a negotiable financial instrument for sustaining the liquidity of the market.

The *Silver Purchase Act* of 1934, which was passed by the US Congress on 19 June, declared it to be the policy of the United States to increase its stocks of silver until they equalled one-fourth of the total monetary stocks of silver and gold. The sudden and massive rise in the price of silver caused by heavy US purchases just as quickly raised the price of silver abroad. This precipitated a massive flow of silver out of China and upset the Chinese silver standard economy. In the middle of these paralyzing monetary and financial conditions, the Shanghai real estate market, which had begun to slow before the summer of 1934, crashed.

After September 1934, the silver drain and the uncertain future of the yuan ushered in a rush for liquidity. Concerned about the rapid drain of silver, people withdrew their bank deposits and hoarded the metal. As a result of large exports, the silver reserves shrank. Facing the rapid dwindling of their silver stocks, foreign banks began to restrict and later to refuse collateral loans signed against real estate. This practice pressured Chinese banks, which called in their outstanding credit, restricted the amount of advances, demanded additional collateral, and refused to renew loans on maturity. In this financial climate, the real estate market collapsed. The volume of transactions in the real estate market in Shanghai had dropped in 1932 when the Japanese attacked the city. After rebounding in 1933, it declined 69 percent in 1934, and a further 42 percent in 1935 (see Table 4.2). Once the real estate market crashed, people lost their trust in land as secure collateral. In the credit crunch that followed, the management of enterprises that were heavily dependent on loans became almost impossible.

Table 4.2: Volume of Transactions in the Real Estate Market in
Shanghai, 1930–October 1935

Year	(Millions of yuan)
1930	84.4
1931	183.2
1932	25.2
1933	43.1
1934	13.0
1935 (to October)	7.5

Source: Data furnished by the Shanghai Civic Association and Bankers' Cooperative Credit Service and cited in Weiying Lin, *The New Monetary System of China: A Personal Interpretation* (Shanghai: Kelly and Walsh, 1936), p. 64

Bankers were most concerned about the crash of the real estate market because the title deed was the most important negotiable item in the financial market. To secure the liquidity of the financial market, they decided formally to institutionalize the previous ways of extending credit with collateral items by establishing the Shanghai Acceptance House. F. W. Gray, a foreign employee of Bank of China, criticized the House's plan to make godown warrants of a certain kind into negotiable instruments by the addition of a bank acceptance. He argued that this would only facilitate the holding rather than the marketing of commodities in the absence of a provision connecting the proposed system of financing with the actual demand for a stated quantity of commodities.

Answering Gray's critique, Zhu Bochuan, the manager of the Joint Reserve Board, argued that the plan was a way to cope with the stagnation of the market:

> In theory, there is no doubt that a pure commercial bill is better than the form we propose to adopt. The futile attempts however must be attributed to the peculiar financial conditions and business environment in Shanghai [...] The underlying purpose of the scheme under discussion is twofold. While originated with a view to rendering liquidity to the credits now semi frozen, it is intended to pave the way for the creation of a discount market for commercial bills in the future. The general business depression in the past few months has resulted in large quantities of commodities kept in stock, a large part of which are now in the hands of the banks which have granted loans to the merchants against these securities. In face of the stagnant market condition these loans became more or less semi frozen and although there is no immediate danger attached to the loans which are amply secured by the commodities of readily marketable nature, yet the banks not being able to make use of their full resources to face the stringent financial situation are reluctant in granting further new loans to the merchants who may warrant every consideration of a lender. The consequence of such a phenomenon is a stringent money market, further business depression and, worst of all, a general breaking down of confidence.

Zhu expected that the bills accepted jointly by a group of banks would be credit instruments of a high standing. Many such would be bought for short-term investment, not only by financial institutions, but also by individuals who regarded the bills as sound investments. Zhu concluded that if drawers of bills were thoroughly investigated and the commodities properly evaluated, strictly inspected and safely stored, the bills would command confidence on the part of investors and, as a result, the bills would be exchanged frequently before maturity, which would increase the liquidity of bank funds as well as the velocity of money and credit available in the market. Although the practice of bank acceptance was new to the Shanghai financial market, as Zhu stated, the banking institutions regarded the Federal Reserve Board in the United States as a model of the joint acceptance of a group of banks with joint control of credit extension.

Admission to the acceptance house was restricted to the members of the Joint Reserve Board and the Clearing House. Only bills issued by member banks as drawers and those issued on the security of property or commodities deposited with the house were accepted.[24] As the Chinese economy recovered from the depression after the currency reform on 4 November 1935, the Shanghai Acceptance House did not have to cope directly with a financial crisis. Nevertheless, the rehabilitation of the long-term credit market proved difficult, despite the general recovery of the economy. Moreover, the Central Bank did not monopolize the right of issuing notes or centralizing bank deposits. Under the circumstances, the Joint Reserve Board and its two adjacent institutions played critical roles in maintaining the Shanghai financial system.

Conclusion

Defeated during the Opium War, China, at Britain's request, opened five ports to the Western powers for trade. In terms of the global economic regime in the nineteenth century, this 'free-trade' regime has been regarded as vitally important. At the same time, it is well known that realizing the idea of free trade with the outside world required political and military intervention; as early as 1953, Ronald Robinson and John Gallagher referred to the situation in China as involving 'the imperialism of free trade'.[25] It should be noted that recent studies re-evaluate the existence of free trade, particularly in Asia, arguing that even if the free trade regime was enforced from outside, the positive effects of increased trade opportunities were enjoyed by the local Asian merchants as well as the Western traders.[26] The key question for this re-evaluation is how the foreign merchants themselves could relate to the local merchants. In analysing the dynamics of the Shanghai financial market, this chapter has examined an aspect of this issue.

After the opening of the Shanghai port in 1842, not only Western traders, but also bankers, came to Shanghai. As Shanghai developed into the centre of trade and, later, of the light manufacturing industry, financial institutions of both foreign and domestic origin increased. The rapid growth of the Shanghai financial market in the early twentieth century meant that more business was conducted with 'strangers'. Instead of the traditional Chinese way of offering loans based upon personal credit, the foreign banks requested their Chinese counterparts present tangible collateral real estate for long-term loans and certificates of godown for short-term ones. Because the foreign banks were the major supplier of funds to the market, their decision induced the shift from personal credit to collateral loans among participants in financial transactions.

The new way of lending money worked during the years of mild inflation in the early twentieth century. However, the turbulence of the silver price and the Japanese aggression led to the large and rapid drop in the value of collateral, which critically undermined the lenders' trust in the debtors. In China, currency reserves were scattered because there was no central control over the issuance of notes or the expansion of credit. Competition among financial institutions tended to expand note issuance and credit when money was easy; tight money, on the other hand, produced a disastrous scramble for cash.[27] At that point, the financial institutions in Shanghai collectively secured the liquidity of the market by setting up the Joint Reserve Board and its adjacent organisations. Through those institutions, they sought to resume credibility backed by the collateral items. Although the foreign banks did not formally participate in the scheme, they played a key role in its management. Given that the Chinese national government did not lead the transformation of the credit market even after the currency reform in November 1935, the importance of those collective actions by the banks in Shanghai cannot be overestimated.

Because China was not colonized, the status of the foreign banks was not backed by the political authority of the Western powers and, thus, the roles that they played differed from those of the colonial banks. Nevertheless, they had a significant impact in shaping the modern Shanghai financial market. In the course of making inroads into China, foreign banks tackled the problem of how to assess the credibility of their local counterparts and lessen the risks involved in the transactions with them. This question was relevant in the past and is still relevant today. Thus, the solutions devised by Western bankers are not just of historical interest but are pertinent to today's economies as well.

It can be perceived that this chapter's perception of imperial banking is somehow different from the others. Actually, the assumption of the absence of central banking is controversial and the predominant role of foreign banks in China has changed since the early 1930s. Foreign banks in China are now considered to play a less important role than ever before, due to the Chinese government establishing a series of banking reforms, such as the Central Bank of China in 1928; negotiating for the return of customs sovereignty in 1929; setting up the Clearing House in 1933; increasing the funds to Bank of China and Bank of Communications; and establishing the new currency, *fabi* [legal tender] in 1935. As such, examining this area from an alternative perspective suggests that the modern Chinese banks are flourishing, whereas the foreign banks are diminishing. The categorisation of native banking, modern banking and imperial banking thus has to be assessed using subtle criteria in order to avoid misleading perceptions of the strength of imperial banking in China, despite its hegemony in the foreign concessions and their surroundings. Nuances are to be respected and we are well aware of this necessity, so as to avoid mixing realities from different areas and neglecting the ever active balance in China between trends towards economic patriotism and autonomy, and submission to foreign powerful companies and financial flows.

Appendix 4.1

Table 4.3: The Composition of Loans, Fukang Native Bank, 1896–1937, sourced from Zhongguo renmin yinhang Shanghai shi fenhang ed. Shanghai qianzhuang shiliao, pp. 780–3

Year	Personal	Silk and Cocoon	Raw Cotton and Cotton Yarn	Rice	Gold	Real Estate	Others	Sub Total	Total
					Collateral				
1896	189,211	–	–	–	–	–	–	0	189,211
1898	256,679	–	–	–	–	–	–	0	256,679
1899	521,756	–	–	–	–	–	–	0	521,756
1900	302,893	236,880	–	–	–	–	–	236,880	539,773
1901	554,600	–	–	–	–	–	–	0	554,600
1902	571,675	150,593	–	–	–	–	–	150,593	722,268
1903	478,685	681,712	–	–	–	–	–	681,712	1,160,398
1904	499,858	788,767	–	–	–	–	–	788,767	1,288,625
1905	622,784	476,269	122,865	–	–	51,246	8,424	658,805	1,281,588
1906	862,049	126,360	259,740	–	–	–	114,426	500,526	1,362,575
1907	757,351	437,968	151,632	–	–	–	0	589,600	1,346,951
1925	1,295,467	269,221	283,303	–	141,383	498,528	1,173,771	2,366,206	3,661,673
1926	1,615,948	693,389	144,831	–	1,502,280	356,616	1,720,709	4,417,825	6,033,773
1927	1,015,390	42,269	695,556	–	–	409,870	1,623,983	2,771,677	3,787,067
1928	2,088,026	235,011	926,797	–	–	664,991	1,712,612	3,539,411	5,627,437
1929	2,046,027	250,138	343,980	–	1,012,452	618,225	2,019,936	4,244,731	6,290,758
1930	1,904,984	493,477	648,933	–	113,317	1,100,273	2,944,868	5,300,867	7,205,850
1932	714,265	207,090	481,937	–	–	1,496,449	3,062,826	5,248,302	5,962,568

Collateral

Year	Personal	Silk and Cocoon	Raw Cotton and Cotton Yarn	Rice	Gold	Real Estate	Others	Sub Total	Total
1933	805,111	8,039	403,296	212,334	–	1,922,206	915,789	3,461,664	4,266,775
1934	862,493	–	125,637	219,023	975,045	2,274,757	1,562,113	5,156,575	6,019,068
1935	409,502	–	400,459	241,705	472,402	1,906,197	913,382	3,934,145	4,343,647
1936	1,125,849	–	165,973	–	–	1,664,160	616,230	2,446,363	3,572,212
1937	282,942	–	41,156	–	–	813,898	641,492	1,496,546	1,779,488

Appendix 4.2

Table 4.4: The Composition of Loans, Shunkang Native Bank, 1905–35, sourced from Zhongguo renmin yinhang Shanghai shi fenhang (ed.), Shanghai qianzhuang shiliao, pp. 818–19

			Collateral				
	Personal	Silk	Other Commodities	Securities	Real Estate	Sub Total	Total
1905	406,002	202,679	27,948	–	–	230,627	636,628
1906	977,564	–	52,201	–	–	52,201	1,029,765
1907	658,782	–	–	28,371	–	28,371	687,153
1908	592,189	–	204,035	–	–	204,035	796,224
1909	874,250	–	386,398	127,184	–	513,582	1,387,832
1910	246,611	–	318,888	402,222	–	721,110	967,721
1911	157,876	–	228,758	259,740	–	488,498	646,374
1925	1,097,000	–	1,202,683	–	–	1,202,683	2,299,683
1926	956,429	–	1,424,588	–	28,080	1,452,668	2,409,097
1927	935,248	–	1,632,463	–	369,652	2,002,115	2,937,363

	Personal	Collateral				Sub Total	Total
		Silk	Other Commodities	Securities	Real Estate		
1928	1,279,886	–	1,894,303	–	1,037,445	2,931,749	4,211,635
1929	885,939	–	1,448,946	–	881,174	2,330,121	3,216,060
1930	692,989	–	2,409,343	–	1,845,543	4,254,885	4,947,874
1935	92,607	–	1,145,118	–	1,003,011	2,148,129	2,240,736

Appendix 4.3

Table 4.5: The Composition of Loans, Fuyuan Native Bank, 1925–37, sourced from Zhongguo renmin yinhang Shanghai shi fenhang (ed.), Shanghai qianzhuang shiliao, pp. 800–1

	Personal	Collateral					Total	
		Commodities	Securities	Real Estate	Others	Sub Total	Sub Total	Total
1925	1,132,885	–	–	730,080	1,996,759	2,726,839	2,726,839	3,859,724
1926	966,370	–	–	647,408	2,355,875	3,003,284	3,003,284	3,969,654
1927	692,054	–	–	28,114	3,962,892	3,991,006	3,991,006	4,683,060
1928	955,334	–	–	875,415	2,875,448	3,750,863	3,750,863	4,706,197
1929	926,387	–	–	1,028,634	3,296,409	4,325,043	4,325,043	5,251,430
1930	1,154,043	–	–	1,235,443	3,068,988	4,304,431	4,304,431	5,458,474
1932	652,840	–	–	2,140,659	2,902,863	5,043,522	5,043,522	5,696,362
1933	734,000	–	–	2,259,094	4,384,030	6,643,124	6,643,124	7,377,124
1935	394,500	–	–	2,568,495	2,209,984	4,778,479	4,778,479	5,172,979
1936	1,243,583	803,799	824,225	3,187,815	118,459	4,934,298	4,934,298	6,177,881
1937	588,109	773,615	38,998	3,229,242	216,947	4,258,802	4,258,802	4,846,911

Table 4.6: The Composition of Loans, Henglong Native Bank, 1919–27, sourced from Zhongguo renmin yinhang Shanghai shi fenhang (ed.), Shanghai qianzhuang shiliao, p. 841

	Personal	Collateral			Total
		Commodities	Real Estate	Sub Total	
1919	886	1,244	–	1,244	2,130
1920	484,887	680,781	145,300	826,081	1,310,968
1921	1,086,382	1,525,280	–	1,525,280	2,611,661
1922	1,184,288	1,662,740	–	1,662,740	2,847,028
1923	2,178,576	3,058,720	–	3,058,720	5,237,296
1924	2,858,180	–	–	0	2,858,180
1925	3,354,441	4,709,635	–	4,709,635	8,064,076
1926	3,830,053	5,377,394	280,800	5,658,194	9,488,247
1927	1,376,630	1,932,789	1,088,100	3,020,889	4,397,520

5 BRITISH BANKS AND THE CHINESE INDIGENOUS ECONOMY: THE BUSINESS OF THE SHANGHAI BRANCH OF THE CHARTERED BANK OF INDIA, AUSTRALIA AND CHINA (1913–37)

Man-han Siu

This chapter examines the business of the Shanghai branch of the Chartered Bank of India, Australia and China (hereafter Chartered Bank) from 1913 to 1937, using time series analysis in order to investigate the relationship between British banks and the indigenous Chinese business community in Shanghai and assess some aspects of 'imperial banking' in China. The business environment of foreign banks had changed significantly during this period. World War I had disrupted the world economic order and led to the collapse of the international gold standard. The Great Depression of 1929 saw an unprecedented severe worldwide depression. At the same time, tensions between the foreign powers in China grew and the apparent political unification of the Republic of China by the Nanjing National Government had made remarkable progress in state building. In the banking sector, the growth of Chinese joint-stock banks after 1914 and the creation of the Central Bank of China had limited the role played by foreign banks in regard to the handling of governmental funds after 1928. Moreover, the implementation of the Currency Reform in 1935, which nationalized the silver stocks held by banks and instituted a managed currency, had changed the operating environment of foreign exchange business drastically.

How did these changes affect the relationship between British banks and the Chinese business community? How did the balance between 'imperial banking' and 'native banking' change? What kind of strategies did British banks adopt in the face of a changing business environment? Research on British banks operating in China can roughly be divided into three groups, as follows. The first group focused on the role played by British banks in the British foreign policy towards China.[1] Policies involved long-term capital movement such as International Consortium and the currency reform of 1935 in China are the representative examples for examination. The second group tried to analyse foreign banks from the perspective of the development of Chinese financial market. In regard to the question of domination of the foreign banks in Chinese financial market in the early twentieth century, Frank Tamagna pointed out that, though foreign banks lost their absolute control over some spheres in the 1930s, foreign banks remained a decisive factor in China's international financial relations.[2] On the other hand, Linsun Cheng suggested that the effective competition from modern Chinese banks was one of the main factors that caused the decline of the influence of the foreign banks.[3] However, what exactly led to the decline of foreign banks in China remained unclear, as a close examination of the China business of foreign banks had not been undertaken until now. The third group tried to examine British banks from the perspective of business history. British banks were the earliest foreign banks to establish in China and, until 1941, were in a predominant position among foreign banks. In 1936, there were seven British banks operating in China, including the Hong Kong and Shanghai Banking Corporation (hereafter HSBC) and Chartered Bank. Geoffrey Jones examined the major British overseas banks operating in Asia and located them in British international business history, but the impact of foreign banks on host economies was not his focus.[4] Both HSBC and Chartered Bank published their business history. Though the banking history of HSBC enhances our understanding in Chinese financial history,[5] the lack of empirical data on individual branches leaves many questions unanswered. On the other hand, the commissioned banking history by Chartered Bank was not an academic study.[6] Most of the foreign banks operating in China were multinational banks with extensive branching networks all over Asia. Branches were virtually single-unit banks joined in a federation under the control and supervision of the head office. The published financial statements of these multinational banks did not show the performance of individual branches. With only scarce and incomplete data, it has been difficult to understand the business performance of foreign banks in China. Therefore what really happened to Shanghai branches of British banks in the interwar period is still an enigma in Chinese banking history and has much room for exploration.

The archival collections used in this chapter include the balance sheet of Chartered Bank deposited in the London Metropolitan Archives, London, and records of Chartered Bank deposited in the Chinese Business History Resource Center, Shanghai Academy of Social Sciences, Economics Institute, Shanghai (hereafter SASSEI).

Banking Resources of the Shanghai Branch of Chartered Bank: A Comparison with HSBC and Bank of China

With the grant of its Royal Charter in December 1853, Chartered Bank was established in London and eventually began its business in February 1858, the year in which it opened its Shanghai branch. In 1936 there were 8 branches and sub-branches – Hong Kong, Canton, Shanghai, Hankow, Peking, Tientsin, Tsingtao and Harbin – in China. The Hankow and Tsingtao sub-branches were under the control of the Shanghai branch. On the other hand, HSBC was founded in March 1865 in Hong Kong. In 1866, a special enactment of Ordinance No. 5 of the Colony of Hong Kong meant that the bank could place its head office in Hong Kong. As a result, HSBC became the largest foreign bank in China in the 1880s and held its predominant position until the 1930s. Though exchange business was its core business, the business activities of the bank included local business such as receiving deposits, granting advances, underwriting Chinese government loans, and issuing bonds for companies. In 1936, it had more than ten branches and agencies in China (including Manchuria). The Shanghai branch, which was established in 1865, controlled branches and agencies in Tsingtao, Tientsin, Hankow, Peiping and Chefoo. The Shanghai branches of British banks were the most important branches in North and Central China.

The modern Chinese joint-stock banks developed rapidly after 1914. Bank of China[7] was established in September 1905 as a state bank. It was granted with the right to issue banknotes and act as the custodian of the funds of the central and provincial governments. It also had the privilege of managing official funds and, as a result, was involved in a lot of official financial activities, such as issuing government bonds. In 1928, with the establishment of the Nanjing regime, Bank of China moved its head office from Peking to Shanghai. From its inception, it was the largest bank in terms of deposits, loans and total assets among Chinese joint-stock banks. With its special status and financial ability, it was virtually the leader of modern Chinese banks. In 1936, it had more than 200 branches and agencies in China. Unlike foreign banks that had worldwide branching networks, Chinese banks developed national branching networks.

**Table 5.1: A Comparison of the Financial Resources of
Chartered Bank, HSBC and Bank of China**

	Total Assets (in £1,000)			Total deposits (in £1,000)			Deposits of Shanghai Branch (in Ch. $1,000)		
	HSBC ‡	Chartered Bank ‡	Bank of China §	HSBC ‡	Chartered Bank ‡	Bank of China §	HSBC ¶	Chartered Bank **	Bank of China ††
1890	25,571	15,923		17,615	6,882				
1913	39,466	27,243	3,074	28,805	17,128	1,829	37,133*	7,319	8,707†
1928	71,792	60,991	55,783	55,371	44,005	36,352	110,366	25,265	44,141
1936	70,101	64,508	102,965	51,935	48,184	49,086	81,300	29,060	143,406

*   Deposits at March, 1911
†   Deposits at the end of 1914
Sources:
‡   G. Jones, *British Multinational Banking, 1830–1990* (Oxford: Oxford University Press, 1993), pp. 394–400.
§   Zhongguo yinhang and Zhongguo dier lishiz dang'anguan, *Zhongguo Yinhang Hangshi Jiliao Huibian, 1912–1949* [Compiled Material of the History of the Bank of China of the Chartered Bank] 3 vols (Beijing: Dang'an chubanshe, 1991), vol. 3, pp. 1833, 1985, 2231.
¶   Inspector's Report on Shanghai Branch, 1915, Hong Kong and Shanghai Banking Corporation Archives, SHG 70; Letter from the Manager of the Shanghai Branch to the Chief Manager, 5 February 1929, Hong Kong and Shanghai Banking Corporation Archives, GHO 12.7; and Balance sheet of the Shanghai Branch of 31 December 1936, Hong Kong and Shanghai Banking Corporation Archives, SHGLEDG 128.
**   Balance Sheet of the Shanghai Branch of the Chartered Bank, 1913, 1928 and 1936, Standard Chartered Bank Collection, CLC/B/207/CH04.
††   Zhongguo yinhang Shanghai guoji jinrong yanjiusuo, *Zhongguo Yinhang Shanghai Fenhangshi, 1912–1949* [History of the Shanghai Branch of the Bank of China, 1912–1949] (Beijing: Jingji kexue chubanshe, 1991), Appendix, Table 2.

How did the financial strength of Chartered Bank change in comparison of that of HSBC and Bank of China? According to Table 5.1, if the data for 1913 is taken as 100 percent, the total assets of HSBC, Chartered Bank and Bank of China increased between 1913 and 1928 to 181 percent, 224 percent and 1,814 percent respectively, while their deposits in the same period increased to 192 percent, 257 percent and 1,987 percent respectively. The performance of Bank of China was remarkable. The statistics for the Shanghai branches of the three banks, however, reveal a different trend. Though the deposit growth of the Shanghai branch of Bank of China had the best performance among the three banks, its growth rate was not as large as the whole bank while the Shangai branches of HSBC and Chartered Bank had better performance than the whole bank. If the data for 1928 is taken as 100 percent, the total assets of HSBC, Chartered Bank and Bank of China between 1928 and 1936 changed to 98 percent, 106 percent and 184 percent respectively, while their deposits in the same period moved to 94 percent, 109 percent and 135 percent respectively. In comparison, the deposits of the Shanghai branches of HSBC, Chartered Bank and Bank of China in the same period, again if 1928 is taken as 100 percent, shifted to 74 percent, 115 percent and 324 percent. While Chartered Bank did not expand as much as Bank of China, it performed better than HSBC, which saw an unprecedented decline. In the case of Bank of China, though the deposit of the bank flattened out, the Shanghai branch showed considerable growth, which was important for the bank. A reverse in position of these British banks and Bank of China revealed that changes in business environment during the new regime of Nanjing Nationalist Government after 1928 worked in favour of Bank of China but adversely affected the British banks. This issue will be examined further later on in the chapter.

The Shanghai Branch's Activity in the Deposit-taking Business

All exchange banks operated in China were dominated by the change in gold–silver prices. The decline in the price of silver on the world market after 1873 affected all of the foreign banks operating in Asia. In order to cope with the situation, Chartered Bank instructed all overseas branches and agencies to remit home the whole of their allotted capital in 1885. After that time, with a few exceptions, the working funds of all branches in Asia were entirely reliant upon the deposits they held for their local customers.[8]

The fixed deposits dropped during World War I but grew enormously in 1918 and 1919. After that, while there were some fluctuations, it stayed at a broadly constant rate. On the other hand, the current deposits showed continual growth after 1917 (see Figures 5.1 and 5.11). The number of fixed deposit accounts decreased from a little over 600 in 1913 to less than 600 in 1928, while the number of current deposit accounts increased from a little over 1,400 to more than 2,700 during the same period. The increase in both the number and amount of the current accounts epitomized the business development of Chartered Bank in Shanghai.

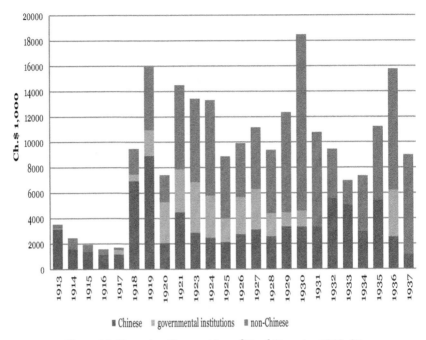

Figure 5.1: Depositor Composition of Fixed Deposits, 1913–37

Source: Half-yearly Balance Sheet of the Shanghai Branch, Chartered Bank, 1913–37. The calculation is based on accounts categorized by Man-han Siu, the criterion of which is explained in n. 9, pp. 208–9.

The depositors of the Shanghai Branch can be divided into three groups: Chinese depositors, governmental institutions and non-Chinese depositors[9] (see Figure 5.1). Chinese depositors held most of the fixed deposits in 1913. At that time, Chinese banking was in its infancy stage and native banks did not receive deposits from the general public; a lot of wealthy Chinese had confidence in foreign banks because of their financial resources, as well as the belief that foreign banks provided security from government inquiries into their accounts. However, in the course of World War I, the amount of fixed deposits from Chinese depositors diminished to a great extent. Although the Chinese increased their fixed deposits in 1918 and 1919, most of these deposits were denominated in British pounds due to the fact that the value of silver was high in terms of gold during World War I.

The competition between foreign banks and modern Chinese banks for deposits from Chinese depositors became keen during the interwar period. The Chinese banks, in general, offered higher interest rates on both fixed and current deposits, even after 1935.[10] In spite of this, the Chinese depositors continued to play an important role in fixed deposits. In the 1920s, the aggregated amount of fixed deposits from Chinese depositors was about 20–30 percent of the total fixed deposit of Chartered Bank. The deposits from Chinese fluctuated in the 1930s, reflecting the fluidity of international and domestic conditions. The foreign banks showed their consideration towards Chinese banks by not accepting new deposits from Chinese depositors right after Shanghai's incident in February 1932, a time when Chinese banks were under financial crisis.[11] Foreign banks made the same decision right after the second Sino-Japanese War broke out in July 1937.[12]

Although the Chinese mainly placed their money in fixed deposit accounts, the change in the amount of current deposits from Chinese depositors as compared to the total amount of current deposits still deserves our attention. As shown in Table 5.2, the aggregated amount of current deposits from Chinese depositors was around 16 percent of the total current deposits in 1913. This dropped to 4.2 percent in 1923, but rose to 13.3 percent in 1936. Though this upward trend shows that the business relationship between Chartered Bank and the Chinese firms and individuals had improved during these years, the Chinese did not play an important role in this sphere of banking activity.

Table 5.2: Ratio of Current Deposits from Chinese in Total Current Deposits

	Current Deposits (Ch.$ 1,000)		
	Chinese	Total	% of Chinese
1913	522	3,418	16.2%
1918	183	2,734	6.7%
1923	285	6,809	4.2%
1928	990	12,416	8.0%
1933	1,906	20,943	9.1%
1936	1,717	12,874	13.3%

Current accounts in taels have been converted into Chinese dollars at Ch. $1 = 0.715 Tael
Source: Half-yearly Balance Sheet of the Shanghai Branch, Chartered Bank, 1913–37.
    The accounts of Chinese depositors are identified with the criterion explained in n. 9, pp. 208–9.

The second group of depositors that greatly affected the amount of deposits were the governmental institutions, either British or Chinese. Chartered Bank became the custodian bank of the funds of the Imperial Maritime Customs, the Custodian of Enemy Property and the Whangpoo Conservancy Board when it was included in the British Group of the International Consortium led by HSBC in December 1916. Founded in 1911, the first consortium was ultimately composed of six national groups. In 1912, a British financier that was not a member of the British group concluded the *Crisp Loan* with the Chinese government. This caused the British Foreign Office to change its policy on giving exclusive support to HSBC, the head of the British Group. Being pressured by the Foreign Office, HSBC enlarged the British Group and offered Chartered Bank an equal participation in the British Group. Chartered Bank rejected the offer on the grounds that it would not be allowed a share in the loan servicing nor the exchange.

In 1916, the British Group was enlarged again, and this time Chartered Bank was accepted the offer to become one of the custodian banks with a custody of 25 percent of the loan fund, while HSBC held 75 percent.[13] After an agreement on 7 December 1916, the reconstituted British Group included HSBC (33%), the Baring Brothers & Cº (23%), the London County & Westminster Bank (11%), Parr's Bank (11%), J. Henry Schröder & Cº (11%), and Chartered Bank (11%).

The Imperial Maritime Customs

The Imperial Maritime Customs was a Chinese governmental institution established in 1854 to collect maritime trade tax. From its establishment, it was administered by a British Inspector-General and had been completely under foreign control since the outbreak of the revolution of 1911. As some of the foreign loans and the Boxer indemnities were secured with customs revenue, the Chinese government was forced to deposit the collected customs revenue at the three customs custodian banks: *Deutsch-Asiatische Bank*, the Russo-Asiatic Bank and HSBC. By the end of World War I, only the Russo-Asiatic Bank and HSBC remained as custodian banks, and most of the funds were deposited in HSBC. At the end of 1928, the national government carried out a re-organization of the Salt Inspectorate and the Customs General Inspectorate. The custody of the revenue, which was entrusted to the Inspectorates, was then transferred to the Ministry of Finance, which, in turn, deposited the main portion of the funds with the Central Bank of China.

The Custodian of Enemy Property

The Custodian of Enemy Property was an institution that handled property claims created by war by the British government.

The Whangpoo Conservancy Board

The establishment of the Whangpoo Conservancy Board originated in the Peace Protocol signed at Peking in 1901. It was re-established in 1912 under a new agreement made between the Chinese Government and the Treaty powers. The purpose of the Board was to direct and control the works of the Whangpoo River for improving the course of the river. The Board, directed by its foreign directors, had entire control of its funds and finance.[14]

These government funds were deposited in a couple of fixed deposit accounts and current deposit accounts of the Shanghai branch of Chartered Bank. As shown in Table 5.3, both the funds in fixed accounts and current accounts were important to the deposit-taking business. It accounted for more than 40 percent of the total current deposit in some particular years and constituted more than 20 percent of the total fixed deposit of the Shanghai Branch of Chartered Bank in the 1920s.

Table 5.3: Deposits from Governmental Institutions

	Fixed Deposits					Current Deposits	
	Custodian in China of Enemy Property (CCEP)	Whangpoo Conservancy (WC)	Chinese Maritime Customs (CMC)	Sub-Total	% of Total	Chinese Maritime Customs (CMC)	% of Total
1917	0	26	0	26	2%		
1918	58	0	320	378	4%		
1919	1,302	0	165	1,467	9%		
1920	1,917	250	144	2,311	31%	1,553	21%
1921	1,606	568	265	2,439	17%	2,201	34%
1923	1,788	651	422	2,861	21%	1,896	28%
1924	839	250	1274	2,363	21%	4,802	44%
1925	875	250	200	1,325	15%	4,922	42%
1926	1,005	550	550	2,105	21%	7,551	46%
1927	940	650	700	2,290	21%	3,556	25%
1928	0	600	700	1,300	14%	2,982	24%
1929	0	800	0	800	6%		
1930	0	900	0	900	5%		

Source: Half-yearly Balance Sheet of the Shanghai Branch, Chartered Bank, 1913–37

Undoubtedly, to be a member of the British Group of the International Consortium greatly enhanced the prestige of Chartered Bank amongst the foreigners in China. Whilst the amount of money in fixed deposit accounts opened by foreigners was less than 10 percent in 1913, it increased to 43 percent in 1926 and 66 percent in 1931 (see Figure 5.1). With the urbanization and industrialization of Shanghai, the foreign population in Shanghai doubled between 1915 and 1930. But the increase in fixed deposits was not only affected by the domestic changes. The sudden increase in 1929 was caused by the enormous amount of deposits held for British banking institutions. Most of these deposits were set at very low interest rates with a duration of less than one year. Unlike fixed deposits accounts, the current accounts were mainly opened by foreign residents and firms in Shanghai. Current accounts enabled businessmen to conduct their business transactions smoothly. The significant increase in the number of accounts and their aggregated amount shows that the bank became quite successful among foreigners in Shanghai.

Figure 5.2: Currency Composition of Fixed Deposits, 1913–37

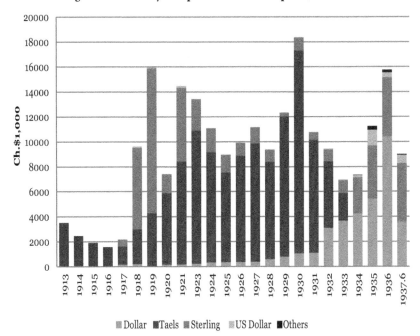

Deposits were made and accounted in various currencies (see Figure 5.2). As a consequence, changes in the amount of deposits partially reflected the changes in the exchange rates between the official currencies adopted by the banks and any other currencies in which deposits were accounted. The amount of fixed deposits made in foreign currencies ran up to a very huge figure on two occasions. One was influenced by the changes in international monetary systems and the other was influenced by the crisis in domestic monetary systems. Before 1914, most of the deposits of the Shanghai branch were denominated in silver currencies. The increase in value of silver after World War I led to a rise of the Chinese currency against both US dollars and British pounds. This caused the amount of fixed deposits denominated in sterling to increase rapidly in 1918 and 1919. However, confidence in the British pound decreased when the British government abandoned the gold exchange system in 1919, which led to a heavy drop in fixed deposits made in sterling. Although Britain re-adopted the Gold Standard, the amount of sterling deposits did not recover to 1919's level.

In 1931, the British went off the Gold Standard again, but its impact on fixed deposits was limited. The increase in deposits denominated in British pounds and American dollars after 1933 was brought about by the *American Silver Purchase Act*. It gave rise to an increase in the value of silver and caused an exodus of large quantities of silver from China. As a result, China was forced to reform its currency system and adopted a managed currency system in November 1935. In the course of establishing this new currency regime, many depositors moved their money from Chinese dollars to foreign currencies. After the new currency was stabilized in the early 1937, Chartered Bank found a decrease in fixed deposits in Chinese national currency as their counterpart Chinese banks offered a much higher rate in deposits (See Figures 5.1 and 5.2).

The Shanghai Branch's Activity in the Exchange Business

The Shanghai Branch of Chartered Bank was mainly orientated towards internationalized business, at the service of the imperial banking connections (UK) or of the American field.

Trade Finance

Trade finance was the core business of foreign exchange banks in China before World War I. In order to understand the development of the trade finance business at the Shanghai branch, it is important to know how banks financed the imports and exports. Richard Feetham concisely described the methods of business of general imports in a report about the present position and future prospects of the Shanghai International Settlement, written in 1931:

> The bulk of the general import trade - under which heading are included piece goods, metals and general merchandise - is done on an Indent basis: that is to say, the Chinese dealer or merchant places his order for his requirements with the importing house, which purchases from makers in foreign countries, and accepts full responsibility for the correct execution of the order placed, and attends to the financing, and vis-à-vis the supplier, accepts full responsibility for payment of the goods ordered. In this business, as a rule, no credit is given to the Chinese buyer, who is required to pay cash before delivery, and usually does by means of a Native Bank Order of from five to ten days' usance. The dealer is usually required to pay Customs duty on arrival of the goods, and interest up to date of payment [...] In the case of exports, the goods are contracted for delivery to the exporter's godown [stockyard] or packing house, and heavy cash advances are made thereon prior to delivery being made by the seller. Goods are not delivered or inspected previous to payment, and the fact that heavy advances have often to be made on account of contracts with Chinese dealers for export, long before delivery of cargo at port of shipment.[15]

Imports from Britain were usually financed by bills drawn under the London acceptance credits. An exporter in the UK had to draw two bills: the first was drawn and accepted by his banker in London; the other was drawn by the exporter on the importer, and was attached to the shipping documents. It was sent out through the bank for collection, and its proceeds would eventually be used by his bank to retire the bill it had previously accepted.[16] Imports from the

USA and Germany had similar arrangements. The amount of these bills bought by the London Head Office, New York and Hamburg branches of Chartered Bank appeared as 'Bills Held for Collection' in both the debit side and credit side of the balance sheet of the Shanghai branch. We can see from Figure 5.3 that bills held for collection decreased in World War I and reached a peak in 1919 when there was a rise in the value of silver. However, the import trade did not flourish in the long run. In regard to exports, the exports bills bought from foreign merchants by Chartered Bank were sent to the importing countries for collection, so they were not recorded in the balance sheet of the Shanghai branch.

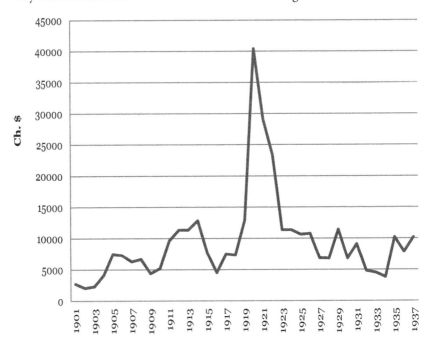

Figure 5.3: Outstanding Bills Held for Collection, 1901–37

In addition to buying and selling bills, the bank offered other forms of credit to importers and exporters to improve their cash flow. In the case of imports, trust receipts were commonly used. A trust receipt was a commercial document whereby the bank released goods into the possession of the entrustee, but retained ownership thereof; upon selling the goods the entrustee then used the proceeds to make full payment of his liability with the bank. In the case of export trade finance, on the other hand, fixed loans and current overdrafts were often made to export merchants and Chinese native banks against exported goods such as cocoons, silk or eggs. By analysing the changes in the amount of fixed loans and current overdrafts using imported and exported goods as security, we can then grasp the trend of trade finance in the Shanghai branch (see Table 5.4). From 1913 to 1928, trade finance was still an important business activity at the Shanghai Branch. However, the trade related advances declined sharply in the 1930s.

Table 5.4: Security of Loans and Current Overdrafts, 1913–33, (Ch.$1,000)

	Current Overdrafts				Loans			
	Trade related	Others	Total	% of Trade related	Trade related	Others	Total	% of Trade related
	A		B	A/B	A		B	A/B
1913	418	1,802	2,220	19%	1,225	160	1 385	89%
1918	425	1,398	1,823	23%	277	329	606	46%
1923	985	5,006	5,992	16%	2,197	37	2,234	98%
1928	1,637	5,632	7,268	23%	2,811	4,122	6,932	41%
1933	533	10,225	10,758	5%	401	13,504	13,905	3%
1936	832	10,101	10,933	8%	289	11,886	12,175	2%

Source: Half-yearly Balance Sheet of the Shanghai Branch, Chartered Bank, 1913–37

Forward Exchange Operations

The forward exchange business was originally derived from trade finance. As the silver price fluctuated enormously, both importers and exporters tried to buy forward exchange when they placed their orders to avoid exchange losses. However, the forward exchange business unrelated to trade finance, but only aimed at arbitrage expanded after 1915. Chartered Bank mainly transacted in British pounds before 1931 (see Figures 5.4–5.7); as Britain went off gold in 1931, the transaction in US dollars took the place of the British pound as the most important foreign currency transacted. The turbulence of the financial market in Shanghai caused by the American silver policy led to a massive scale of transactions in US dollars and British pounds.

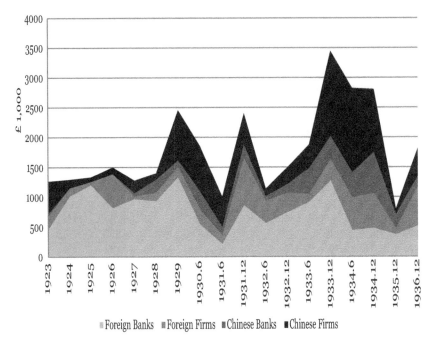

Figure 5.4: Forward Exchange Business: Outstanding Purchase of T. T., sterling (1923–35)

Source: Half-yearly Balance Sheet of the Shanghai Branch, Chartered Bank, 1913–37. The accounts are categorized by Man-han Siu, the criterion of which is explained in n. 20, p. 209.

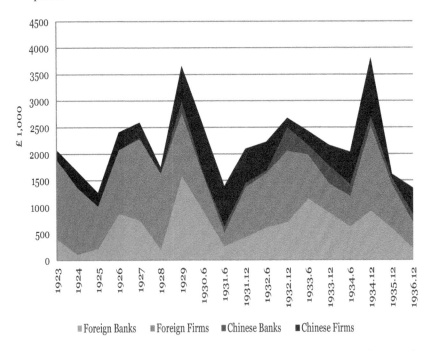

Figure 5.5: Forward Exchange Business: Outstanding Sales of T. T., sterling (1923–35)

In November 1935, China implemented a broad currency reform and moved from a silver standard to a managed currency. This new managed currency had to move within the narrow limits of US dollars and British pounds. The trend of the currency market after the currency reform was described in great detail in the report written by the Shanghai manager of Chartered Bank:

> The controlled currency has behaved very well during the half year. There were one or two occasions when it was subjected to a pretty severe strain and considerable nervousness was shown by the Government finance officials and also the Bankers but on the whole they handled the situation satisfactorily and no serious trouble resulted.[17]

The occasions he mentioned were the 'sky-rocketing rate of the London New York cross-rate' in September, the 'Sino Japanese incident in Shanghai' that also occurred in September, and the Sian Coup in December. In coping with these events, the Chinese government

> immediately shipped to the United States of America silver dollars amounting to 50 million dollars which had been sold by them at 50 cents U.S. currency per ounce and which gave them an available credit of approximately USD 25,000,000. At the same time being afraid of some action by Japan, similar to what had happened in North China, they hastened to ship all their available silver and gold to Hongkong. This created a certain amount of nervousness in the market but strengthened the position of the Government Banks who freely met the demands of the market. [The Sian coup] precipitated a financial panic and would undoubtedly have taxed the Chinese Government Banks' resources to the uttermost had it not been for the assistance of the foreign banks who met all demands on them without calling on the Government Banks for more than a modicum of their clients' requirements. The Japanese Banks and merchants at that time were heavy buyers of sterling and US dollars and were mainly responsible for the heavy drain on the other banks. We sold about £1,000,000, the Hongkong Bank just over £1,000,000, and National City Bank and Chase Bank sold about the same amount each but we believe they drew on the Government Banks for part cover. Most of the other foreign banks also sold smaller amounts while the Chinese Government banks are reported to have sold the equivalent of US$30,000,000. The strong recovery in our rates even before the actual release of Chiang Kai-shek showed that the nervousness was not generally shared by the public and there is obviously much more confidence in the currency now than ever before.[18]

One fact that had been very conspicuous during the last half year of 1937 had been the comparatively small activity of the Chinese speculators.[19] As a result, the exchange transactions for arbitrage decreased to a large extent.

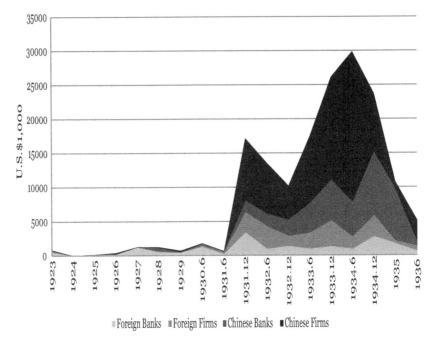

Figure 5.6: Forward Exchange Business: Outstanding Purchase of T. T., US dollars (1923–36)

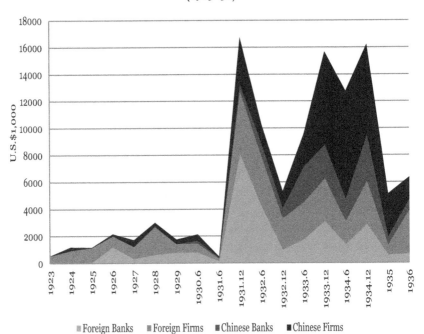

Figure 5.7: Forward Exchange Business: Outstanding Sales of T. T., US dollars (1923–36)

How much did Chinese participate in the exchange operations? As shown in Figures 5.6–5.7, modern Chinese joint-stock banks, Chinese firms and individuals were active buyers and sellers of the forward exchange of US dollars.[20] From June 1933 to December 1935, the total amount of forward US dollars transacted by Chinese banks, Chinese firms and individuals exceeded their foreign counterparts. Undoubtedly, speculation by the Chinese in foreign exchange had accelerated the outflow of silver from China. The increase in Chinese participation in foreign exchange was due to an institutional change in the 1920s.

Before 1929, Chinese banks were not on an equal footing with their foreign bank counterparts in regards to the exchange business. Foreign exchange business was practically in the hands of the members of the Foreign Exchange Bankers' Association, which changed its name to the Shanghai Foreign Exchange Bankers' Association in 1916. In 1921, there were 21 member banks and Chartered Bank was the chairman. The aim of this association was to protect the interests of those banks that are operating in the exchange business. All exchange transactions were to be mediated by the Foreign Exchange Brokers' Association, which was subordinated to the Shanghai Foreign Exchange Bankers' Association. On the other hand, all foreign exchange transaction done by members of the foreign exchange brokers should contain at least one party that belong to the Shanghai Foreign Exchange Bankers' Association, otherwise penal provisions would be applied. Under this rule, exchange business was practically limited to banks that were members of the Shanghai Foreign Exchange Bankers' Association and non-members were prevented from entering the exchange market.

After 1917, Chinese banks began to operate in foreign exchange business.[21] Though they tried to set up their own foreign exchange brokers association, it suffered the setback of small business scale. In order to stand on an equal footing with their foreign counterparts in foreign exchange operations, the Shanghai Bankers' Association wrote to the Shanghai Foreign Exchange Bankers' Association at the end of 1920 to request for some possible measures for participating in foreign exchange market. As there was not any response from the Shanghai Foreign Bankers' Association, they wrote again to make a request that eight Chinese banks that operated exchange business be allowed to become members of the corresponding association in May 1921.

Notwithstanding that the Shanghai Foreign Exchange Bankers' Association turned down this request to accept non-foreign banks into their association, they agreed to consider setting up a new organization that all banks operating in Shanghai, regardless of which banking association it belonged to, could participate in, so as to promote Sino-foreign co-operation. The idea was shelved from June 1921 to March 1926, as the Shanghai Foreign Exchange Bankers' Association did not want to compromise as to the number of Chinese in the committee, in allowing the chairman to be Chinese and in the quota of Chinese to be foreign exchange brokers. However, after 1925, the foreign banks were willing to be more conciliatory and a new foreign exchange, the Shanghai Chinese Exchange

Brokers' Association, consisting of both Chinese and foreign brokers, was established in September 1926.

As the political situation was unsteady after 1926, it took two more years for the foreign and Chinese bankers to reach their agreement on the establishment of a new banking organization. The nationalist government implemented a reform of the banking system and authorized Bank of China to become the government exchange bank. The Association of Shanghai Banks finally formed in March 1929, with a Committee made up of eight members from the Shanghai Foreign Bankers' Association, five members of the Shanghai Bankers' Association and three members of the Shanghai Native Banks Association.[22]

The Shanghai Branch's Activity in Current Overdrafts and Loans

The business activities of Chartered Bank corresponded to two different business communities: the Western one and the Chinese one. British managers lent to Westerners while Chinese compradore acted as an intermediary of Chartered Bank and the Chinese community. The compradoric system was started from the time the bank established its Shanghai branch in the nineteenth century, but it was still essential for the business activities of the Shanghai branch in the 1930s. The function of the compradore was to provide information on the market as well as to arrange loans to reliable traders or other banks that the bank Chartered Bank could lend to. A compradore had to compensate Chartered Bank for any loss when his loan was in default. In a few cases, the compradore shared part of the interest, about ½ percent, of the loan to be received from the borrower. Although he had to deposit his title deeds of the property situated in the International Settlements in the bank as security, his liability was unlimited.

Advances of Chartered Bank were made in the form of fixed loans[23] as well as current overdrafts. The amount of fixed loans was small until 1927 and started to grow after 1928 (see Figure 5.8), to the point where, in 1937, the amount of fixed loans was about six times of that of 1927. Security against loans showed changes in the nature of business (see Table 5.4). Before 1927, most of the fixed loans were made for the purpose of financing foreign trade. Most of the borrowers, including the foreign importers, exporters and Chinese native banks, were lent on demand. However, the ratio of the imported and exported goods as security to the total amount of security provided decreased as the security provided by borrowers changed. The duration of these fixed loans ranged from on demand to one or two years, depending on the nature of the transaction and the credibility of the debtors. Undoubtedly, the lending policy had changed after 1928. The ratio of loans to Chinese firms and individuals to the total fixed loans dwindled between 1924 and 1928 but increased rapidly after 1932.[24] From 1933 to 1937, more than half of all fixed loans were made to Chinese firms and individuals. In some cases, the guarantee was not limited to the compradore. Some first-class native banks acted as an additional guarantor, too. While fixed loans with the guarantee of a compradore continued in the 1930s, loans to Chinese companies that did not require any guarantee emerged too. It was this kind of new, fixed loan that pushed up the whole amount of fixed loans. Table 5.5 shows a list of the Chinese loan borrowers in 1934. Out of the nine Chinese loan borrowers in 1934, two of them borrowed without any guarantors. One of these unguaranteed loans was given to Mow Sing & Foh Sing Flour Mills and Sing Sung Cotton Mills, which were controlled by the Rong Brothers Company.

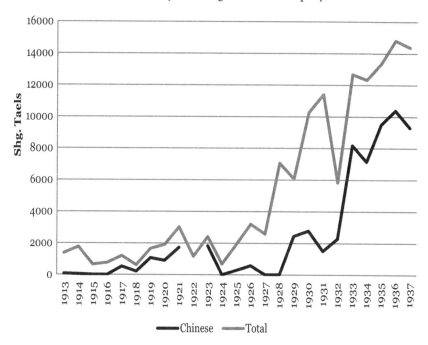

Figure 5.8: Proportion of Chinese Borrowers in Fixed Loans, 1913–37

Table 5.5: List of Chinese Borrowers of Fixed Loans and Current Overdrafts in 1934

Name of the borrowers	Title	Amount	Term	Interest rate	Guarantor
Fixed Loans					
Shen Chen Ku	retired official	5	O/D	7%	British American Tobacco C°
Yien Tuck Dong	Merchants	1400	Hold over	8%	Compradore, first class native bank
Mow Sing & Foh Sing Flour Mills and Sung Sing Cotton Mills	–	4 196	2 years	8%	–
Li Dah Investment Co.	Bankers	900	1 year	6,5%	Compradore
Chow Ken Kee	Merchants	450	1 year	6,5%	Compradore
Yao Pah Kua	Retired Government Official	250	1 year	7%	Compradore
Yung Kong Bank	Bankers	90	O/D	10%	Compradore
Dah Tuck Bank	Bankers	200	O/D	10%	Compradore
So. Brothers & Co.	Merchants	5	3m	7%	–
Current Overdrafts					
Chang Yuan Chi	Late Assistant, Commercial Press, Ltd.	14	–	8%	–
Fu Chung Corporation	Coal Merchants	36	–	8%	–
Great China Co.Ltd.	Department Store	1 772	–	8%	–
Hutchison & Co.	Merchants	12	–	8%	–
So. Brothers & Co.	Merchants	19	–	8%	–
Wing On Co. (Shanghai)	Merchants	500	–	10%	(Head Office Limit $1,400,000)
Cheng Yun Cheong	Compradore, Butterfield & Swire C°	11	–	7%	–
Overseas Banking Corporation	–	499	–	7%	–

The Rong Brothers Company was one of China's most important flour and textile manufacturers. In 1919, it had eight flour mills, which were built in Shanghai and the Lower Yangtze Region and, in 1921, its flour mills held 31.4 percent of the overall capacity of the industry. The Rong Brothers Company built its first cotton mill in 1915 and it had nine cotton factories and twelve flour factories up to 1931. Its total assets were valued at more than 60 million Chinese dollars in 1931. However, the financial loss in 1930–31 forced it to obtain loans from both Chinese and foreign banks.[25] In 1933, Chartered Bank advanced $4.2 million to the company on a two years contract.[26] This amount was more or less the same as those advanced by Bank of China, one of Rong Brothers Company's main creditors.[27] After the contract with the company was due, Chartered Bank acquired the property from the Rong Brothers Company and leased it back to them.[28] This loan appeared in the balance sheet as leased property account. This has been included in the fixed loans category for convenience in comparison.

In contrast, the Rong Brothers Company's loan from HSBC did not get on so smoothly. The interest due prompted HSBC to put the security placed by Rong Brothers Company on auction and led to the interference of the Chinese Government.[29]

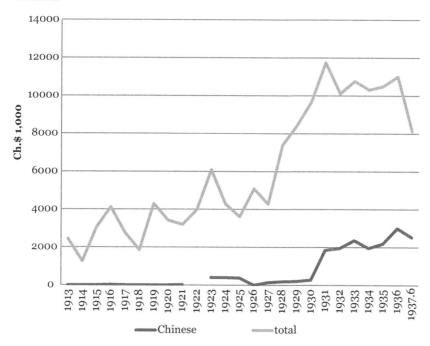

Figure 5.9: Proportion of Chinese Borrowers in Current Overdrafts, 1913–37

The proportion of the current accounts opened by foreigners were much higher than those opened by the Chinese at Chartered Bank. Before 1929, most of the current overdrafts were made to foreigners. However, current overdrafts showed a similar trend as that of fixed loans in the 1930s. The current overdrafts made to the Chinese increased rapidly after 1930 (see Figure 5.9) and, at the end of June 1937, the amount of overdrafts made to the Chinese was around 30 percent of the total amount. Unlike fixed loans, borrowers of current overdrafts did not require a compradore's guarantee. There were about 200 current overdrafts accounts in total, yet, as can be seen in Table 5.5, the number of Chinese current overdrafts accounts was limited to eight. Among these eight accounts, the Great China Co. Ltd and Wing On Co., the department stores in Shanghai were included. Such department stores developed rapidly after 1917 and became some of Shanghai's most influential businesses in terms of capital and turnover. The overdraft limits set by the head office on the Great China Co. and Wing On Co. in 1934 were 1,265,000 taels (equal to Ch.$1,769,230) and Ch.$ 1,400,000 respectively. The aggregate amount of these overdraft limits was 36 percent of the total fixed deposits in that year.

After 1910, the Chinese economy expanded rapidly. World War I gave the indigenous entrepreneurs ample opportunities to expand in the modern sector. Industrialization based upon import substitution developed mainly in Shanghai, the Lower Yangzi region and other treaty ports. Light industry such as flour mills, cotton mills and silk filature flourished. Along with the development in industry, the population growth fostered urbanization in Shanghai. In spite of all these developments, Chartered Bank only began to take advantage of this structural change in the Chinese economy in the 1930s.

The Profit and Loss of the Shanghai Branch, 1915–36

The net profit/losses was made up of net income from foreign exchange operations and net interest income. As it is shown in Figure 5.10, Chartered Bank did not perform well before 1929. During these years, the bank either made losses or earned only a small profit. The trend changed from 1929, but was seriously affected by Britain going off the Gold Standard in 1931.The profit recovered after 1932 and reached its peak in 1934. However, after the *Currency Reform*, the profit of Chartered Bank dropped sharply, although it picked up again after the second Sino-Japanese War.

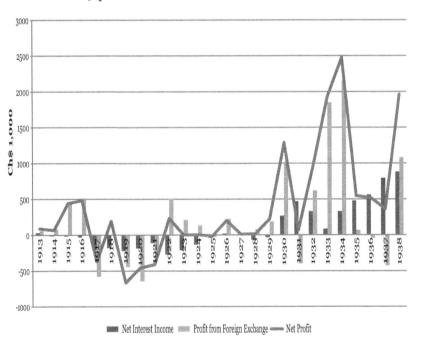

Net Interest Income ▬▬ Profit from Foreign Exchange ▬▬ Net Profit

Figure 5.10: Net Profits, 1913–38

Aside from 1918, between 1917 and 1921 the bank had been continually losing money in foreign exchange operations. In spite of the decline in import trade finance from 1922, the foreign exchange business brought profits to Chartered Bank throughout most of the period 1922–35. It is noteworthy that the extraordinary profit gained from the foreign exchange business in 1933 and 1934 was brought by the financial crisis occurred at that time. The *Silver Purchase Act* of 1934 followed an unprecedented decline in the price of silver during the Great Depression. The fluctuation of gold–silver prices induced frenzied speculations in foreign currencies that increased the volume of foreign exchange business substantially and gave rise to an enormous profit for the bank. However, the steadier foreign exchange environment after the *Currency Reform* kept Chartered Bank's forward differences narrower and interest in trade related overdrafts and loans had therefore been lower and led to a decrease in profit.

Net interest income showed losses in most of the years from 1914 to 1929. The heavy losses in net interest income led to continual losses in net profit. Although Chartered Bank had been the custodian of official funds from 1917 to 1928, it could not utilize its fund fully when restricted by conventional policy in lending (see Figure 5.11). It was only after the Bank began to increase its advances to the Chinese business community that expanded advances and substantial profits were gained.

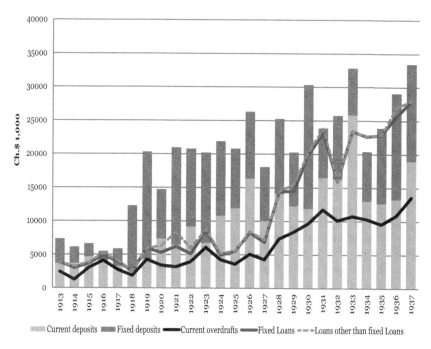

Figure 5.11: Advances and Deposits, 1913–37

The Re-orientation of Policy in Banking Business

The imperial banking system evolved towards more cooperation with the native Chinese banks in order to favour embeddedness and cooperation.

Joint-venture Plan in the Early 1930s

The establishment of the Shanghai Bankers Association symbolized the relationship between the Chinese banks and foreign banks. The breakdown of the monopoly in exchange business held by foreign banks meant that competition could develop. W. E. Preston, the Chief Manager of Chartered Bank, showed his anxiety of the development of foreign banks in China in his talk with Zhang Jiaao, the General Manager of Bank of China in 1929. Preston told Chang that he was looking forward to the Sino-foreign cooperation, an idea that was particularly asserted by Archibald Rose, a former British diplomat in China who became a director of Chartered Bank in 1925.[30] Sino-foreign cooperation was not a new idea at that time. The change in strategy was in line with a new diplomatic policy devised by the British government.[31] The Sino-foreign cooperation of Chartered Bank took a more concrete form as it made a plan to form a joint venture with a Chinese bank in 1930.[32]

The idea of having joint ventures was examined by quite a lot of foreign companies in Shanghai.[33] In 1932, W. J. Evans Thomas, the Manager of the Peking branch of Chartered Bank, made a trip to the interior with Chen Guangpu, a prominent Chinese banker who had established the Shanghai Commercial and Savings Bank, a modern joint-stock bank with a branch network throughout China. They visited the branches and agencies of Chen's bank in Nanjing, Anqing, Jiujiang, Hankou, Kaifeng and Xuzhou, and Thomas came to realize that

> certain branches were almost entirely deposit agencies whose funds were lent to other branches for financing trade. Advances were principally made against produce and raw materials, the latter for small mills and factories. Finished products could then be financed to their markets for sale with an additional profit to the bank on the inland exchange [...] Raw materials and produce were a good banking security, and there was money to be made if business were run on sound banking principles.[34]

Regarding business collaboration, Thomas wrote that 'at that time we had several ideas in common and were exploring the possibilities of linking the activities of a Chinese bank with interior branches to those of a foreign bank with world-wide connections.'[35] However, 'herein we saw possibilities for the future in co-operation between Chinese and foreign banking; but, unfortunately, the course of events in China proved our ideas to be too sanguine.'[36] The joint venture plan was not realized.

After China's Currency Reform of 1935

After China's *Currency Reform*, the monetary system made significant changes that affected Chartered Bank's exchange business to a large extent. Firstly, the forward exchange business decreased substantially as the exchange rates became less fluctuated. Secondly, in the process of coping with the financial crisis, the Chinese Nationalist Government implemented a banking reform that nationalized Bank of China and Bank of Communications, the two most important official banks in China in 1934. After the currency reform, the National Government intervened in the field of foreign trade through the official banks.

With the accumulation of funds in the hands of official banks by selling silver stock to the US Government, the official banks were able to gain a foothold in the foreign trade finance business. By strengthening its overseas network, Bank of China could transact directly with banks in New York, London and other financial centres.[37] The Chinese official banks intervened in the export bills market by obtaining them regardless of price,[38] and by being extensive buyers of certain commodities such as peanuts, sesamum seeds, hides, and wood-oil. One of the reasons was that the Chinese government had to fulfill the agreement concluded with Germany in bartering industrial goods and primary goods in 1936.[39] Moreover, they were trying to gain control over foreign trade.[40] As a result, foreign banks could hardly buy any export bills in a profitable way.[41] However, the problem was more serious in a long run.

A letter from the Shanghai manager to the chief manager showed his anxiety in coping with the structural problems faced by the Shanghai Branch:

> We are no longer able to make large profits in exchange. We are anxious, however, to keep up the profits of this Branch and it is therefore necessary for us to explore other spheres with a view to maintaining our profit earning capacity. With the large quantities of machinery which have been and are still being imported into China, the country is rapidly becoming industrialised, and with the exception of proprietary articles, most of our needs can now be satisfied by the products of local factories. The Japanese cotton industry is rapidly being transferred to China through large imports of Japanese machinery and the country during the course of the next few years is likely to become practically self-supporting. In connection with the large import of textile machinery above referred to, it is generally considered that, with the improvement in the relations between China and Japan, supplies of machinery and other equipment for industrial enterprises will tend to come more and more from Japan instead of Europe and America, and thus one more source of exchange business will pass out of our sphere.
>
> It therefore behoves us to re-orientate our policy to the changed conditions, and show our willingness to participate freely in the finance of sound local enterprises at attractive rates of interest. Up to the present, this field has been confined almost entirely to Chinese banks and is their main source of profit, for with their branches inland, they are able to finance crops and to retain control of raw materials through the process of manufacture right up to the sale of the finished article. Modern facto-

ries are being erected in the large towns all over the country and there are signs on every hand of increasing activity [...]. It is evident therefore that the present activity in imports cannot continue indefinitely and our usefulness to the community in the financing of imports will of necessity become increasingly less. If therefore we are to remain a powerful institution in China, we can only do so by lending to good Chinese concerns, and with the ever growing feeling of confidence and stability, we are of opinion that we should not be running more than an average business risk.[42]

The proposal of the Shanghai manager was to re-orient their policy by financing the sound local enterprises that changed the business of the Shanghai branch from that of an exchange bank's to that of a local bank's. With the industrialization of China, financing the Chinese industry became a natural option to Chartered Bank. Though it had begun to adapt to the changing situation after 1929 and had made advances to the Chinese business community at an unprecedented level, the proposal by the Manager of the Shanghai Branch showed that the currency reform had forced foreign banks to further their strategy in more thoroughly penetrating Chinese business environment. However, Harold Faulkner of the Peking Branch strongly opposed the proposal while the board of directors in London also took his side.[43] The conflicting views within Chartered Bank show the difficulties in forecasting the prospects of the Chinese economy in the 1930.

Conclusion

After the Nanjing regime was established, the government carried out a series of reforms in the banking sector. This caused foreign banks to lose some of the privileges that they had enjoyed before 1928. For example, foreign banks lost their monopoly on carrying out foreign exchange business. Moreover, they could no longer continue to be the custodian of official funds related to the Chinese government. Even though the changes that took place seemed to have adverse impact on foreign banks, far from being contracted, the business of the Shanghai Branch of Chartered Bank expanded both in scale and scope.

In regards to the local business, deposits increased four times while advances progressed seven times from 1913 to 1936. In regards to exchange business, foreign exchange purchases increased four times whilst foreign exchange sales increased two times between 1923 and 1936. The growth in the volume of the business was rapid, particularly after 1928. At the same time, the customer base of the Shanghai Branch became more diverse. After World War II, not only did the bank receive deposits from companies, individuals and public institutions, but also from governmental organizations. On the other hand, in regard to advances and exchange businesses, although Chartered Bank operated within the traditional framework that transacted mainly with Western enterprises and Western residents, changes took place. The relationship between Chartered

Bank and the indigenous Chinese business community limited to taking deposits from Chinese depositors and making advances to Chinese native banks, the traditional financial institutions in order to finance trade previously. After 1928, credit facilities were provided to business spheres besides trade finance. Moreover, the bank tried to break loose from an almost exclusive dependence on Western customers, extending its lending activities to Chinese enterprises and Chinese residents. Transaction with Chinese joint-stock banks and Chinese residents also grew significantly in the 1930s.

The closer relationship between Chartered Bank and the Chinese business community was one of the main reasons of the expansion in the scale and scope of the Shanghai Branch. The implementation of the currency reform of 1935 brought structural changes to financial markets in China and pushed the bank to accelerate its penetration into Chinese indigenous economy. The fact that the business of Chartered Bank expanded after 1928 showed that the foreign and Chinese banks were by no means locked in a zero-sum game in which one party's loss is the other's gain. Foreign banks also benefited from the development of the Chinese modern economy and although Chinese banks became powerful competitors, they could also be counterparts of alliance in new spheres.

Despite these advances, the outbreak of the second Sino-Japanese War made it impossible for foreign banks to implement its strategy and thus a realignment of the relationship between foreign and Chinese banks could not be realized. Instead of co-operating with Chinese banks in local business, Chartered Bank, as a representative bank for the Chinese Currency Stabilization Fund, jointly established by the Chinese and British governments in 1939, co-operated with Chinese official banks to defend Chinese currencies. The strategy of strengthening economic relations with Chinese indigenous economy could only be adopted in Hong Kong after World War II.

6 RUSSIAN AND SOVIET IMPERIAL BANKING IN ASIA IN THE 1890s–1920s

Sofya Salomatina

This chapter analyses the transformation of Russian pre-revolutionary imperial banking in the activity of Soviet banks in Asia in the 1920s. Generally, colonial banking was a part of the economic expansion of major powers in the 19th century and at the beginning of the 20th century, when the metropolitan banking system spread to economically less developed and often dependent territories to serve metropolitan businesses. However, this movement could have included political aspects, and in this case, we can speak about imperial banking as part of the imperial policy. The example of the Russian Empire clearly shows this trend.

Before World War I, the powerful Russian Empire had interests along its Asian border, but above all in Persia and China. In most cases, banks supplemented government policy, acting as its economic agents. After the Russian Revolution in 1917, there was a formal rejection of the imperial policy, including the imperial practice of banking. At the same time, in the 1920s, Soviet Russia established some Soviet banks in Asia and their network largely coincided with the pre-revolutionary Russian banking system abroad. However, to what extent did the Soviet banking practice of the 1920s correlate with imperial banking before the revolution? Was there any succession in imperial banking? Was it due to imperial ambition or economic reality? Could a foreign bank influence local conditions or did this bank depend on them? Finally, could a foreign bank be an agent of local financial modernization?

The Soviet banking institutions in Asia, affiliated with the State Bank of the USSR and the Bank for Foreign Trade of the USSR (*Vneshtorgbank*), are the main focus of this chapter, with particular attention to the Russo-Persian Banking-house (*Ruspersbank*), the Mongolian Trade and Industrial Bank (*Mongolbank*), the Tuvinian Trade and Industrial Bank (*Tuvinbank*) and the Far Eastern Bank (*Dalbank*) in Harbin. The study is based on archival materials of the Vneshtorgbank in the 1920s from the Russian State Archive of the Economy (RSAE). Three types of documents were investigated: general statistics on foreign trade and its crediting, balance sheets of Soviet banks abroad, and analytics on Asian markets. Published reports of the Vneshtorgbank were also used in this study. For comparison, some of the published and archival materials about pre-Revolutionary banks (the Discount and Loan Bank of Persia, the Russo-Chinese Bank and the Russo-Asiatic Bank) were also added.

In 2010, Kazuhiko Yago began the comparative study of Soviet banks in the Far East.[1] However, in general, the study of the Soviet banking system is in its infancy, partly because it is considered to be a non-classical system, without commercial credit and free capital markets. On the other hand, the main effort in Soviet economic history studies has been focused on the principles of the command economy, but its financial issues have remained out of the mainstream. This chapter is one of the first attempts to investigate the archives of Soviet banks, but it focuses on the New Economic Policy (NEP) period, when commercial credit still existed, and the experience of pre-revolutionary banks' studies may be useful for this subject. The general information on the Soviet banking system of the 1920s was derived from A. Blum's study released in 1929.[2] The jubilee volume on the *Vnesheconombank*,[3] the successor of the Vneshtorgbank, was published in 1999. This was based on archival documents, but it paid little attention to Soviet banks in Asia.[4] In 2011, Nikolai Krotov released another jubilee publication with some sections about Soviet banks in the Far East in the 1920s.[5]

This chapter includes five main sections, all devoted to the 1920s: an analysis of Imperial banking in pre-revolutionary Russia; a brief outline of the Soviet banking system; Soviet international banking transactions; Soviet exports to Asia and imports from Asia; and the history of the Russo-Asiatic Bank and Soviet banks in Asia. Thus, this study investigates not only Russian and Soviet 'imperial' banking, but also the Soviet banking system.

Imperial Banking in the Russian Empire, 1890–1917

Research on Russian imperial banks has a long tradition, based on archival studies. These banks were investigated uppermost in connection with Russian foreign policy in Persia, China and Mongolia. The principal issues concerned the ownership and control of these banks (the ratio of private and public holding of shares, Russian and foreign forces in their management), details of the negotiations on loans to Asian governments and the acquisition and exploitation of concessions.[6] At the same time, these banks are much less studied as business institutions. In 2012, K. Yago published a chapter on the commercial operations of the Russo-Chinese Bank from a regional perspective.[7] Boris Anan'ich devoted some pages in his book on the Discount and Loan Bank of Persia to the economic conditions of banking in Persia.[8] A brief overview of Russian banks in China was included in the book by Ji Zhaojin.[9] Nevertheless, the accumulated knowledge allows us to make generalizations about Russian imperial banks and raise new issues relating primarily to their commercial activities.

The Milestones of Russian Imperial Banking

Before WWI, the Russian Empire competed with Great Britain over Persia, with Japan over Manchuria and Korea, had trading outposts in China, and established protectorates over the northern territories of China (Mongolia and Tannu Uriankhai[10]), which were not recognized by other states. Government policy was reinforced by a special bank in most cases. Russian imperial banks emerged from the 1890s, as a part of the policy of the Minister of Finance Sergei Witte.

The Russo-Chinese Bank acted in China in 1896–1909 and from 1910, the Russo-Asiatic Bank (1910–26) took over some of its 'imperial' duties. Thanks to these banks, Russian business had a stable position in Asia before WWI. Russia virtually ceded Korea to Japan in the late 1890s; therefore, the project of the Russo-Korean Bank (1897–1901) actually failed. The situation in the protectorates - Mongolia and Tannu Uriankhai - called for the creation of a modern financial institution. For these purposes, the Mongolian Bank (1914–18) was established, but it did not really start its operations because of war and revolution in Russia.

In Persia, the private Moscow International Trade Bank, a member of Polyakovs' business group, was trying to gain a foothold during the early 1890s. The bank's branch was opened in 1892 and operated with some success,[11] but gradually the Persian direction was completely taken over by the Discount and Loan Bank of Persia (1891–1921). Russian exports and imports in Persia were higher than English ones (see Figure 6.4), while the Discount and Loan Bank of Persia gradually lost to the British the Imperial Bank of Persia in competition for loans and concessions.[12] Thus, there is a discrepancy between the political and economic results of Russian penetration into Persia, which deserves further study. It is also worth mentioning the Istanbul (Constantinople) branch of the Russian Bank for Foreign Trade, which has not yet been studied, but which apparently served southern Russian foreign trade. The results of the Russian colonial expansion differed in two control milestones: before World War I and after it. By 1914, Russia had certain economic positions along its Asian borders. World War I strongly influenced this situation. Russian trade with Asian countries stopped; all imperial projects were frozen. The ruble depreciated abroad as did local currencies. Foreign branches were separated from Russia and began to lose their assets, property and personnel. By the end of the war, all these institutions were in serious crises and all Russian imperial conquests had been lost.

The Model of Russian Imperial Banking

What was the difference between Russian imperial banks and the foreign branches of Russian private banks? A private bank entered a foreign market with purely commercial objectives, primarily to service the settlements of domestic entrepreneurs with a foreign financial centre. At the same time, a foreign bank's branch could take advantage of the local financial market for a profit. In any case, the branch made efforts to adapt to the local business conditions. Russian imperial banks were also institutions designed for payments between Russian and Asian financial centres as well as being engaged in other banking operations in local financial markets abroad. However, unlike private banks, these banks were created by the Russian government primarily for political objectives, which were just supplemented by economic tasks. Imperial banks had to respond quickly to requests from the state, so they were distinguished by two main features.

Firstly, all imperial banks were in a different form under the control of the government, and only the Russo-Asiatic Bank was a fully private institution. The boards of banks were located in St. Petersburg, and their Asian branches were headed by officials who were diplomats rather than financiers. Government control enabled this bank to be entrusted with projects that were considered to be unprofitable by private business. On the other hand, the Russian state was generally distrusting of private initiatives. There is a remarkable case on this subject in Sergei Belyaev's book: in the 1910s, the Ministry of Finance tried to return the Russo-Asiatic Bank to Mongolia, where the Russo-Chinese Bank had suffered heavy losses some years before because of the difficulties of the Russian gold-mining concession company 'Mongolor' and defaults on loans by Mongol princes.[13] The Russo-Asiatic Bank rejected the government's project, not seeing the commercial benefits in it, and preferred to stay in those Chinese regions where its business had already been adjusted. The Russian Ministry of Finance decided to engage in Mongolian financial modernization and drafted the Mongolian Bank, but it did not dare charge with this project the private Siberian Commercial Bank, which had agreed to start business in Mongolia under its own risk. However, the government itself did not have the resources for this project in the war period.

Secondly, imperial banks were generally created under a much freer charter in comparison with private Russian banks. Imperial banks enjoyed the benefits of less stringent requirements for liquidity, securities and the terms of loans, and they had the right to issue their own bank notes and mint local coins. They could also purchase foreign and private securities without limits, i.e. securities of obscure reliability in Russian contemporary banking terminology. They could even receive tax payments in Asian countries and provide Asian treasuries with banking services, gain and develop concessions and go into commodity trade. The government, for political and economic expansion in Asia, used imperial banks, which were a part of a system of unequal relations between the Russian Empire and neighbouring Asian states in which it sought to extend its influence. It is important to note that areas adjacent to Russia had centuries-old traditions of nationhood; therefore, it was impossible to dominate directly or to impose European institutions there. In addition, the local population had its own consumption standard, and they did not need Russian goods very much. The Russians had to form a market of its products in these countries and pay for local goods in gold or silver. Trade relations gradually formed its own infrastructure, such as sales offices, warehouses, dealers and traders' settlements.

The Russian government led a diplomatic struggle to lend to local governments and concessions for the construction and management of transport, communications and mining companies, for participation in the control of the local currency, for tax and customs systems and for the conquest of local commodity markets. The government also sought other privileges such as trade, tax and transport agreements advantageous to Russia. Imperial banks managed loans to local government. They could act as direct resellers and as managers for concessions. For example, the Russo-Chinese Bank financed and managed the Chinese Eastern Railway (CER) before this obligation was passed to the Russo-Asiatic Bank. The Discount and Loan Bank of Persia controlled the construction and operation of the Tehran-Anzali Highway and construction of the Tabriz railway (this list of projects could be continued).

Russian Imperial Banks as Business Projects

As already noted, these banks have mainly been studied from political perspectives, and their commercial operations are still underestimated and they deserve further study. The size of their business must be estimated for a start. The Russo-Chinese Bank and Russo-Asiatic Bank published regularly their reports according to Russian law. The assets of the Discount and Loan Bank of Persia are more difficult to evaluate, because the bank had a special legal status and was not obliged to publish reports. The bank's archive in the Russian State Historical Archive in St. Petersburg holds a lot of financial statistics, but these materials have almost never been studied. Table 6.1 presents the first attempt to compare the data on three banks. The problem is that we encounter three types of consolidation of financial statements in the branch accounts. The aggregate account included in the balance sheet as turnover in both debit and credit, whereas other principal accounts are included as balances. Thus, the financial statements contained double counting in the branch account, which was standard accounting practice between the head office and regional divisions. This difference in accounting is mentioned in the notes to Table 6.1.

Table 6.1: Russian Imperial Banks and the Russo-Asiatic Bank, thousands of rubles

	Date of financial statements	Number of branches		Assets	
		Total	In Asia	Total	Abroad
Discount and Loan Bank of Persia ††	01.01.1912	22 ‡‡	14 ‡‡	68,424 *	28,825 §
Russo-Chinese Bank §§	01.01.1906	38 ¶¶	15 ¶¶	323,717 †	161,083 ¶
Russo-Asiatic Bank ***	01.01.1914	87 †††	10 †††	828,741 ‡	149,283 **

* Excluding the branch accounts: 36,512 thousand rubles.
† Including the branch accounts and working capital of branches: 91,966 thousand rubles.
‡ Including the branch accounts: 82,969 thousand rubles.
§ Persia.
¶ Paris and Asia.
** London, Paris and Asia.

Sources:
†† Russian State Historical Archive (RSHA), fond 600, opis 9, delo 1230, list 36ob–37.
‡‡ Data on Discount and Loan Bank of Persia branches on 1 July 1913 from V. V. Lavrov (ed.), *Akcionerno-paevye predprijatija Rossii po oficial'nym dannym* [The Russian joint-stock companies according to official data] (Moscow: M. Lavrov, 1913), p. 479.
§§ *Otchet po operatsiiam Russko-Kitaiskogo banka za 1905 g.* [Report on operations of the Russo-Chinese bank in 1905] (Sankt-Petersburg: [n.p.], 1906).
¶¶ Data on Russo-Chinese Bank branches, made by the author, based on annual reports: S. A. Salomatina, 'The Statements of the Russo-Chinese Bank, 1897–1910', in *www.hist. msu.ru/Dynamics/data/12_017.xls*.
*** *Vestnik finansov, promyshlennosti i torgovli: Otchety kreditnyh uchrezhdenij, torgovyh i promyshlennyh predprijatij,* [The bulletin of finance, industry and trade: annual reports of credit institutions, trade and industrial enterprises] (Sankt-Petersburg: The Ministry of Finance of the Russian Empire, 1914), n. 31, p. 1727.
††† Data on Russo-Asiatic Bank branches on 1 July 1913 from *Akcionerno-paevye predprijatija Rossii* [The Russian joint-stock companies according to official data], pp. 474–5.

In 1912–14, the Discount and Loan Bank of Persia had maximal assets before the period of war inflation. According to its total assets, it looked like an average regional bank that yielded to the major universal banks of Petersburg and Moscow. Its branch network was divided between Russia and North Persia. The issue of the bank's adjustment to the Persian business environment has been little studied. Unlike private banks, it was allowed to run pawn operations, habitual to the local population. The largest account in the financial statements concerned foreign currency exchange.

The Russo-Chinese Bank is presented in Table 6.1 according to its maximal balance on 1st January 1906, i.e. the report for 1905. Even if we subtract the branch accounts from its assets, the result is 232 million rubles, which exceeds the assets of Russia's largest private joint-stock bank - the Volga-Kama Commercial Bank (202.5 million rubles on 1 January 1906).[14] In 1905, the largest item of the bank's income was also foreign currency exchange in foreign offices: 4.45 million rubles from 12.8m of gross income.[15] The bank practiced some local types of lending (chop loans)[16] and issued their own banknotes, like other banks in China. The Russo-Chinese Bank appeared as a major international business in the first period of its history, and then the focus of its activities gradually began to shift to the Asian branches inside the Russian Empire.[17] Firstly, the bank's branch network was divided into three groups: offices in Eastern Siberia; Far Eastern offices abroad, led by Shanghai branch; and the Paris office. Later, offices in Central Asia, along the Trans-Siberian railway and in Manchuria were established.

The Russo-Asiatic Bank was larger than the Russo-Chinese Bank. Its history has to be written in superlative degree: it was the largest commercial bank of the Russian Empire, had a branch network of 87 offices (in 1913) and was the largest group of affiliated industrial enterprises, including a powerful military/industrial complex. The bank was studied as a centre of a military industry group even though its other fields have hardly been investigated.[18] There was also an international payment network, which these banks managed. The network of foreign branches of the Russo-Chinese Bank and Russo-Asiatic Bank included in their heyday branches in global financial centres (with some variations): London, Paris, New York, San Francisco, Hong Kong, Shanghai, Bombay (Mumbai), Calcutta (Kolkata) and Yokohama.[19]

The trading operations of Russian imperial banks are insufficiently explored. Russian private commercial banks were not allowed commodity trade; they could only lend to trade or to go into the commission business. However, government-controlled imperial banks could be direct resellers, bypassing private business, thus developing the market for Russian goods abroad or carrying out assignments for the Russian government. The Russo-Chinese Bank practiced commodity trade, for which it developed its own warehouses and cargo barges in Vladivostok. However, its share of commodity transactions (4.8 million rubles by 1st January 1906) was still insignificant compared with its basic discount and loan operations (90.3m).[20]

There was a remarkable example of competition between the Discount and Loan Bank of Persia and Russian private trade and industrial enterprises.[21] In the 1890s, Russian textile firms, headed by Emil Tsindel from Moscow, began gradually to enter the Persian market. The Ministry of Finance strongly encouraged them, but then decided to carry out its own trading operations in Persia through the Discount and Loan Bank. Thus, the governmental bank started to act as a direct competitor to Russian companies and merchants. At first, the bank's own trading went well and it expanded its trade infrastructure in Northern Persia.[22] When the bank, having available large and cheap credit from the government, engaged in lending to Persian merchants, Russian private firms went under and had to leave the market after heavy losses, such as Emil Tsindel and another large textile enterprise from Moscow Province, the Company of N. N. Konshin's Textile Mills, which is mentioned in the archival documents. The economic ties of Russian and Persian merchants, established in the previous decade, began to break. In the end, the bank overstocked the market and suffered great losses.[23] The issue of the competition between state and private institutions in Persia in the first half of the 1900s noted in Boris Anan'ich's research,[24] however, is cited as a much tougher version of this story, as it is derived from the report of 1924, i.e. of Soviet period, from the Vneshtorgbank's archive. This interesting subject is in need of verification by quantitative data.

Causes of the Troubles for Russian Imperial Banks

The degree of the success of Russian governmental banking projects in Asia has not been evaluated. At present, the prevailing view is that the misfortunes of the Discount and Loan Bank of Persia and Russo-Chinese Bank were caused by political and financial difficulties, associated with the Russo-Japanese War and the revolutionary events of 1905–1907.[25] This position undoubtedly deserves attention because the resources of the bank in Persia were largely dependent on public funds,[26] while the Russo-Chinese Bank operated partly in a warzone and funded the military spending of the Russian government.[27] However, an analysis of the literature and review of the archives of both banks allow us to assume that the version of commercial nature of the troubles of these banks is in need of further development. The bank in Persia returned to 'normal' banking after 1904: it established agencies in Russia and focused on commission trade with Persia, providing favourable conditions for Russian companies. However, low-quality loans, problems of adaptation and political projects went on to be sources of troubles to the bank in the 1910s.[28]

The major problem for imperial banks was lax credit to local elites. In fact, they were bribes and the Ministry of Foreign Affairs insisted on these credits, explaining them by political reasons, and the Ministry of Finance always gave way to this pressure. However, both the bankers and the diplomats understood that the repayment of these credits would be very unlikely and that the political benefits would be worse than the ministry expected. If the government controlled the bank, the bad loans were secured by governmental funds. The case of the private Russo-Asiatic Bank differed, and political projects were separated from the business: for example, the Beijing branch of the Russo-Asiatic Bank issued loans to Mongol princes in the 1910s from funds of secret expenditures of the Russian embassy rather than from the bank's own funds.[29]

The Russo-Chinese Bank declared large losses in the report for 1907; in financial statements on 1 January 1908, it showed 7.2 million rubles of losses: a net profit of 3m was written off to cover a part of it, but a net loss of 4.2m remained.[30] As to the report of the auditing committee, the bank was faced with a large default payment caused by the local economic situation as well as with mistakes in dealing with local customers, but the total loss in China was about 2.27m. The rest of the debts occurred in Russia. A large number of purely managerial violations were revealed in Russian branches: bad credit ratings, excessive overdrafts, unreliable loans, overdue debts, the misuse of capital and so on.[31] Long and difficult negotiations on the future of the Russo-Chinese Bank ended in 1910. The bank merged with the Northern Bank, affiliated with French *Société générale*. The new private bank, based on the ordinary Russian charter, was the Russo-Asiatic Bank.

In summary, we can say that Russian imperial banks were 'ready for anything' or 'more than a bank'. Within the empire, the government sought to limit private banks, whereas abroad it tried to get away from any limits of governmental imperial banks and entrusted to them special missions of the Ministry of Finance, the Ministry of Foreign Affairs and the Ministry of War. In Asia, the Russian government was constantly trying to impose political ahead of economic expansion. It sought to act through state institutions and distrusted private business.

The troubles of Russian imperial banks were largely caused by a contradiction between the political and economic tasks given them. Loans could be non-marketable and concessions could be unprofitable, but these projects were supported by political considerations. Another problem was the banks' management: a challenge of adaptation to local conditions was assigned to officials, who were not always equal to the task. However, all the risks of imperial banks were assumed by the government, whose solvency was superior to any private bank, and this consideration cannot be ignored in the analyses of their effectiveness. After the collapse of the Russian Empire, its zone of influence was lost, but the resumption of Russian foreign trade was on the horizon. Would Soviet Russia repeat the imperial approach or develop new relations in Asia? The next section is devoted to this issue.

Vneshtorgbank of the USSR as a Part of the Soviet Banking System of the 1920s

In the 1920s, a completely new banking system was sent to Asia from Russia. This has to be outlined briefly. The Soviet banking system began to form almost immediately after the October Revolution of 1917, although the previous banking system had been gradually transformed by wartime factors from 1914 and this process did not stop after the revolution. However, the transformation became systemic from October 1917. State monopoly on banking was introduced. Private banks were nationalized and merged with the State Bank. The mortgage system and stock market were abolished and public debts were cancelled. Eventually, the Russian banking system failed to bear the difficulties of the war, revolutions, civil war and 'war communism' and finally collapsed at the beginning of 1920. The symbol of the collapse was the abolition of the People's Bank of the Russian Federation, which served as the State Bank of the Russian Empire at that time. This was in the first period of Soviet banking history from October 1917 to January 1920.

The next period, associated with the 'NEP' (New Economic Policy or *Novaya Ekonomicheskaya Politika*), began in October 1921 when the new State Bank of the Russian Federation was established.[32] This NEP banking system was based on the commercial credit principal but almost without private property, staying in other economic sectors. Another bound of NEP banking was the credit reform in 1930–1931, which was similar to industrialization and collectivization in the banking sector. From the 1930s, mature Soviet banking institutions acted without commercial credit in the form of a 'non-classical' banking system. The NEP banking system adopted pre-revolutionary short-term credit and cooperative institutions and rejected mortgaged ones. Table 6.2 presents its structure. Half of its assets belonged to the State Bank of the USSR on 1 October 1928. The rest of its hierarchy lined up as follows: state joint-stock banks for trade and industry, cooperative banks, municipal banks as well as numerous agricultural credit societies and mutual credit societies.

The principal joint-stock banks were the Industrial and Commercial Bank of the USSR (*Prombank*), the Bank for the Electrification of the USSR (*Elektrobank*) and the Bank for the Foreign Trade of the USSR (*Vneshtorgbank*). The Vneshtorgbank's case can be used to outline the peculiarities of the Soviet banks of the 1920s.

Table 6.2: Soviet Banking Assets on 1 October 1928

	Millions of rubles	%
State Bank	5,933	49
Joint-stock commercial banks for trade and industry	1,920	16
Cooperative banks	465	4
Municipal banks	1,642	14
Agricultural credit institutions	2,062	17
Mutual credit societies	41	0.3
Total	12,062	100

Source: A. Blum, *Istorija kreditnyh uchrezhdenij i sovremennoe sostojanie kreditnoj sistemy v SSSR* [The history of credit institutions and the current state of the credit system in the USSR], (Moscow: Gosfinizdat USSR, 1929), p. 208

The Vneshtorgbank's history began in August 1922 when the Russian Commercial Bank was established as a concession of *Swenska Ekonomie Aktiebolaget*, led by a 'red banker' Olof Aschberg (1877–1960). The bank's founder was one of the famous adventurers of the early Soviet period, a Jewish banker from Sweden, the head of the Stockholm '*Nya Banken*'. Aschberg sympathized with European socialists, was close to the influential Bolsheviks and took part in their financial projects. Among other things, he brought a collection of about 250 icons from Russia, which is currently at the Swedish National Museum in Stockholm.[33]

In March 1924, the Russian Commercial Bank was transformed into Vneshtorgbank as an export and import bank for the Soviet Ministry of Foreign Trade, namely the People's Commissariat of Foreign Trade of the USSR (*Narkom-vneshtorg* or NKVT). In the 1920s, the bank took part in the interdepartmental rivalry between the NKVT and the State Bank, which was common in the Soviet administrative system.[34] Nevertheless, Vneshtorgbank was gradually evolving toward the de facto status of a department of the State Bank.[35] Vneshtorgbank as an early Soviet bank combined the features of 'classical' and 'nonclassical' banking. Tables 6.3 and 6.4 represent the Vneshtorgbank's financial statements on 1ˢᵗ October 1924 and its 'classical' features, based on discounts and accounts secured by goods. The bank held securities, but there was no stock market in the USSR and this portfolio included shares of affiliated state banks and companies. The bank's liabilities were also traditional and based on its own funds and deposits.

Table 6.3: The Vneshtorgbank's Assets on 1 October 1924

Accounts	Millions of rubles	%
Cash and own current accounts	1.65	3
Securities	1.66	3
Foreign currency and bills	1.13	2
Discounted bills of exchange	23.20	36
Credit accounts against goods	13.10	20
Correspondents foreign nostro	8.61	13
Correspondents domestic nostro	1.17	2
Correspondents domestic loro	3.81	6
Branch accounts	6.05	9
Total		93
Total assets	65.25	100

Table 6.4: The Vneshtorgbank's Liabilities on 1 October 1924

Accounts	Millions of rubles	%
Own funds	18.87	29
Deposits	19.16	29
Loans from the Ministry of Finance	3.06	5
Special accounts and rediscounting in the State Bank	8.80	13
Correspondents domestic nostro	2.41	4
Correspondents foreign loro	5.20	8
Branch accounts	6.45	10
Total		98
Total assets	65.25	100

Source: *Bank dlia vneshnei torgovli SSSR. Otchet za 1923/24 gg.* [The Bank for Foreign Trade of the USSR. Report], (Moscow: Gosizdat USSR, 1925), pp. 26–7

Vneshtorgbank was conceived as a foreign trade bank. The indebtedness of Soviet foreign trade trusts was 85 percent of the assets at the head office and 55/58 percent at branches, totally about 70 percent.[36] Important deposit customers were Soviet trade missions. Foreign currency accounts amounted to 60 percent of deposits on 1 October 1924.[37] At the same time, major Soviet banks were not really special institutions in the 1920s. Their specialization depended on the customers that these banks had managed to attract and for which banks competed. The 'non-classical' features of Soviet banking concerned the dominance of state institutions as shareholders. On 1st October 1924, the bank's principal shareholders were the NKVT (62%) and the State Bank (32.6%). Governmental institutions amounted to almost 90 percent of deposits by 1924.

The goal of the banking reform held in 1927 was to make Soviet joint-stock banks strictly specialized in services to different sectors of the economy. The reform was not entirely successful, but customers were greatly 'redistributed' among the leading Soviet banks, which would have been impossible in the classical banking system.[38] The particular problem of the Soviet financial system of the 1920s was a foreign currency issue, although such a currency problem existed in the overall context of world economic development in the 1920s. Although the gold standard era had gone, many governments tried to return to the previous order. There was monetary reform in Soviet Russia in 1922–4. It planned a new ruble based on the gold standard. The reform had a positive effect on the financial system, notably overcoming hyperinflation, but it was seemingly impossible to introduce a gold ruble as in the pre-revolutionary period. Moreover, it became clear that the ruble exchange rate would not be kept in external payments from the end of 1925. Soviet Russia returned to its strict regulation of foreign exchange transactions, rooted in the governmental policy of World War I. This policy included the withdrawal of all currency earnings, their concentration in the State Bank and distribution between organizations. This procedure was under strict control at the highest level of political and economic power. From February 1926, the major Soviet banks that served foreign trade became participants of this currency redistribution.[39]

The new rules for foreign exchange, as well as other reorganizations in 1926–7, brought Vneshtorgbank under the control of the State Bank.[40] Thus, the Soviet banking system of the 1920s was characterized, firstly, by the complete dominance of state ownership; secondly, banks were not completely separated from each other and there was a redistribution of resources and customers between them; thirdly, from 1926, banks were completely subordinate to the State Bank in terms of foreign currency operations. At the same time, Soviet banking kept the principles of commercial credit and there was competition for customers among banks, annoying utterly Soviet leaders.

The Organization of International Transactions in the USSR During the 1920s

Soviet banks' international operations were distinguished, firstly, by the state foreign trade monopoly and, secondly, by the foreign currency centralization outlined above. Soviet public trusts were engaged in export and import operations, although there were also few concession companies. The Soviet trust of the 1920s, headed by a board, was a self-financing association of enterprises in industry or commodity trade. Banking support for trusts comprised a two-level system of institutions: a group of Soviet domestic banks and a group of Soviet banks abroad. Soviet foreign trade financing was entrusted mainly to the State Bank (62/70 % of all transactions) and then to Vneshtorgbank (23/35%) and *Prombank* (3/9%). Other banks were involved in these operations to a small extent, but the consolidated reports on foreign trade were composed of these three major banks (Table 6.5).

Table 6.5: The Structure of Soviet Foreign Trade Crediting, %

	1 October 1925	1 October 1926	1 October 1927
State Bank	70	65	62
Vneshtorgbank	23	26	35
Prombank	7	9	3
Total	100	100	100

Source: A. P. Zabaznov, J. P. Golicyn and A. G. Sarkisjanc, *VEB: Vneshekonombank: 75-letiju Vneshekonombanka posvjawaetsja* [Vnesheconombank: To the 75th anniversary of Vnesheconombank], (Moscow: Typo graphic design, 1999), p. 41

The Soviet banking system kept in touch with world finances through Soviet banks abroad (Soviet foreign banks, or '*zagranbanks*'). These were full-fledged commercial banks based on local laws, but their majority were owned by the State Bank or the NKVT, namely Vneshtorgbank. The subordination of zagranbanks varied between the NKVT and the State Bank in the 1920s. Table 6.6 provides a list of Soviet banking institutions operating abroad in the 1920s.

Table 6.6: Soviet Banks Abroad in the 1920s

Europe	Moscow Narodny Bank, Ltd (London)
	Arcos Banking Corporation, Ltd (London)
	Banque commerciale pour l'Europe du Nord (Paris)
	Garantie und Kredit Bank für den Osten 'Garkrebo' (Berlin)
	Svensk Ekonomiebolaget (Stockholm)
	Nordiske Kredit Akcie Selscab 'Nord-Credit' (Copenhagen)
	Sokrabank (Oslo)

Asia	Russo-Persian Banking-house (Teheran)
	Mongolian Trade and Industrial Bank (Urga)
	Tuvinian Trade and Industrial Bank (Kyzyl)
	Far Eastern Bank (Dalbank) in Harbin
	Branches:
	Istanbul Branch of the Vneshtorgbank of the USSR
	Kobe Branch of the Far Eastern Bank (DVBank) in
	Khabarovsk
	Banking office in embassy in Kabul
	Banking offices in trade missions in Western China (Urumqi,
	Kashgar, Yining, Chuguchak)

The system of zagranbanks and its functions are poorly studied. These banks were founded in the early 1920s, when the Soviet banking system had no credibility abroad. Apparently, these banks were planned for credit blockade breaking, but following the diplomatic recognition of the USSR, it became clear that the State Bank and Vneshtorgbank could provide greater guarantees to foreign partners, because they were larger and closer to the centre of decision making. Soviet foreign banks were entrusted with international settlements, lending to Soviet export buyers and collecting economic information.[41] The diversification of foreign trade crediting between the State Bank and Vneshtorgbank was dependent on the distribution of customers, i.e. export and import trusts, between them. However, because this distribution was unstable, banks' specialization in commodities was very volatile. Nevertheless, we have enough data to explain why the State Bank prevailed in Soviet foreign trade credits. Its customer list included major trade trusts dealing with the export of grain, Siberian and Karelian timber and plywood and furs as well as the import of metals and rubber.[42] Before the redistribution of customers in 1927, Vneshtorgbank credited a substantial proportion of the export of furs and hides and provided services to the Soviet Oil Syndicate. After the reform of 1927, it got various exports of foods and agricultural products.[43] Both banks were also actively engaged in the export of plywood and hardwood, furs and flax as well as the import of rubber, tea, technical felts, industrial equipment and agricultural machines.[44] Vneshtorgbank concentrated on most export and import operations in Asia, primarily in Turkey and Persia.[45]

The financial terms for Soviet banks abroad changed during the 1920s. Soviet Russia started out as a rogue state, but over the next decade, the Soviet Union entered the system of international payments. In the early 1920s, Soviet customers paid abroad in cash or with large deposits, and then foreign companies started to lend to the Soviet exports in foreign ports under the guarantees of the State Bank and Vneshtorgbank. From the early 1930s, financial arrangements completely moved to the Soviet Union and these were carried out via letters of credit, payable at the State Bank and Vneshtorgbank.[46] Thus, in the 1920s, the Soviet Union tried to establish a system of banking in which domestic institutions would be separated from volatile global finance, but internal ones could become members. This system was lined up for foreign trade crediting in the first place. The results of foreign trade development, as reflected in internal Soviet statistics, are analysed in the next section.

Soviet Exports and Imports in the 1920s in Asia

Soviet exports and imports to neighbouring Asian countries at the end of the 1920s, represented in Figure 6.1, are based on the Asian foreign trade statistics in the Vneshtorgbank's archive. Foreign trade statistics were compiled in rubles and tons. In this case, we use the data in rubles, because Soviet economic policy was directed to a trade surplus in money terms, as it became clear in the Vneshtorg-bank's analytics. This goal had been achieved in trade with Turkey, Persia, Japan, Tuva and Western China. Imports dominated trade with the rest of China, Mongolia and Afghanistan (Figure 6.1).[47]

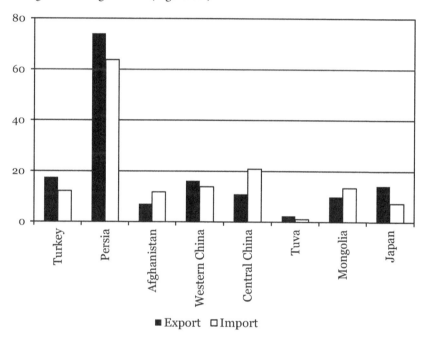

Figure 6.1: **Soviet Exports and Imports in Asia in 19²⁸⁄₉ (financial year), millions of rubles**

Soviet foreign trade statistics were divided into four categories: food (vital supplies), raw materials and semi-finished materials, livestock and industrial products. The structure of exports and imports is presented in Figures 6.2 and 6.3,[48] and data on the livestock trade are skipped as insignificant. According to these data, Soviet industrial exports were important in Asia, except, of course, Japan. It is noteworthy that Soviet-Persian trade held a leading position in the 1920s.Persia was the main destination for food and industrial exports in Asia as well as food and raw material imports in the USSR.

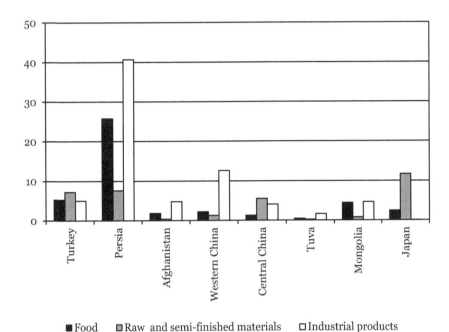

Figure 6.2: The Structure of Exports to Asian Countries in 1928/9 (financial year), millions of rubles

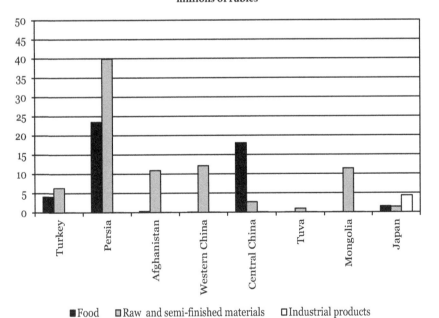

Figure 6.3: The Structure of Imports to Asian Countries in 1928/9 (financial year), millions of rubles

The evolution of Russian foreign trade can be illustrated by its trade with Persia (Figure 6.3). Export and import development were similar in major trends; therefore, we can pay more attention to imports to Persia. The Vneshtorgbank's archive stores the statistical reports on foreign trade in Persia during 1901–23 in Persian qirans. In this period, 80–90 percent of total exports and imports were from Great Britain and Russia. These data were appended by the figures on exports from the USSR to Persia in 1925/6 (financial year) and 1928/9, recalculated from rubles to qirans at a fixed rate of Ruspersbank at the end of the 1920s (1 ruble = 4.5 qirans). However, the rates of ruble and qiran were very volatile in this period, and the black market rate was 30/35 percent lower than the official one. As a result, the additional data in Figure 6.3 very roughly fix a recovery of trade after the period of the wars and revolutions in Russia. Figure 6.3 is a very clear illustration[49] that all Russian foreign trade achievements had been lost in 1914–21 and that the closest competitors took the place of Russia in the market. However, it is noteworthy that Russia's foreign trade began gradually to return to the previous level in the 1920s.

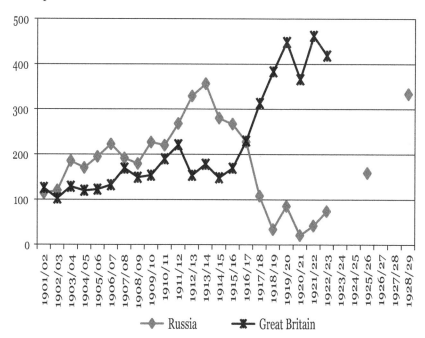

Figure 6.4: Exports to Persia from Great Britain and Russia in 1901–23 and Additional Data on Soviet Exports in 1925/6 and 1928/9, millions of qirans

Unlike in Persia, Russia had no strong trade positions in other countries. Britain and Japan dominated Chinese trade (Figure 6.4).[50] Britain played an important role in Afghanistan. Mongolia's and Tuva's markets were still very weak. The Japanese competition in Mongolia was much weaker than in Manchuria, and Russia had a chance of gaining a foothold there.

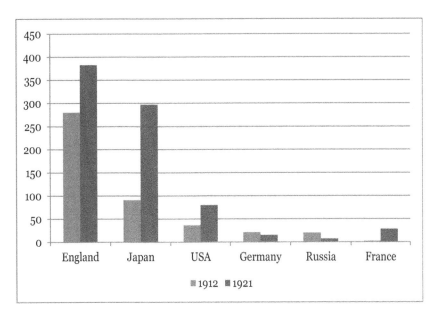

Figure 6.5: Exports to China in 1912 and 1921, millions of customs taels

Banks of the Former Russian Empire and Soviet Banks in Asia in the 1920s

The fate of the banking institutions of the Russian Empire abroad was usually sad after the October Revolution. In the war period, they gradually dropped into a deplorable financial position, but foreign branches seemed to have an uncertain legal status after the revolution and bank nationalizations in Russia. A serious struggle began for the property of the Russian Empire abroad (both public and private). Three forces were involved in this: the new Soviet government, previous owners and local authorities abroad. The outcome of this struggle depended on the combination of many factors. During the struggle for the ownership of the Russian Empire abroad, Soviet Russia rejected imperial traditions and began to form a new system of banking institutions in Asia. This system accepted the same functions as the imperial banks of the Russian Empire but under new conditions.

This section is devoted to the analysis of this new system and its differences from the system in the pre-revolutionary period. Its material is divided into three directions of foreign trade: the Far Eastern direction (North and East China, Japan); Mongolia and Tuva; and the southern direction (Turkey, Iran, Afghanistan, Western China). The commercial operations of leading Soviet banks are the focus of attention as well as the issue of the transformation of pre-Revolutionary imperial practices.

The Fate of Russian Imperial Banking in the Far East

The history of Russian banks in North and East China as well as in Japan in the 1920s implies a gradual fading of the Russo-Asiatic Bank and an attempt by Soviet banks to take its place. The Russo-Asiatic Bank was nationalized on 14 December 1917, as were the other private banks inside Russia; however, it still kept branches abroad. The chair Alexey Putilov escaped from Russia through Siberia and China, arrived in Paris in October 1918 and headed the *Comité de Paris*, i.e. the bank's board abroad.[51] Then, a significant part of the remaining bank's assets was invested in projects that depended on the success of the Russian White movement. There is information on the bank's investment in trading companies in Southern Russia in 1919–1920, namely in the territories controlled by General Anton Denikin and later Baron Pyotr Wrangel.[52] The White movement in Siberia, headed by general Alexander Kolchak, also received funds from the bank through the board of the CER, in which both Kolchak and Putilov were members in that period.[53] The defeat of the White movement meant another significant loss of assets after the nationalization in 1917. From then, the London and Paris branches were not able to continue full-fledged operations.[54] Chinese branches, headed by Shanghai, were kept from bankruptcy 'because of skilful foreign exchange transactions of Blächer (Blyakher)', one of its directors.[55]

Moreover, there was an important area of branch activity in the right of way of the CER, including the centre in Harbin, where the Russian population lived. Chinese Eastern Railway (or CER 中东铁路; also known as the Chinese Far East Railway) was a railway in northeastern China (Manchuria) linking Chita with Vladivostok in the Russian Far East. The administration of the CER and the Chinese Eastern Railway Zone was based in Harbin. The CER was the last major asset of the bank, and the French government supported the bank in its struggle for control over the railway. This backing was considered to protect French shareholders' rights. During these years, the French government also tried to use the bank for transferring funds for French interventional troops in Russia in 1918–19; however, French participation in intervention was quite marginal compared with other states.[56] Unfortunately for the Russo-Asiatic Bank, several forces at once submitted claims to control the railway in different forms. There were the 'White' (counter-revolutionary) Kolchak and 'Red' Soviet governments, the Chinese government in Beijing and the autonomous government of warlord Zhang Zuolin in Mukden as well as interventionist forces (the US, Japan, Britain, etc.).[57]

On 20 October 1920, the Russo-Asiatic Bank concluded an agreement with the Beijing government affirming the bank's rights to the CER. However, on 31 May 1924, the victory was on the side of Soviet diplomacy, and the railway became joint-managed by the USSR and China. In 1924, Soviet Russia was able to negotiate not only with the Chinese government, but also with Zhang Zuolin who actually controlled the territory of North-Eastern China. The CER's control stock, owned (partly) by the Russo-Asiatic Bank, was ignored despite the protests of the French government.[58] The loss of the CER was a serious blow to the bank, because it meant the loss of its client base in China. This point should be clarified. The railway was the economic base of Russian settlements in Manchuria. Russian Harbin and the right of way were territories that retained the governance and lifestyle of the Russian Empire after the October Revolution. By 1917 in Manchuria, there were about 50,000 railroad workers and their families as well as the people engaged in the trade and service of Russian settlements. After the revolution, especially after the defeat of the White movement in the Civil War, Harbin became the largest centre of White emigration, and there were many professional soldiers among the refugees from Russia.[59]

By 1923, there were around 200,000 'White Russians' in China, including 165,000 in Harbin, 15,000 in Shanghai and the remainder that lived mainly in the right of way of the CER. At this point, the Russian population was maximal, and this figure gradually declined because Russian citizens left China as the political situation deteriorated there.[60] Under the agreement of 1924, Soviet and Chinese citizens could only work on the railway. As a result, some Russians took Soviet citizenship. In 1929–30, there were almost 110,000 Russians in Manchuria (125,000 in China totally), among them 50,000 were the Soviet citizens, including about 37,000 in Harbin. In Shanghai, Soviet citizens amounted to no more than 500 people; the others were White emigrants.[61]

The political situation was very severe in China in the 1920s: the everlasting conflicts between the Soviet and Chinese administrations went on the CER; White and Red Russians were totally irreconcilable with each other; and Japan strengthened its presence in North-Eastern China. In addition to internal Chinese conflicts, relations between the USSR and China were deteriorating permanently, especially in 1927, after the Kuomintang's accession to power accompanied by a rupture of relations between the Kuomintang and the Chinese Communist Party, backed by the Soviet Union and the Comintern.

The Far Eastern Bank in Harbin (*Dalbank*) composed a memorandum on the situation to the Chinese branches of the Russo-Asiatic Bank in February 1926. It was a memo to the foreign department of the State Bank's direction. A copy of this document was also kept in the Vneshtorgbank's archive. However, it is important to bear in mind that this memo expresses the view of the direct enemy of the Russo-Asiatic Bank in China. The memo states not only that the CER was a major customer of the Russo-Asiatic Bank, but also that most of the other customers were in some way connected with the railway: 'The bank was valuable for China by its ties with Russia and the CER; as the bank had lost these ties, it lost its meaning.' As a result, the previously profitable offices (Tianjin, Beijing) 'do not justify their existence', while the offices in Western

China (Xinjiang) brought great losses; the customers of the rest branches 'don't deserve confidence'. In addition, 'foreign citizens had presented a number of lawsuits against the bank for old days' payments', which the bank lost in court and it would have a number of very large payments.[62] The chain of events that led to the collapse of the bank is insufficiently explored. It is known only that it was closed on 26 September 1926 after losing five million sterling pounds in currency speculations in Paris and that Chinese branches were burdened with a debt of 2.69 million yuans in silver dollars, of which 1.67m was accounted for by the Shanghai office.[63]

Soviet Banks as Imperial Banks in the Far East

Soviet banks tried to occupy the niche of the Russo-Asiatic Bank in the 1920s. In this regard, the term Dalbank (*Dal'nevostochnyi Bank* or Far Eastern Bank) is often mentioned. This bank's name is found in the literature on the history of the CER and the activity of the Comintern and Soviet intelligence in China in the 1920s, but the bank is not a subject of these studies. In fact, two Dal'nevostochnyi banks were mixed in these cases: the Far Eastern Bank in Khabarovsk and the Far Eastern Bank in Harbin. This confusion is largely due to the intricate system of subordination within the Soviet banking system in the 1920s.

The Far Eastern Bank in Khabarovsk (Dalbank in Khabarovsk or DVBank)[64] was founded in Chita on 7 March 1922 as the Bank of the Far Eastern Republic, i.e. the central bank of the Far Eastern Republic, a nominally independent state in 1920–2 dependent on Soviet Russia. The republic's government owned 55 percent of the bank's control stock and the remainder was divided between cooperatives and local authorities. After the Far Eastern Republic joined the Russian Federation, the bank was renamed the Far Eastern Bank in 1923 and later transferred to Khabarovsk. There is a memo about Dalbank in Khabarovsk, which the financial and credit department of Vneshtorgbank prepared for the foreign department of the Direction of the State Bank of the USSR on 26 April 1926. The memo reports that DVBank had a branch in Harbin in the early years, but that the situation in April 1926 was characterized 'being closely associated with Dalbank in Harbin and having an office in Kobe (Japan), Dalbank [in Khabarovsk] also finances import-export operations of our Far Eastern economic organizations, operating in China'.[65] Thus, a separate bank acted in Manchuria instead of the Harbin branch of DVBank by 1926. By the way, the Kobe branch of DVBank was engaged in financing the fish and seafood supply from the Soviet Far East to Japan.[66]

An important part of DVBank's specialization was gold transactions. It sets out in a memo the following:

In its early years, before the opening of branches of the State Bank, in additional to ordinary banking, Dalbank also controlled money circulation in the Far East, in connection with this it widely developed purchasing of gold and was a monopolist in these operations in 1922–23 financial year. Now the Dalbank's gold operations greatly expand not only in a quantity but also in types of activity, the bank is charged with the task off financing of the Far Eastern gold mining within special funds allotted to it.[67]

In addition to gold operations, Dalbank in Khabarovsk lent to local trade and industry. By 1st October 1925, its share capital amounted to five million rubles, with total assets of about 40m, discount and loan operations of 11m and current accounts, excluding the deposit of gold operations, about 8m. Its profit in 1925 was 945,000 rubles, and dividend 12 percent. The memo also states that 'in the Far East, both Soviet and foreign, the bank enjoys a well-deserved reputation as a solid bank and the Dalbank's guarantees enjoy the full confidence of the foreigners'.[68]

In June 1930, the Far Eastern Bank in Khabarovsk was reorganized into the Far Eastern Communal Bank. In May 1939, it was liquidated after changes in the political division of the region. However, another Dalbank - The Far Eastern Bank in Harbin - is much more interesting for the subject of our study, but is also studied very weakly. It operated from 1923 as a joint-stock bank based on a Chinese charter and under the Chinese jurisdiction.[69] Generally, we can say that DVBank inherited the area of the Russo-Asiatic Bank in the Russian Far East and Japan, while Dalbank in Harbin operated in its territories in North and Eastern China. The Harbin Dalbank's branch network included just six offices, while the Russo-Asiatic Bank had 11 there. Compared with the Russo-Asiatic Bank, there were no Dalbank branches in Western China.

For any study of banking, balance sheet data are very important as the starting point of the work. Tables 6.7–6. 9 show the calculations based on the balance sheet of 1st January 1927. According to these data, Dalbank in Harbin is a full-fledged commercial bank, whose resources were formed by deposits (54%) as well as discount, loan and trade operations (44%). In addition, 21 percent of its assets were in branches (Table 6.7). Shanghai (43%) and Tianjin (23%) dominated these, as they were in major financial centres to the south of Manchuria. The branch network's structure also indicates that the bank was a Soviet 'door to China' (Table 6.8). Every branch operated in the local currency (Table 6.8), and the bank's consolidated balance sheet was presented in yens. However, during this period, the monetary situation in China was even more complicated, and the bank's operations (head office and branches) were divided into different currencies. As a result, 42% of its assets were in yens and 31% were in US dollars compared with 50% and 20% in liabilities. The bank's third largest currency was the Harbin dollar (Table 6.9). In contrast to Persia, attempts to put rubles into circulation were very limited, because this project was seen as obviously hopeless.

Table 6.7: Consolidated Balance Sheet of the Head Office and
Branches of Dalbank in Harbin on 1 January 1927*

Operations	Yens (1)	% of assets (liabilities) (2)	The share of head office (without branches), %, (1) = 100% (3)
Assets			
Cash, current accounts and other highly liquid assets	4,745,401.95	11	57
Discount, loan and trade operations	18,943,471.57	44	78
Correspondent accounts	11,058,868.63	26	95
Account with the branches	3,405,800.54	8	78
Paid interests and commissions	2,847,502.75	7	76
Other assets	1,631,835.76	4	56
Balance	42,632,881.20	100	79
Liabilities			
Fixed capital and reserves	4,262,832.12	10	100
Deposits	23,025,984.40	54	87
Correspondent accounts	5,437,298.67	13	98
Interests, commissions and other revenues	3,992,119.25	9	70
Other liabilities	5,914,646.76	14	21
Balance	42,632,881.20	100	79

*   Balance until final profit-and-loss account.
Calculated from RSAE, fond 7590, opis 3, delo 144, list 1–12.

Table 6.8: Branch Assets of the Dalbank in Harbin on 1 January 1927

Branch	Assets	Currency of assets	Share in consolidated balance in yens, %
Calgan	411,745.31	Yen	5
Manchuria	973,170.77	Harbin dollar	9
Peking	337,330,92	Silver dollar	3
Tianjin	2,882,286.75	Beijing dollar (?)	23
Hailar	1,581,165.38	Dayan	17
Shanghai	3,052,388.84	Tael	43
All branches *	8,891,653.48	Yen	100

*   RSAE, fond 7590, opis 3, delo144, list 1–12
Source: RSAE, fond 7590, opis 3, delo147, list 167, 179, 191, 203, 215, 227

Table 6.9: Breakdown of the Transactions in Different Currencies in the Consolidated
Balance Sheet of Dalbank in Harbin on 1 January 1927, %

	Assets	Liabilities
Yen	42	50
US dollar	31	20

Harbin dollar	12	11
Gold ruble	5	9
Mexican dollar	5	4
Tael	3	4
Pound sterling	2	-
Other currencies	0,1	2
Total	100	100

Source: RSAE, fond 7590, opis 3, delo 144, list 1–12

Dalbank in Harbin provided banking services to the CER and Soviet-Chinese trade customers. Numerous Soviet citizens in China were the bank's clients. The bank also distributed Soviet loans among the Russian community in Harbin and all over in Manchuria.[70] Dalbank in Harbin is usually mentioned in studies of the CER, the White movement, the Comintern and Soviet intelligence in China. In the 1920s, Soviet political leaders considered China to be a country of potential revolution of the October type.[71] They supported the Communist Party of China through the Comintern, using legal and illegal means. In addition, any political force in China could receive weapons, equipment, military instructors and money if it met the Soviet interests. The published Comintern's documents proved the active Soviet participation in the Chinese internal policy in the 1920s.[72] In this regard, the reports of S. L. Wilde, the Comintern's messenger in Shanghai in 1923, are often cited. His official position was a chief accountant in the Shanghai office of the Central Union of Consumer Societies of the USSR. Wilde sent detailed reports to Moscow about money that he distributed as an estimate and stated that Dalbank was a channel of transfers in some cases. However, the sums reported by Wilde were not very large. In fact, there are just two published reports, and they include nominal total sums of about 20,000 in various currencies, circulated in China and Japan. Wilde passed to one recipient from 1,000 to 10,000.[73]

The set of estimates for the support of Soviet political projects in China, published in the same volumes, are much more interesting from a financial point of view. The Executive Committee of the Comintern approved these estimates, and its hearings include considerably larger sums in comparison to Wilde's reports. It is clear that these means were transferred to their recipients, but their posting has never been studied, although Dalbank in Harbin was obviously the main financial agent of the intended operations. It is worth noting that the archives of Soviet banks, available in the RSAE, contain information only on economic activity, but not on political projects. However, the endorsement of large payments through Dalbank was found among the published documents on Chinese affairs, but at a higher level, in the Political Bureau of the Central Committee of the All-Union Communist Party (Bolsheviks): 'It decided by the polling of the Politburo's members on 6 April 1927: to issue immediately a loan of two million rubles to the Central Bank of Hankou through the Shanghai Branch of Dalbank.[74]

The history of the Comintern in China is closely linked to the history of the Soviet foreign political and military intelligence, institutionalized as the Foreign Department of the Joint State Political Directorate (OGPU) and Fourth Directorate of the Red Army Staff. This connection is clearly visible from the published Comintern's materials and it has been repeatedly analysed in studies.[75] Victor Usov summarises data on Soviet resident agents in China.[76] The collected evidence demonstrates that fixed-post spies more often nominally worked in Soviet economic agencies abroad than in banks and that Dalbank was less a 'bank ready for anything', as pre-Revolutionary imperial banks, but rather a bank ready for any money transfer.

Dalbank in Harbin had a reputation as a financial agent under Soviet influence. In this sense, Piotr Balakshin's testimony is often cited. He was an historian of Russian Far Eastern emigration as well as a witness of these events in the 1920s. Notably, he typically mixes Dalbanks in Harbin and in Khabarovsk in his study:

> The branch of Dalbank, headquartered in Khabarovsk, was opened in Harbin [...] Dalbank was used to operations of the Comintern in Manchuria and China. Dalbank bought gold bullions to be sent to Moscow, sold valuables, confiscated in Russia, for foreign currency abroad and kept current accounts for a Comintern's secret agents.[77]

This evidence is valuable, however, because it reflects the bank's image in the eyes of contemporaries. It should also be noted that the phrase 'bought gold bullion to be send to Moscow' in this context has a 'spy' connotation; however, from the above quoted memo of Vneshtorgbank to the State Bank, it is clear that these operations of Dalbank in Khabarovsk were primarily economic.

Dalbank in Harbin closed in 1934 after the Japanese occupation of Manchuria and the sale of the CER to Manchukuo. The Shanghai branch of the bank came under the control of *Moscow Narodny Bank*, the Soviet bank in London, which operated until 1950.[78] In other words, the need for the bank was no longer because of the loss of the CER, and it was enough to have access just to Shanghai in a new political and economic situation.

Soviet Imperial Banking in Mongolia and Tuva

The fortunes of Mongolia and Tuva were very close in the 1920s, and their banking development cannot be analysed beyond the general historical context. The Mongolian People's Republic was proclaimed in 1924. The Tuvinian People's Republic (*Tannu-Tuva in*, 1921–6.) existed in 1921–44. Until the end of World War II, both republics were recognized by the USSR only, and they were parts of China to the rest of the world. In 1944, Tuva became a part of the Soviet Union as the Tuva Autonomous Region within the RSFSR. The USSR and Comintern had a decisive influence on the Mongolian and Tuvinian internal situations, including the creation of local communist parties and provision of military and economic aid in their struggle for power. As a result, Soviet-style states were set up there, in which all institutions were developed with the assistance of Moscow advisers. Both Mongolbank and Tuvinbank were parts of this project of Sovietization.[79]

Mongolbank could be conventionally considered to be an implemented project of the pre-Revolutionary Mongolian bank, whose concession was called back by the Mongolian government in September 1918, because the bank failed to start the projects for which it had been created. It would lend for the export of raw materials, create a market for Russian goods, develop the local industry and modernize financial institutions (i.e. implement currency and fiscal reforms) as well as start the construction of the railway from Russia to Mongolia.[80] In the 1920s, the project for a central and commercial bank for Mongolia was renewed under these new conditions.

The Mongolian Trade and Industrial Bank (*Mongolbank*) opened its doors in Ulan Bator (Urga) on 2 June 1924. Now, it is the Bank of Mongolia. In the 1920s, the bank was a joint-stock company; its shares were divided between the People's Commissariat of Finance and the State Bank of the USSR, on the one hand, and the Government of the Mongolian People's Republic, on the other. Soviet citizens occupied most of the bank's key positions. Mongolbank directly reported to the State Bank of the USSR within the Soviet banking system, but there is a lot of material about this bank in the archive of Vneshtorgbank.[81]

Mongolbank was a monopolist in an area where there were no strong traditions of banking. The bank took over the functions of the central bank: it serviced the accounts of the Mongolian Ministry of Finance, participated in the state budget's estimation, and developed tax and customs rates. From December 1925, the bank began to issue the Mongolian national currency, the *tugrik*. Bank notes were printed in the USSR. Until the spread of tugriks, the base currency in Mongolia was the Mexican silver dollar circulating in China. The gold ruble was another currency permitted in Mongolia (currency regulation also followed the Soviet model).[82]

Tables 6.10–6.12 provide an overview of the bank's operations and structure of customers on 1st January 1926. It was a small bank, but it grew strongly from its opening. Its resources were based on its own funds, borrowings and correspondent accounts. A large part of resources had a Soviet origin, but local deposits gradually grew. The Mongolian Ministry of Finance owned 42 percent of deposits; further, 11 percent of depositors were Chinese, whereas there were few deposits by Soviet institutions. By the end of 1927, Mongolbank had five permanent and two temporary offices for stocking raw materials.[83] Branches were still weak, however, and most operations were carried out by the head office. Credit accounts against goods dominated among credit operations (approximately 25 percent of assets) were created, partly because the bill's law was established in Mongolia in 1925. Discount and loan customers were mostly Mongolian (49%) and Soviet (42%).[84]

Table 6.10: Balance Sheet of Mongolbank on 1 January 1926

Operations	Mexican dollars	% of assets (liabilities)	Percentage of head office (without branches), %, (1) = 100%
	(1)	(2)	(3)
Assets			
Cash, current accounts, securities, foreign currency and precious metals	2,180,747.23	35	88
Discount, loan and trade operations	3,043,530.96	49	90
Correspondent accounts and branch accounts	784,791.20	13	60
Other assets	198,550.87	3	91
Balance	6,207,620.26	100	85
Liabilities			
Fixed capital and reserves	1,012,680.00	16	100
Issued banknotes	176,126.72	3	100
Deposits	1,423,436.62	23	75
Lends	1,221,056.09	20	100
Correspondent accounts and branch accounts	1,744,560.73	28	74
Profits	169,628.17	3	100
Other liabilities	460,131.93	7	76
Balance	6,207,620.26	100	85

Branches in total assets on 1 January 1926: Altan-Bulak -60.8%, Tszain-Shabi -8.3%, Uliastaj - 14.0%, San-Beise- 6.3%, Kobdo- 6% (RSAE, fond 7590, opis 3, delo 92, list 35).
Source: RSAE, fond 7590, opis 3, delo 92, list 41–2

Table 6.11: Deposits of Mongolbank on 1 January 1926

Number of accounts	455	
Sum in thousands of Mexican dollars, including	1,420.9	100%
Ministry of Finance of Mongolia	590.1	42%
Montsenkop *	76.7	5%
Soviet economic institutions	98.2	7%
Chinese customers	152.7	11%
Other customers	503.2	35%

*   The Mongolian People's Central Cooperative (*Montsenkop*), the largest cooperative organization in Mongolia.
Source: RSAE, fond 7590, opis 3, delo 92, list 16

Table 6.12: The Mongolbank's Discount and Loan operations on 1 January 1926

Customers	Mexican dollars	Mexican dollars, total	%

Soviet customers		1,360,449.53	46
Industry	20,000.00		
Cooperative institutions	61,731.08		
State economic institutions	1,271,986.47		
Noneconomic institutions	6,731.98		
Mongolian customers		1,442,205.18	49
Cooperative institutions	1,441,005.18		
Noneconomic institutions	1,200.00		
Chinese private firms	1,150.20	1,150.20	0.04
Other private firms	154,580.55	154,580.55	5
Total		2,958,385.46	100

Source: RSAE, fond 7590, opis 3, delo 92, list 19

The bank was engaged in financing local trade, export/import operations with China and the Soviet Union and lending to industry and agriculture. Its main customers were the largest Mongolian People's Central Cooperative (*Montsenkop*) as well as large Soviet economic organizations: Company 'Wool', Siberian Trade Trust, Far Eastern Central Cooperative Association and Soviet trade missions. Large Mongolbank customers were mainly engaged in the purchase of wool, furs and cattle. The bank dealt with commodity trade, such as tea, textiles, cereals, sugar, tobacco, confectionery and farm implements, for the Russian population in Mongolia.[85]

Like Mongolbank, Tuvinbank was the only bank in the area where financial institutions needed to be created from scratch, and it was necessary to start with the introduction of money circulation instead of traditional commodity exchange. The Tuvinian Trade and Industrial Bank (*Tuvinbank*) in Kyzyl opened in September 1925. Now, it is the National Bank of the Tyva Republic (or Tuva), affiliated with the Bank of Russia. In the1920s, it was a joint-stock bank; two-thirds of its stock (300,000 rubles) belonged to the State Bank of the USSR and the remaining third was owned by the government of Tanna-Tuva. The director, who actually determined the bank's policy, was always a representative of the State Bank of the USSR, and the chair of the council was from Tanna-Tuva.

It was a very small bank: its total assets amounted 1,107,400 rubles on 1 October 1926. Tuvinbank acted as a central bank and provided settlements on behalf of the Tuvinian Ministry of Finance. However, attempts to issue a national currency failed, and the Russian ruble was put into circulation in 1928. The bank acted with great support from the State Bank of the USSR. This support included human, technical and financial resources. The Tuvinbank's debts were written off from time to time. The bank's main function was lending to the economy, but the economy itself was still very weak and not needed in modern banking. Therefore, it was forced to engage in economic and commercial activities. 'Non-banking' departments gradually grew into large state enterprises, which later became the bank's customers. In the 1920s, Tuvinbank established enterprises in gold mining and cattle breeding. It delivered and distributed food and equipment and it financed the construction of small industrial enterprises.[86]

Thus, Mongolbank and Tuvin bank were essentially projects run by Soviet banks in areas where financial institutions had to be upgraded and Soviet goods markets created. These 'imperial banks' were not only banking institutions and the financial agents of the government, they also acted as trade and economic organizations if it was necessary to create customers for themselves and markets for Soviet products.

The Southern Area of Soviet Imperial Banking Abroad

This section focuses on the Ruspersbank in Persia (Iran) and the foreign operations of the Central Asian Bank (Asiabank). However, the Istanbul branch of Vneshtorgbank also worked southerly from March 1925. The branch was simultaneously a division of the Soviet Bank and a subject of Turkish law.[87] The Vneshtorgbank's archive keeps many materials on the Istanbul branch, but this issue was not included in this study. Before the Russian Revolution, there was a branch of the Russian Bank for Foreign Trade in Constantinople, but it did not survive the war turmoil and it was liquidated in 1915.[88]

Ruspersbank

The Russian Federation transferred the remains of the Discount and Loan Bank of Persia without compensation to Iran in 1921 under an interstate treaty. Russia also renounced loans granted by the bank to the Iran government. Iran obtained the entire public and private economic infrastructure of the Russian Empire on its own territory, such as roads, railways, wharves, warehouses, telegraph lines and industrial enterprises.[89] However, a question arises about the condition of Russian property at the time of the transfer, because all the previous years, Russian businesses were gradually losing assets in Iran.[90] Ruspersbank was created in Tehran in 1923 to replace the Discount and Loan Bank of Persia. Its founders were the Russo-Asiatic Stock Company with a board in Moscow (an early Soviet concession, similar to the one from which Vneshtorgbank grew), the Russian Commercial Bank (the future Vneshtorgbank) and Iranian merchants. In the 1920s, Ruspersbank had a charter from the Iranian government and simultaneously subordinated to the People's Commissariat of Foreign Trade and to Vneshtorgbank. This bank, known later as the Russo-Iranian Bank, lasted until 1979 when banks in Iran were nationalized.[91]

In the 1920s, Ruspersbank developed a network of 13 branches in Northern Iran, which almost completely coincided with the branch network of the Discount and Loan Bank of Persia in 1913.[92] It had a difficult state in the 1920s. Its serious problems are described in the report for 1925/6. In the previous 19²⁴/₂₅, the State Bank of the USSR was trying to bring the Russian gold currency (*chervonets*) into the Iranian market as a stable convertible currency with the rate keeping at a nominal level. On behalf of the State Bank, Ruspersbank bought gold *chervontsy* in exchange for British pounds, which were provided by the State Bank. Sellers of the currency were Persian merchants trading with the Soviet Union. Then, it transferred chervontsy to the State Bank's branches in Baku and Moscow and sold British pounds to the Imperial Bank in Tehran or to individuals through the sale of postal and telegraphic transfers to London.[93]

Table 6.13: The Ruspersbank's Reformed Balance on 1 October 1926*

Operations	Thousands of qirans	% of assets (liabilities)	Change to 1 July 1927, %, (1) = 100%
	(1)	(2)	(3)
Assets			
Cash, current accounts and other highly liquid assets	5,003	8	134
Securities	7,250	11	–
Discount and loans against bills	6,379	10	320
Loans against goods	12,839	20	181
Correspondent accounts	25,307	39	64
Purchased transfers	2,725	4	170
Other assets	5,756	9	95
Reformed balance	65,259	100	121
Liabilities			
Fixed capital	25,000	38	106
Reserves	5,417	8	106
Deposits	21,330	33	120
Correspondent accounts	5,573	9	88
Profit-and-loss account	1,569	2	630
Other liabilities	6,370	10	103
Reformed balance	65,259	100	121
Off-balance accounts	17,882	–	216
Balance before reformation (in previous accounting system)	83,141	–	142

*　Reformed balance means that the accounting system had changed and some accounts were transferred into 'off-balance' items from 1 October 1926. The difference between these two accounting systems is shown in the last rows of the table.

Source: RSAE, fond 7590, opis 3, delo 98, list 8, 48

However, in late 1925 and early 1926, it became clear that the rate of chervonets could not be kept. At the beginning of 1926, the State Bank refused to buy the Russian currency in Iran due to a foreign currency crisis in Russia.

Ruspersbank also stopped currency operations. Thereafter, two Russian currency rates appeared in Iran: firstly, the Ruspersbank's rate, caused by the qiran rate to the British pound and the pound's rate to ruble in Moscow, and secondly, the black market rate in Iran. These two rates were significantly different. While the Ruspersbank's rate was 4.5 qirans per 1 ruble (45 qirans per 1 chervonets), the black market rate was 2.9 qirans per 1 ruble (29 qirans per 1 chervonets). In December 1927 and January 1928, the black market exchange rate fell to the worst level (2.6/2.7 qirans). In other months, the difference between the official and black market rates always remained between 30 percent and 35 percent.[94] In the issue, Iranian private merchants and even Soviet economic institutions refused to take currency to Ruspersbank, preferring to exchange it in Iranian private banks at a favourable rate.[95]

Table 6.14: The Ruspersbank's Regional Structure on 1 October 1926

Branches	Thousands of qirans	% of assets
Tehran direction	49,883	76.4
Tehran office	2,159	3.3
Other branches	13,217	20.3
Total	65,259	100.0

Source: RSAE, fond 7590, opis 3, delo 98, list 9

The currency depreciation led to a strong reduction in the prices of Soviet goods. The situation was discussed at a closed meeting of the Foreign Trade Section of the Council of the Congresses of the State Industry and Trade in early 1928. The consolidated opinion was not to leave the market and not to free up space for competitors.[96] The currency crisis struck the bank more seriously than it seems at first glance. The bank's own funds included 25 million qirans (or 5m rubles) of basic capital and 5,417,000 qirans in reserves on 1 October 1926 (Table 6.13). However, half of the capital was not in Iran, but in the USSR, and this share was up to 80 percent in the last quarter of 1925–6, the most difficult period of the crisis.[97] Thus, most of the bank's capital was immobilized in Moscow. The report for 1926–7 mentioned that the bank failed to obtain lending from foreign banks, so Ruspersbank acted completely on Soviet resources.[98]

Ruspersbank focused primarily on foreign currency transactions in the period of the 'struggle for chervonets', but discount and loan operations, based on Soviet-Iranian trade, seemed to be poorly developed, in opinion of the reports' compilers.[99] Table 6.13 shows the balance on 1 October 1926. There is a crisis balance sheet, but it doesn't well demonstrate the essence of the bank's problems, analyzed in additional materials to the report. The balance sheet just indicates a relatively low proportion of discount and loan operations, a high proportion of fixed capital in the liabilities, the large debit correspondent account and weak credit one (i.e., large debts to banks, but weak bank resources in the correspondent accounts). Most operations (75%) were concentrated at the Tehran head office (Table 6.14).[100]

The share of Iranian merchants did not grow or tended to decrease according to the bank's report in 1925/6. Iranian merchants accounted for approximately 82 percent of discount customers, but 90 percent of credit accounts against goods were opened by Soviet organizations. The overall ratio of Iranian and Soviet customers was 1:2.[101] In liabilities, Soviet customers amounted to 70/80% and Iranian ones possessed 18/27 percent of accounts. The largest deposits in nine branches on 1 October 1926 were in Mashhad (44%), Tabriz (15%), Pahlavi (11%) and Rasht (13%).[102]

Soviet-Iranian trade was transferred to the barter system for a while because of the crisis. In the second quarter of 1927, the barter system was cancelled and a new relationship was established, which improved the situation of the bank and Soviet-Iranian trade as a whole (Table 6.13). The new policy aimed to attract Iranian merchants to the bank, and financial conditions for them became equal to those for Soviet organizations. The bank began to promote Soviet exports to Iranian regions. The bank's operations began to grow, and the share of Iranian merchants increased by 12 percent from 1 October 1926 to 1 July 1927.[103]

However, problems remained. The lucrative offices were only in Tehran direction, Rasht and Pahlavi, but all other branches including the Tehran office were unprofitable on 1 July 1927. The reason was their expensive executive personnel, which accounted for up to 40 percent of gross income. For example, executive expenses exceeded the gross income in Hamadan and Qazvin and were equal to income in Barfrush and Tabriz. The loss in Isfahan consisted of the following operational expenditures: service benefits, travelling and daily allowances. The same disproportionate personnel costs were observed in the *Sabzevar* branch. At the same time, the report pointed out that when interest on current accounts was fully charged, Tabriz, Tehran office (Bazaar) and, perhaps, *Sabzevar* would only be unconditionally unprofitable.[104] Thus, the Ruspersbank's report explained the difficulties caused by currency problems and high operational expenditures, but it deadened its main business problem: the inability to attract enough solid customers. This subject needs further research.

Foreign Trade Operations of Asiabank

In areas that had a weak tradition of modern banking and Soviet influence was weak, Soviet banking penetration took place in the form of accounting departments of embassies, consulates and trade agencies without explicit subordination to any domestic Soviet banks. This was the case for Afghanistan, in Kabul from 1925, as well as in Western China (Urumqi, Kashgar, Yining, Chuguchak) in the late 1920s and early 1930s.[105] In Soviet Central Asia, the Central Asian Bank

(Asiabank) specialized among other things in transactions with Afghanistan, Western China and Khorasan (Eastern Iran) in the 1920s.[106]

Asiabank was established in 1924 as a joint-stock company with a capital of 7.5 million rubles and with a board in Tashkent. Its shareholders were the People's Commissariat of Finance of the USSR, the Central Cotton Committee, Bukharan SSR, Turkestan ASSR and Khorezm SSR.[107] These banks were also called 'special banks', as every bank had a certain specialization. In this case, the bank dealt with banking services to Soviet Central Asia. It was also attributed as a 'bank for outlying districts' ('okrainnyi bank').[108] The term 'okrainnyi bank' is very close to the discourse of traditional colonialism. Further, DVBank was also considered to be a bank for outlying districts. Statistics on the Asiabank's foreign trade operations indicate that the bank dominated Soviet operations in Afghanistan. In the Iranian Khorasan, the bank apparently shared the market with Ruspersbank. In Western China, the institutional organization of Soviet operations are still poorly studied, and the fact that a quarter of operations there were serviced by Asiabank is the first attempt to clarify this issue (Table 6.15).

Table 6.15: The Asiabank's Foreign Operations in 1928/9

	Afghanistan		Western China		Khorasan	
	Loans, thousands of rubles	Percentage of all Soviet foreign trade operations in the region, %	Loans, thousands of rubles	Percentage of all Soviet foreign trade operations in the region, %	Loans, thousands of rubles	Percentage of all Soviet foreign trade operations in the region, %
Exports	6,516	93	4,427	27.6	4,396	38.3
Imports	9,296	79	2,860	20.8	6,877	49.1
Total	15,812	84.50	7,287	24.4	11,273	44.3

Source: RSAE, fond 7590, opis 3, delo 77, list 29

Table 6.16: The Asiabank's Foreign Trade Customers in 1928/9, %

Customers	Afghanistan	Western China	Khorasan
Soviet economic institutions in the USSR	99.12	57.38	93.19
Soviet economic institutions abroad	0.04	10.61	–
Orient merchants in the USSR	0.30	11.98	6.81
Orient merchants abroad	0.54	14.17	–
Domestic trade	–	5.86	–
Total	100	100	100

Source: RSAE, fond 7590, opis 3, delo 77, list 30

Foreign trade customers in Afghanistan and Khorasan were typically Soviet and located in the USSR. A different situation was observed for the bank's operations in Western China, where one-third of operations were loans to foreign merchants (Table 6.16). This small case of Asiabank, based on archival material, shows that other Soviet banks engaged in foreign trade services, except the State Bank, Prombank and Vneshtorgbank, and we still do not have the complete picture of this process.

The sparse cases of Soviet banks in Asia allow us to draw a preliminary conclusion about two models of banking. Firstly, the model of Mongolbank and Tuvinbank, based on the Soviet political control over Mongolia and Tuva, when the transfer of the Soviet economic model became possible in these countries. Therefore, the development of modern banking in Mongolia and Tuva occurred as a part of the modernization process, but within the Soviet model. Mongolbank and Tuvinbank were institutions with significantly larger power than traditional banks, because they were assigned the task of organizing industrial enterprises and trade development. Secondly, two dissimilar institutions, Ruspersbank and Dalbank in Harbin, had similar features: there was no Soviet political control over the territories of their activity and the direct imposition of Soviet institutions was impossible. This Soviet bank thus had to adapt to local conditions.

For Ruspersbank, the Soviet economic authorities were not able to find the optimal structure of operations in the 1920s. Currency issues, customers' network development and the management of expenditure in branches were all failing, but all the resources of the Soviet banking system behind Ruspersbank allowed it to keep this project afloat. In China, the position of Dalbank in Harbin was somewhat better. On the one hand, the local political and economic situation excluded any attempts of direct Soviet-type banking; on the other, the bank had guaranteed customers associated with the CER, the Soviet population in Manchuria and the services to Soviet-Chinese trade. In this regard, the fate of the pre-Revolutionary Russo-Asiatic Bank is extremely significant: the rupture of ties with Russia created the conditions for the bank's collapse.

Conclusion

These special banks attended to the expansion of the Russian Empire in Asia. They were under governmental control, with significantly freer charters compared with private banks, which make it easier to adapt to the conditions of another country or to the demands of the Russian government. The state control over these banks allowed using them in regions where Russian private banks did not want to take risk or where the government wanted to maintain maximal control over the Russian expansion. Russian imperial policy in Asia was driven by ideology, typical of the powers of the age, which meant that some Asian areas should be fixed as Russia's sphere of political and economic influence. As part of imperial policy, special banks were engaged in lending to local governments, developing concessions and forming markets for Russian goods, but the basis of their activities was purely banking: providing foreign trade with credits and payments as well as operations in local financial markets. The operations of imperial banks were not always successful, but the issue of their effectiveness as commercial enterprises turned out to be less important compared with their participation in the struggle for the political and economic influence of the Russian Empire. All losses of imperial banks could always be written off at the expense of public resources.

In the 1920s, in the Soviet period, imperial banking transformed into new forms of participation in the economic expansion. Foreign trade became a state monopoly in the USSR, and state property dominated the economy, meaning that the economic component of the Soviet foreign banking system was more important than in the pre-revolutionary period. In other words, there were no other institutions, except public ones, for the development of foreign trade. Asian trade was always important for Russia, because these countries had good opportunities for Russia's industrial exports, not only exports of food and raw materials, as in Europe. This conclusion does not apply to Japan, which was a country for industrial imports from Russia in the 1920s. On the other hand, the situation for Russian exports was not favourable in all countries. The best situation was in Iran; the market in China was very competitive; in Afghanistan, Western China, Mongolia and Tuva, the Russian goods' market was still very weak and it was necessary to continue its formation. A network of Soviet banks appeared in Asia in the 1920s and these banks tried to capture an economic niche that had been occupied by Russian private and imperial state banks before WWI and the Russian Revolution.

The functions of Soviet banks abroad have not been well investigated yet. This system began to develop during the period of political and economic isolation from the Soviet Union; these institutions had to seek foreign credit in the first place. However, Soviet foreign banks failed to cope with this task, as explained in Table 6.17, which compares the assets of Soviet banks, the State Bank of the Russian Empire, the Russo-Asiatic Bank and imperial banks. The calculations are based on the exchange rates available in publications. Even though these calculations cannot be entirely accurate in the comparison of the ruble's purchase power in 1914 and at the end of the 1920s, Table 6.17 still implies that Soviet foreign banks were very small institutions in comparison with Soviet domestic banks. The State Bank of the USSR, which absorbed nationalized private banks, was much larger than Vneshtorgbank, which was a rather small-sized bank from the perspective of the banking system of the Russian Empire.

Three very important conclusions follow from the data in Table 6.17. Firstly, the breakup of credit's blockade of the USSR could happen through the Soviet State Bank in the first place, because it could give maximal guarantees to creditors, and then through Vneshtorgbank. Secondly, the foreign success of Vneshtorgbank was in inverse proportion to its independence from the State Bank: more dependence meant more guarantees to creditors. Indeed, Vneshtorgbank gradually became a department of the State Bank. Thirdly, Soviet foreign banks could not be independent institutions; they could serve as branches, because they had to be dependent on their sources of larger Soviet banks.

Table 6.17: Comparison of Banks' Assets, US dollars

	Date	Assets in millions of currency units	Currency of assets	Balance in millions of US dollars, 1927–9
State Bank of the USSR *	01.10.1928	5,933.1	ruble	11,569.5
Vneshtorgbank †	01.10.1927	162.3	ruble	316.4
Dalbank in Harbin ‡	01.01.1927	42.6	yen	20.8
Mongolbank §	01.01.1926	6.2	Mexican dollar	2.7
Ruspersbank ¶	01.01.1927	70.4	qiran	30.4
State Bank of the Russian Empire **	01.01.1914	3,040.5	ruble	5,898.6
Russo-Asiatic Bank ††	01.01.1914	828.7	ruble	1,607.8
Russo-Chinese Bank ‡‡	01.01.1910	287.7	ruble	558.0
Discount and Loan Bank of Persia §§	01.01.1912	68.4	ruble	132.7

Sources:

* A. Blum, *Istorija kreditnyh uchrezhdenij i sovremennoe sostojanie kreditnoj sistemy v SSSR* [The history of credit institutions and the current state of the credit system in the USSR], (Moscow: Gosfinizdat USSR, 1929), p. 208.

† *Bank dlia vneshnei torgovli SSSR. Otchet za 1926/27 gg.* [The bank for foreign trade of the USSR. Report for the 1926/27 period], (Moscow: Gosizdat USSR, 1925), consolidated balance sheet.

‡ by rate of statement: RSAE, fond 7590, opis 3, delo 144, list 1–12.

§ by rate of Dalbank's statement: RSAE, fond 7590, opis 3, delo 92, list 41–2.

¶ by official rate: RSAE, fond 7590, opis 3, delo 98, list 8, 48.

** *Gosudarstvennyi bank. Otchet za 1916 g.* [The State Bank. Report for 1916] (Petrograd: [n.p.], 1917), pp. 50–1; and S. A. Salomatina, 'The Statements of the State Bank of the Russian Empire, 1861–1917', in *[http://www.hist.msu.ru/Dynamics/data/12_014.xls]*.

†† *Vestnik finansov, promyshlennosti i torgovli: Otchety kreditnyh uchrezhdenij, torgovyh i promyshlennyh predprijatij,* [The bulletin of finance, industry and trade: annual reports of credit institutions, trade and industrial enterprises] (Sankt-Petersburg: [n.p.], 1914), n. 31, p. 1727.

‡‡ *Otchet po operatsiiam Russko-Kitaiskogo banka za 1909 g.* [Report on operations of the Russo-Chinese Bank in 1909] (Sankt-Petersburg: [n.p.], 1910); and S. A. Salomatina, 'The Statements of the Russo-Chinese Bank, 1897–1910', in *[http://www.hist.msu.ru/Dynamics/data/12_017.xls]*.

§§ RSHA, fond 600, opis 9, delo 1230, list 36ob–37

Thus, Soviet foreign banks were actually branches in the entire Soviet banking system. They serviced payments between the Soviet Union and other countries and collected information on foreign markets - there are many business analytics in the Vneshtorgbank's archive. The customers of these banks consisted mainly of Soviet organizations. The idea of supplementing payments and analytical functions with banking operations in local markets simply for the sake of profit was infeasible, because it was against the communist ideology and implied a negative attitude to virtually any type of banking profit. Thus, in contrast to the imperial ideology, communist ideas restricted the operations' pattern of Soviet banks abroad. The Soviet banking system abroad was notable for its strict control over employees and focus on profit on authorized operations, but simultaneously we must always keep in mind that the Soviet banking system as a whole was a source of capital and therefore a cover for any loss.

In the 1920s, the use of banks for political purposes occurred under another ideology compared with the pre-revolutionary period. The Soviet ideology of this decade was based on the idea of world revolution, of uncompromising political struggle for transition to a new social and political order. In 1919, the Comintern was established and the idea of political influence on other countries through the national communist movement became an important part of Soviet foreign policy. Any legal and illegal means were allowed in this struggle. We can see the two versions of Soviet expansion in Asia in the 1920s and correspondingly the two types of Soviet banks abroad. The first type concerned Mongolia and Tuva, where the political influence of the Soviet Union and Comintern was stable and dominant. The exports of the Soviet economic system in whole took place in these countries. The activities of Mongolbank and Tuvinbank, backed by all the resources of the Soviet banking system, had a strong aspect of modernization. These banks took part in the creation of modern monetary and fiscal systems and engaged in the organization of the local industry and commerce, thereby 'growing' customers by themselves.

The second type characterizes Soviet banking in countries where the USSR had no strong political positions, such as Turkey, Iran, Afghanistan and China. The banks operating there had to meet the economic challenge by adapting to the local conditions. As for the cases of Ruspersbank and Dalbank in Harbin, they were based on the local legislation, firstly, to be comprehensible to foreign partners, and secondly, to get away from the rigid rules and restrictions of the Soviet banking system. Ruspersbank was unable to find an effective business model in non-socialist states that would not contradict with the Soviet economic ideology. Nevertheless, Iran remained the largest trading partner of the Soviet Union in Asia. Dalbank in Harbin had a stable group of customers associated with the CER and Soviet diaspora in Manchuria. In this period, there was a civil war in China, and the USSR provided different political forces with various forms of material support as well as tried to export revolution directly through the Comintern and Communist Party of China; however, the victory of the Kuomintang and Chiang Kai-shek in the political battle put an end to Soviet plans. Money for legal and illegal political projects in China was transferred through Dalbank in Harbin, although this issue needs further study.

The idea of political and economic influence on the territories of Asian states remained urgent in the history of the first third of the 20th century. Until 1914, this phenomenon was well described in terms of traditional imperialism, but from the 1920s, it began to transform and it became into the Soviet ideology. It seems as though this economic and political influence could be carried out under various slogans. In the 1920s, the Soviet Union had fewer economic opportunities than the Russian Empire due to the consequences of wars and revolutions, but now all the forces were assembled in the hands of the Soviet state, and the dream of pre-revolutionary high-ranking officials about fully controlled external expansion had come true in a form unexpected for them.

7 CHALLENGING IMPERIAL BANKING IN INDIA: FROM THE LEGACY OF EMPIRE TO NATIONALISTIC RULES

Ashok Kapoor

The history of Indian banking was closely associated with that of foreign banking as the initiative towards formation of banks in the modern sense was taken by the Europeans in India. Banking in India originated in the last decades of the eighteenth century, from the early stages of the British overseas empire. The first foreign bank to be established in India was Bank of Hindostan in 1770 followed by the General Bank of India in 1786. The oldest bank still in existence is the State Bank of India, which was established as the Bank of Calcutta (1806) by the Royal Charter of the East India Company. The Bank of Bombay (1840) and the Bank of Madras (1843) were also established by Royal Charter. These three banks were known as the 'Presidency Banks'. The earliest foreign bank to be established in India was Chartered Bank of India, Australia and China at Calcutta in 1853 and it was followed by *Comptoir d'escompte de Paris* in Calcutta in 1860, in Bombay in 1862 as well as branches in Madras and Pondicherry (a French colony in India). Hong Kong & Shanghai Banking Corporation (HSBC) opened its branch in Calcutta in 1869. Calcutta became a hub of the foreign banks because of trade and commerce of the British Empire.

The history of Indian banking can be conveniently divided into four phases:

Phase I (1786–1935): The establishment of foreign banks, referred to as 'exchange banks', which were involved in financing foreign trade and engaged in foreign exchange business.

Phase II (1935–69): 'Imperial banking' was inserted within the rule of the Reserve Bank of India (hereafter the RBI) and, in 1949, of the Banking Regulation Act, which gave the RBI regulatory and supervisory powers, before being constrained by the nationalization of banks.

Phase III (1969–91): 'Social control' over banks intensified, although a pre-liberalization mood took shape; foreign banks diversified in areas where domestic banks were operating and branch expansion witnessed unprecedented growth so as to reach common man.

Phase IV (1991–2005): Foreign banks benefited from the liberalization of the Indian economy and their numbers increased. During this phase the Indian financial system was integrated into the global system. Whilst imperial banking was part of an internationalized system under the dependence of the capital of the Empire and the City, as a first form of what is called sometimes 'first globalisation', the recent system is more a multipolar one (London, New York, etc.), although it still depends on international centres of corporate and investment banking and on 'capitals of capital'.[1]

Until 2004, thirty-one foreign banks in India, with a total of 295 branches, accounted for 0.36 percent of total branch network despite an 8.53 percent share in banking assets.[2] Foreign banks are interested in parking their financial resources in a stable and profitable environment that has minimal risk. However, the foreign banks had been critical of the policies, attitude and approach of the Reserve Bank of India with regards to branch expansion, while the domestic banks criticized foreign banks for concentrating on big cities and niche banking. Nonetheless, during all these years, the experience gained by foreign and Indian banks had been mutually beneficial to both, resulting in assimilation and the diffusion of sound banking practices, which made the Indian banking system healthy, transparent and financially viable, enable its integration into the international financial system. Since the beginning of the twenty-first century, the principles of transparency, liberalization, globalization and innovative information and communication technology in banking have provided a new impetus to the banking system.

Phase I (1786–1935): From Imperial Banking to the Establishment of Native Banks

For a long time banks have been one of the vital instruments for the growth of the economy not only in India but also all over the world.

Imperial Banking Contributing to a National Financial System

In the eighteenth century the borrowing needs of the Indian people were largely met by indigenous bankers and financiers. The concept of borrowing from the public was pioneered by the East India Company to finance its campaigns in the Anglo-French Wars in India. The endeavours of the East India Company to establish government banks were primarily influenced by the necessity of raising both long and short-term financial accommodation from the banks. The origin of modern banking in India dates back to the late eighteenth and early nineteenth centuries when the European agency houses were established in the port towns of Bombay and Calcutta. The early traders who came to India in the seventeenth century could not make use of the indigenous bankers due to their ignorance of the local language as well as the indigenous bankers' inexperience with European trade. As a result, the agency houses started banking, separate from their commercial pursuits; although their primary business was trade, they entered into the sphere of banking in order to facilitate their trade. The agency houses also served as bankers to the East India Company and, since they had no capital of their own, they raised deposits, issued currency notes, financed trade and established joint stock banks. The first bank to be established in India was the Bank of Hindostan in 1770, followed by the General Bank of India in 1786. Subsequently, some joint stock banks were established in India but agency houses are regarded as a harbinger of modern banking in India.

The oldest bank still in existence is the State Bank of India which was established by the Royal Charter of the East India Company as the Bank of Calcutta in 1806. Similarly, the Bank of Bombay (1840) and the Bank of Madras (1843) were established by the Royal Charters of the East India Company. Known as the presidency banks, these three banks acted partially as the central bank of the country for many years, and were merged together to establish the Imperial Bank of India in 1925. Foreign banks in India were established during British rule. In 1836 the Bank of India and, in 1840, the Bank of Asia were established during the rule of the East India Company but they could not make much headway due to the opposition of the agency houses and the East India Company, who feared that their monopoly in foreign remittances and the discounting of foreign bills would be threatened.

The earliest foreign banks established in India were British and French banks as they were engaged in stiff rivalry over trade and commerce in India. Both countries had established colonies in the port towns. The earliest banks were opened in Calcutta as it was the financial capital of India and the hub of international trade. Chartered Bank of India, Australia & China was the first foreign bank to establish its branches at Calcutta, Bombay and Shanghai in 1858. The bank was keen to capitalize on the huge expansion of trade with India and China and other British possessions in Asia, and on the handsome gains it could make from financing the movement of goods from Europe to India. Subsequently, as a sequel to the removal of protectionist policies in trade and commerce by the British and the French, *Comptoir d'escompte de Paris* (CEP) established branches at Calcutta in 1860 and at Bombay in 1862, along with branches in Madras and Pondicherry. The antecedents of the Hong Kong and Shanghai Banking Corporation (HSBC) could be traced to India in 1853 with the opening of Mercantile Bank of India, London and China, which was established at Bombay. It subsequently opened branches in Madras and Calcutta. HSBC has operated in India since 1867 with the opening of its first branch in Calcutta.

During the second and third quarter of the nineteenth century, two events adversely affected the growth of banking in India. The first event was the commercial crisis of 1829–32 which put an end to the business of agency houses until about 1860; the second was the American Civil War. The Civil War stopped the supply of cotton from the American states to Lancashire, England during 1861–5, and, to fill the new gap in the market, many promoters opened banks to finance trade in Indian cotton. In a few years the boom collapsed and, with large exposures to speculative ventures, many of the banks established during these years failed. The depositors not only lost their money but their trust in the banking system. Subsequently, banking in India remained the exclusive domain of Europeans for several decades, until the beginning of the twentieth century.

Imperial Banking as Leverage to Indian International Banking

It is interesting to note that there was no law limiting liability and so all joint stock banks operated on the basis of unlimited liability. In 1860 legal recognition was given to the limited liability of the banks. Many companies had registered themselves as banks and, when they failed, they were included in the statistics of bank failures. With the passage of the Indian Companies Act (1913) a few sections relating to joint stock banks were included in it. Before the establishment of the Reserve Bank of India (the RBI), there were three types of banks operating in India, namely: 'presidency banks', amalgamated in 1921 as the Imperial Bank of India; foreign-owned 'exchange banks'; and Indian joint stock banks. The compartmentalization of banking in India prompted Lord George Curzon, Viceroy of India, to remark that it seemed we were behind the times. The banking system in India was like an old-fashioned sailing ship, divided by solid wooden bulkheads into separate and cumbersome compartments.

Table 7.1: Commercial Banks in India (1870–1937)

	Presidency Bank		Indian Joint Stock		Exchange Banks		
	Total Deposits	No of Banks	Total Deposits	No of Banks	Total Deposits	No of Banks	Total
1870	118.3	-3	1.4	-2	5.2	3	124. (8)
1900	156.9	3	80.8	9	105	8	342.7 (20)
1913	423.6	3	241	41	310.4	12	975.0 (56)
1919	799.9	3	612.7	47	743.6	11	2,156.2 (61)
1921	725.8	1	801.6	65	752	17	2,279 (83)
1930	839.7	1	986.6	88	681.1	18	2,197.3 (107)
1937	2,716.7	1	7337	690	1,812.8	15	11,866.6 (706)

Banking and Monetary Statistics of India, Reserve Bank of India (Figures in million rupees)

During this period small banks were established with a view to finance trade and commerce but their growth was slow and banks faced periodic failures. In 1870, only three exchange banks had established their agencies in India. By 1913 their number increased to twelve, out of which more than half had their head offices in London, while the rest belonged to various other countries including

Japan, France, Germany, Russia and the USA.[3] 'Presidency banks' and, later on, the Imperial Bank of India were legally barred from participating in the foreign exchange business and the Indian joint stock banks showed no interest in financing foreign trade. As a result, the field was open for the Europeans to establish near monopolistic control over the foreign exchange business in India.

World War I disturbed the proportion of India's foreign trade with various countries and led to the closure of some of those countries' banks, yet at the same time, a few countries established new branches of their banks in India. *Deutsche-Asiatische Bank* and Russo-Asiatic Bank closed their agencies in India while five new banks opened branches in 1918–20, of which two were from Japan, two from the Netherlands and one from Portugal. Exchange banks were engaged in providing foreign exchange for trade and commerce; financing internal trade, especially for the transportation of goods to port towns and the interiors; and taking deposits from the public.

Initially the exchange banks depended primarily on home funds for meeting their additional financial requirements and had to bear the criticism of being unsound and undesirable for the Indian money market. Subsequently, these banks developed an Indian deposit business which gave rise to complaints of unfair competition from the Indian banks! The foreign banks operating in India during this period can be conveniently divided into two groups. In the first group were the British banks, such as Chartered Bank of India, Australia & China (1853), the National Bank of India (1863), the Mercantile Bank of India (1893) and the Eastern Bank (1910). These banks financed the bulk of funding for Indo-British and Indo-China trade. To some extent they promoted internal trade which in-directly helped their exports to Britain. In the second group were foreign banks that specialized in the trade of their respective countries, such as CNEP, the Yokohama Specie Bank, *Deutsche-Asiatische Bank*, the Russo-Asiatic Bank, and the First National City Bank.

Two important factors helped the exchange banks to acquire more or less a monopoly in the field of financing the external trade of India. The presidency banks and, after the amalgamation of the presidency banks, the Imperial Bank of India, had been prohibited from dealing in foreign exchange and from borrowing money from abroad. Some of the banks like the Alliance Bank of Simla and the Tata Industrial Bank, which were engaged in this business, did not, however, attain anything like even a partial success, due mainly to their lack of access to the London money market and partly to their comparatively small resources.

The old classification of the exchange banks was based on the extent of business done by them. According to this, five banks were doing considerable business while the remaining thirteen were merely agencies of large banking corporations doing business all over the East. Another interesting classification was based upon the nationality of the banks. Eight banks were British while the remaining ten were from Japan, the USA, Holland, China, France, Portugal and Singapore. Business done by the non-British banks was much less significant than that of the British banks. For example, the total deposits and total advances (including bills discounted) in India and Burma of the ten non-British banks were 16 percent and 19 percent, respectively, of the total deposits in 1935.[4]

The business of the exchange banks can be divided into exchange business and ordinary banking. Within the exchange business, the bulk of the bills dealt in were export bills. The bills were purchased by the banks' Indian branches and were held by their London offices until they were retired or paid on maturity. They were usually discounted in London, immediately following their acceptance. Exchange banks also financed the import of trade through their head offices and branches outside India. The purchases of export bills by them represented transfers of funds to London. To bring these funds back to India, they used to buy India council bills sold by the Secretary of State for India. Other methods of raising funds were by cashing import bills; selling drafts to Indian students and travellers abroad; buying rupee notes in London and selling them in India; and the import of gold and silver.

Within the ordinary banking business, exchange banks also established a majority of their branches in the port towns, while maintaining inland centres in the four provinces of Bengal, Punjab, the United Provinces and the North West Frontier Province. Approximately seventy-five branches belonged to eight British banks and the remaining twenty-five belonged to non-British banks. The inland branches played some part in the financing of inland trade mainly on account of goods or produce in transit prior to export or immediately after import. The support, which the piece-goods trade in Delhi and Amritsar, and leather trade in Kanpur, received from them, was well known. In Calcutta they made advances against Hessian delivery orders and inland bills or *hundis* (promissory notes), while in Bombay they did practically every type of banking business. Significantly, in Assam, Bihar, Central Provinces and Berar and Orissa, the exchange banks had no branches either at the ports or in the interior.

The statistics regarding the operations of exchange banks were meagre as revealed from the weekly returns: The *Statistical Tables Relating to Banks in India* was the only source of information regarding banks' deposits and cash, but it hardly provided any information on banks' investments in India. About demand and time liabilities, exchange banks received deposits both in current and savings bank accounts and also received fixed deposits. The rate of interest offered by them was higher than the Imperial Bank of India but lower than those of the Indian joint stock banks. The aggregate deposits of the exchange banks showed a steady rise until 1921. Starting from a meagre Rs.5.2 million in 1870 and increasing to Rs.105m by 1900, Rs.750m had been deposited by 1921.[5] During the next thirteen years, the deposits of the exchange banks declined, presumably because of the establishment of the Imperial Bank of India and competition from other Indian joint stock banks. The total demand and time liabilities in India and Burma of the exchange banks on 15 August 1941 amounted to Rs.954m. Out of this about Rs.820m was accounted for by the eight British exchange banks and about Rs.90m by the two US banks. The balance of Rs.44m belonged to the remaining ten banks.[6]

About advances and bills discounted, an absence of information regarding the investments of the exchange banks in India led to a general belief that exchange banks took money out of the country for use elsewhere. The evidence given before the Central Banking Enquiry Committee proved that there was no foundation for such an assumption. According to the figures collected by them for the year 1929, the advances and bills discounted in India by exchange banks amounted to Rs.460m and their investments in government and other securities totalled Rs.260m.[7] The total of these two items was Rs.720m whereas total deposits in India amounted to Rs.660m in the same year. Very little was known to the outside public concerning the extent to which they employed their funds in various countries in which they were operating. Their business was so fluid and governed by such a variety of considerations – including trends in international trade, differences in interest rates in various countries, seasonal factors and international political developments – that it is difficult to generalize or to correctly judge the matter.

The Hegemony of Imperial Banking

Provisions for controlling non-national banks in foreign countries and India were to be found in the laws of various countries. In the USA, Italy, Japan, Belgium and Germany, foreign banks interested in establishing a branch had to obtain a license from the prescribed authority. In Germany, foreign banks, excepting those that had come into existence before 16 January 1920, were prohibited from accepting deposits and security as bails. In Italy, branches of foreign banks were required to make a certain prescribed deposit as a guarantee for the business transacted in Italy and its colonies. In Japan there was a similar provision requiring a deposit of 100,000 yen in respect of each office or agency doing business there. In Belgium foreign banks had to earmark ten million francs for their business in the country. The authorities issuing banking licences in these countries were empowered to impose specific restrictions in order to enable them to treat a non-national bank in the same manner as their own institutions were treated in the country from which the non-national bank in question had originated.

Foreign banks had an inherent advantage over the Indian banks in the foreign trade business as they had the support of capital resources, efficient management, access to London money market and, last but not least, experience in the foreign exchange market. The foreign trade of India was regarded as a very lucrative business and all foreign banks wanted to share a major slice of the pie while the Indian traders and exporters had a meagre share of just 15–20 percent. The Indians had a lot of grievances against exchange banks, some of which are detailed here: exchange banks held a monopolistic position in foreign trade and the exchange business, which was detrimental to Indian business; Indian customers were required to deposit 10–15 percent of the value of merchandise with exchange banks in order to open a confirmed letter of credit; exchange banks discriminated against Indian steamships and insurance companies; responsible posts were not offered to Indians; exchange banks were not bound by any legal restrictions in India and were exempt from even limited statutory obligations imposed on Indian joint stock banks; no protection was afforded to Indian depositors; and import bills were drawn in sterling at a relatively high rate of interest.

Mastering Imperial and Foreign Banking?

The *Indian Central Banking Enquiry Committee Report* (1931) pointed out that the entire foreign exchange business was under the monopoly of exchange banks.[8] Furthermore, to a lesser extent these banks accepted deposits and provided loans. With a view to giving the proposed Reserve Bank of India some control over exchange banks, the committee recommended licensing the Indian offices of exchange banks. To obtain a license the committee also suggested that the banks should be required to furnish the proposed central bank of the country with a statement on their assets and liabilities as well as periodic reports of Indian and non-Indian business handled by them. Other stipulations might also be imposed on them from time to time. The domestic traders and bankers criticized them for favouring the European traders at the cost of Indian business interests. An insistence on having two British signatures as a condition for a rediscount for trading in foreign exchange posed problems for Indian traders.

Keeping in view some of the criticism cited above, the Indian Central Banking Enquiry Committee recommended the extension of foreign connections by Indian joint stock banks and the establishment of an Indian exchange bank, if the Imperial Bank of India was not able to participate in the financing of foreign trade. During the early phase, the number of foreign banks in India increased from three to eighteen and they maintained a substantial share of deposits and credits of the total banking system. However, in the absence of any statutory regulation for the banking industry, it would have been unfeasible, unjustified and even inequitable to regulate only exchange banks.

Before the establishment of the Reserve Bank of India, the position of head offices and branch offices of the banks was as follows: these 1,269 head offices and branches of the banks were located in 475 towns. The remaining 2,100 towns and all villages in the country had no formal banking facilities. Only 22.62 per cent of the population had access to banking while 77.38 per cent had no access to banking facilities.

Table 7.2: The Position of Head Offices and Branch Offices of the Banks in India

Banks	Head Offices	Branches
Exchange Banks	0	98
Imperial Bank of India	3	160
Indian Joint Stock Banks	320	946
Total	323	1,204

Source: S. L. N. Simha, *History of the Reserve Bank of India, Volume 1: 1935–1951* (Bombay: the RBI, 1970), p. 168.

Phase II (1935–69): Challenging the Legacy of Imperial Banking: From the Establishment of the Reserve Bank of India to the Nationalization of Banks

During this period the Reserve Bank of India[9] was established on 1 April 1935 as the central bank of the country, with a share capital of Rs 50 million as recommended by the Hilton Young Commission. The functions of the reserve bank were to serve as banker both to the government and to other banks, to issue bank notes and to maintain the exchange rate. Besides this, the central bank was endowed with extra powers and manoeuvrability in extraordinary circumstances, which could be exercised with the prior approval of the Governor General in Council or the board of directors.

Imperial Banking Without Strict Regulation

In the early phase, in India, there were no regulatory restrictions on foreign banks in respect to their operations. Exchange banks enjoyed a good deal of freedom in their operations and were engaged in multifarious activities, some of them were related to banking while others were related to trade and commerce. Under Section 42 of the RBI Act 1934[10] exchange banks were required to send to the central government and the RBI a weekly report showing: the amount of demand and time liabilities in India, which evolved significantly; the amount held in India in currency notes of the government of India and bank notes; the total amount held in India and Burma; the amount held in India in rupees and coins and subsidiary coins; the amount of advances made and bills discounted in India; and the balance held in the RBI at the close of business each Friday.

The aforesaid information was treated as confidential and a consolidated statement was prepared. James Braid Taylor, Governor of the RBI, felt that

> we consider that a consolidated statement based on the returns collected under clause 42 should be published on the ground that they should be of interest and value to the public. Though the returns of the individual banks must be regarded as confidential, this consideration does not apply to statistical returns complied from the all.[11]

After the establishment of the RBI, the monopoly of exchange banks in foreign exchange business was breached; Indian banks were allowed to deal in it and, slowly and gradually, foreign banks were brought under the regulatory and supervisory regime. The primary objectives of the establishment of foreign banks in India were to develop economic relations with the country so as to avail themselves of opportunities in the import–export trade. The size of the country and its economy, as well as its less restrictive regulatory practices and high interest rates, helped to reap maximum profits with a reduced element of risk.

The entry of foreign banks was regulated: the RBI Act 1934 and the Banking Regulation Act 1949[12] were two key regulatory instruments for governing the Indian banking sector. The RBI Act empowered the RBI to exercise control and regulate the banks, non-banking financial institutions and other financial institutions. For regulating the banking sector, the RBI issued master circulars on a yearly basis to incorporate changes in policy, supervision and regulation of the banking sector. All banks, irrespective of being Indian or foreign, were required to obtain a license for commencing business in India. For the entry of foreign banks in India a capital requirement was fixed at USD $70 million for wholly owned subsidiaries and USD $25 million for branches. The key factors taken into consideration by the RBI for the issue of a license were: the business plan of the foreign bank; the reciprocity offered to Indian banks in the host country; India's economic and political relations with the country in which the bank was incorporated; the history of the foreign bank both in India and globally; and the international ranking of the bank.

Regulating Foreign Banks

After the establishment of the RBI, some steps were initiated to exercise some control over the exchange banks by asking them to provide some information about their business. Prior to this, the Central Banking Enquiry Committee (1931) had discussed the question of increasing the share of the Indian banks in the foreign business and bringing some necessary control over exchange banks.[13] There was growing criticism of the practices of exchange banks in that they were competing with the Indian banks for business within the country, both in respect of attracting deposits and providing credits, as well as the fact that they continued to discriminate against Indian insurers. The RBI was of the view that there could be no discrimination against foreign banks on the principle of reciprocity. According to Section 23(3) of the Banking Companies Act,[14] foreign banks were allowed to operate in India as long as the countries in which they were incorporated did not discriminate against Indian banks and complied with the requirements of the Banking Companies Act. Exchange banks' easy access to London and other European money markets, their ability to attract deposits in India at low rates, and their early start in the business of financing India's foreign trade, gave them an advantage over Indian banks. While their larger resources and wide connections in different countries had fostered the confidence of their clientele, their efficient business method had no small share in it.

Exchange banks were not required to furnish the RBI with any detailed information regarding their assets and liabilities. The only statement they submitted periodically comprised as the weekly returns under Section 42 of the RBI Act;[15] and copies of consolidated balance sheets which did not provide separate figures of their Indian business under Section 277 of the Indian Companies Act.[16] These banks did not come under the purview of the various provisions of the Indian Companies Act relating to Indian Banking Companies. The central board asked Taylor, Governor of the RBI, to find out how the statistics of the exchange banks about their operations in India could be made as complete as those of the Indian joint stock banks.[17] According to Taylor, the exchange banks were functioning as authorized dealers and were providing the RBI with detailed information about their daily exchange operations.[18] He felt that obtaining information about their assets and liabilities would only be of statistical interest. The central board was not satisfied with the governor's views and asked him to obtain information regarding investments and the foreign exchange business of the exchange banks. Taylor reported to the central board in February 1942 that the exchange banks were maintaining assets in India in excess of 75 percent prescribed in the proposed Banking Act.[19] Their resources were distributed as follows: financing of internal trade – 33 percent; cash – 16 percent; government securities – 20 percent; financing of foreign trade – 23 percent; and other miscellaneous areas – 8 percent.

The move towards banking legislation gathered momentum. The exchange banks were in a privileged position in the matter of statutory legislation and, as such, were naturally opposed to the proposed Banking Act. Public opinion, however, was in favour of bringing all foreign banks under stricter control by a system of licensing. Despite this, the management of the RBI suggested that a clause in the 1944–5 bill prescribe that banks incorporated outside British India or the United Kingdom should obtain a license from the RBI for carrying out business in India.[20] This move would have placed British banks on a superior footing and was vehemently criticized, not only by the Indian banks, but also by the other foreign banks. *The Eastern Economist* called this 'politically obnoxious and economically vicious' and added that

> this will not only foster uneconomic competition prejudicial to the growth of national banking institutions, but give rise to presumption, wholly without justification, that the UK banks do not need to be regulated in respect of their capital, liquidity and other standards of healthy banking.[21]

The *Select Committee Report* (February 1947) recognized the validity of the criticism made against the clause as it stood and recommended an extension of the provisions of licensing to all banks incorporated outside India.[22]

Broadening Foreign Exchange to Native Banks

As regards foreign exchange dealings of the exchange banks, all foreign banks were eligible for licenses to deal in the foreign exchange business. A few authorized dealers were given licenses to deal only in sterling. Following in the footsteps of the Bank of England, the RBI also followed a restricted policy of issuing licenses to deal in foreign exchange. The list of banks dealing in foreign exchange remained the same until 1943, apart from when the licenses of three Japanese banks were cancelled in 1941, on the grounds that the banks originated from an enemy country of India. Licensed banks were allowed to transact business at the rates prescribed by the Exchange Banks' Association. During this period the expansion and development of Indian banks took place and some of them were keen to start business in foreign exchange. The RBI liberalized the policy to enable Indian banks to undertake business in foreign exchange and licences were provided under the following conditions: that the bank enjoyed a good reputation and standing; showed good chances of attracting foreign exchange business and appointed agents overseas; and had appointed managers with experience in foreign exchange.

Some banks not able to fulfil the aforesaid conditions were given a license to initially deal in sterling and, after they had developed adequate experience, a general license was given. The following remarks of Shri Chintaman D. Deshmukh, Governor of the RBI, on one application for a licence, showed the paradigm shift in the policy.

> Even if the operations were not large they may yield experience both to the bank concerned and ourselves. These questions are bound to arise as soon as the preoccupations of the War are over and no charge should be laid at our door that we have thwarted Indian bank's efforts to enlarge their experience, unless we have very good reasons of public interest. These do not appear to exist and I would grant the license applied for.[23]

The foreign trade business dealt with by the Indian banks always remained very small and, even in 1948, was just 16 percent of total business. The central board of the RBI was of the view that the RBI could be of little assistance to the banks, which regarded their exchange business merely as a sideline, and the issuance of licences to deal in foreign exchange as a symbol of prestige.

National Regulation vs the Legacy of Imperial Banking

As the move towards the regulation of foreign banks took shape, the Banking Companies Act of 1949, also known as the Banking Regulating Act, was the single most vital legislative initiative.[24] It was instrumental in repainting the whole banking canvas, including the position and function of foreign banks in India. The Act brought domestic and foreign banks to an equal footing. The Banking Companies Act and its subsequent amendments gave the RBI substantial and far-reaching powers to regulate foreign banks in India. The following changes were applied to foreign banks: the bank was in a position to pay its present or future depositors in full as their claims accrued; banks' affairs were not, or were not likely to be, conducted in a manner detrimental to the interest of present or future depositors; in the case of banks incorporated outside of India, the government or the law of the country in which the bank was incorporated did not in any way discriminate against banks registered in India and complied with all the provisions of the law; banking companies already in existence at the commencement of the act were not prohibited from carrying on business until the RBI informed them that the license could not be granted to them; minimum capital for all banks functioning in India was prescribed: for banks incorporated outside India the minimum value of paid up capital and reserves was fixed at Rs.1.5m in any part of the country, excepting Bombay and Calcutta, where it was Rs.2m; the RBI was empowered to issue, cancel and forfeit banking licenses; to inspect, supervise and call for reports and returns; and to issue directives to the banks to maintain a certain portion of assets and liabilities in India; the banks were required to stipulate and change their lending policies; and the supervision and inspection of foreign banks started in 1959.

Commenting on the powers and responsibilities vested in the RBI under this act, *The Eastern Economist* wrote:

> The detailed narration of the duties and powers of Reserve Bank have been given deliberately to impress upon the public the colossal burden that a single institution is being called upon to have in policy making as well as day to day administration of the country's banking system. It is a responsibility which may not weigh on the old lady of the Thread Needle Street. But Reserve Bank is by no means an old lady or even elderly one. It is, in fact, a very young maiden – just fifteen years old – possibly sure of its ability, as young things usually are, but not yet very sure of its experience in a difficult world.[25]

The Act was amended a number of times to include provisions for bringing efficiency in its operation, to create uniformity in practices to be followed by all banks and to establish effective control over banks by regulation and supervision. An amendment of the Act in 1959 authorized the RBI to inspect foreign banks, provide guidelines for lending and to stop business activities that were against the economic interest of the country.

With the desire to strengthen capital funds and raise the liquidity requirements of the bank, the RBI had a meeting with the representatives of the banking
associations in December 1961, in which the following decisions were taken:
all banks should transfer a minimum of 20 percent of their declared profits to
their reserves until such time as the paid-up capital and reserves reach 6 percent
of their deposits; and all banks should maintain a minimum over-all liquidity ratio of 25 percent of their deposit liabilities, which represents an increase
from the present legal minimum of 20 percent.[26] The Bombay and Calcutta
Exchange Bank Associations had asked for certain facilities in the event that the
RBI implemented the liquidity requirement and suggested that the RBI should
allow exchange banks to deposit sterling securities with the RBI, London, to the
extent of 2.5 percent of their deposits towards the asset requirement. The RBI
was of the view that, as branches of international institutions, these exchange
banks stood on a special footing and most maintained high liquidity ratios.
Hence their requests were agreed to.

When the Deposit Insurance Corporation came into existence on 1 January
1962, a Deposit Insurance Corporate Act involving foreign banks was brought
into force.[27] Under the Act, all functioning banks, including foreign banks, were
categorized as insured banks. Insurance protection to a depositor was limited
to Rs.1,500 or the amount deposited, whichever was less, and the premium was
fixed at Rs.0.05 per Rs.100 of total deposits in India less some specified deposits.

In a meeting with the representatives of foreign banks on 28 November 1967,
the Governor of the RBI informed them about changes which the government
of India wanted to impose as part of a policy of social control.[28] The objective of
the RBI was to persuade foreign banks to conform as closely as possible to the
pattern prescribed for Indian banks. Emphasis was laid on the following points:
the Governor pointed out that the local board of foreign banks should not be set
up for public relations but should actively participate in directing the operations
of the banks; the local boards should have more powers than the chief executive
officers of the banks; the local boards should have representatives from banking
professions, industrialists, agriculture, co-operatives and small scale industries;
the chairmen of the local boards should be Indian and all the members of the
board should be Indians, although the chief executive officer could be a member of the board even if a foreigner; the foreign banks were required to submit
information on the amount of foreign funds deployed; banks were to prepare
a programme regarding Indianization and to indicate to the RBI a bank's rate
of Indian recruitment and how much further progress towards Indianization
would be made in the next five years; and foreign banks were to take increasing
interest in lending to the agricultural sector.

Phase III (1969–91): The Indianization of Banking against the Legacy of Imperial Banking

The Indianization of the banking economy followed two main paths: the process of nationalization by itself, as well as the encouragement of native banking. By the time the RBI was established, organized banking had developed to a significant extent and foreign banks or so-called exchange banks were major players in Indian banking. In 1935, there were seventeen exchange banks present in the country with 88 branches. The government took major initiatives in the banking sector after the independence of the country in 1947. Seven banks owned by the princely states were nationalized in 1959 and they became subsidiaries of the State Bank of India. In 1969, fourteen national banks in the country were nationalized and again in 1980, seven more banks were nationalized in order to gain social control over them.[29]

The Impact of Nationalization on the Legacy of Imperial and Foreign Banking

The year 1969 witnessed the nationalization of fourteen commercial banks in the country and seven more banks were nationalized in 1980 with the objective of providing a major thrust to banking in rural and semi-urban areas. The branch expansion programme witnessed unprecedented growth and an effort was made to provide basic banking facilities to the common man. In contrast the business of foreign banks suffered during this period and their share in total assets, deposits and credits witnessed a steep fall. Foreign banks diversified in the areas where they enjoyed an edge over domestic banks: foreign currency loans, investment banking, portfolio management, derivatives and other market related activities. In retail banking they focused on high net worth customers.

Foreign Banks and Social Control

In the beginning of the 1960s, most of the banks in India were concentrated in metropolitan cities and major urban areas, whilst rural areas were 'unbanked'. This led to the conclusion that banks were not tapping rural savings nor were they providing credit to the agricultural sector. Besides, there was a general feeling that the banking system in India was catering to the demands of the urban areas and was insensitive to the needs of society. As such, there was a demand in political circles for state intervention, which ultimately gave birth to the concept of 'social control' over the banks. Describing the late 1960s, the *History of the Reserve Bank of India* states:

> Those were the years when the things were heating up politically and when banking became the focus of political attention. The focus ultimately culminated in the

nationalisation but not before the Bank (the RBI) had fought some rearguard action to force commercial banks to expand to poorly served areas.[30]

In 1969, Indira Gandhi, Prime Minister of India, in her address to the newly appointed custodians of the nationalized banks declared:

> Banks being closely linked with the development of our economy cannot remain entirely uninfluenced by the needs of the political situation. The political situation in our country demands that banking facilities should be extended in increasing measure to backward areas, to agriculture, to small scale industries and so on, and banking operations should be influenced by a larger social purpose.[31]

In 1965 the RBI liberalized branch-licensing norms and it was decided that the focus should be on rural areas. Shri Lakshmi Kant Jha, Governor of the RBI, in his address to the Bombay bankers on 18 August 1967, suggested 'slowing down the branch expansion in urban areas'.[32] The bankers told him that they would welcome this so that their competitors, as well as foreign banks, were kept in check. He observed: 'The foreign banks were obliged to confine themselves to the port towns only' to make profits. The thinking of the RBI at that time was that, so far as port towns were concerned, no new licenses should be given for opening new branches of the foreign banks, except for those banks which did not already have a branch in the port towns. Some foreign banks such as the Japanese, the French and the Dutch banks, who only had one or two branches in the country, benefitted as they had an opportunity to open additional branches in port towns.

Foreign banks operated in port towns and other big cities and were allowed to open new branch offices only if the foreign exchange situation was found to be relatively comfortable. This restrictive policy was followed from 1962 and some foreign banks found it discriminatory. While the branch license issue was being discussed, Cooverji Hormusji Babha, chairman of the Central Bank of India, wrote to the Governor of the RBI: 'For peculiar reasons, foreign banks and other service organization claim it as their birth right to expand in the developing countries like ours. Also, I am afraid our authorities, without deeper consideration and thought, facilitate that'.[33] The RBI responded that, because of the restrictions on bringing in funds from abroad, foreign banks wanted to open new branches in metropolitan/port cities so that they could augment their resources. The central board of the RBI, which met in 1967, did not consider it necessary to suggest any tightening of restrictions on the branch expansion of foreign banks and allowed the existing policy to continue. C. H. Babha wrote to Morarji Desai, Deputy Prime Minister, that foreign banks were at a comparative advantage over Indian banks as they enjoyed certain exemptions. To quote C. H. Babha,

> in certain quarters there is lurking suspicion as to whether in the matter of issuing licences to foreign banks for opening new branches in India, the general criteria con-

tained in Section 23(2) of the Banking Regulation Act, 1949 have been applied as meticulously as in the case of Indian banks, or whether there has been any bias in favour of some foreign banks.[34]

By then, Lakshmi Kant Jha had become the Governor of the RBI, and he pointed out that, since 1962, the RBI had permitted only 43 offices out of 91 applications received from nine foreign banks whilst, in the same period, 2,367 new offices were opened by Indian banks.[35] This showed, in the Governor's opinion, that the licenses were not given liberally and without scrutiny. Jha, in his letter to the Additional Secretary, Minister of Finance, presented his frank opinion about the foreign banks, arguing that foreign banks were not necessary for the Indian economy and that the RBI's policy towards foreign banks should be directed to ensure proper discipline in respect of their activities rather than squeezing them out. He believed that

> even recently when the entire future of banking system in a sense being considered afresh, the view we took in respect of the foreign banks was not that they should be told to pack up, but they should bring in foreign exchange on a long term basis. If we accept the policy of allowing foreign banks to operate in the country, then clearly we cannot freeze their operations. As the economy grows and the banking system develops, they must increase their activities and participation though clearly not to the extent of Indian banking system.[36]

The RBI was to continue putting steady pressure on foreign banks to fall in line with its policies and follow the policy of Indianization as well as to ensure that they did not get any kind of unfair advantage because of their foreign ownership. M. Desai, Deputy Prime Minister, in his letter to Babha dated 19 October 1968, echoed similar feelings: 'I assure you that the branch licensing policy in regard to foreign banks has been restrictive and will continue to be so'.[37]

The policy of diversification in opening branches got structured: In a letter from Indraprasad Gordhanbhai Patel, Governor of the RBI, to Manmohan Singh, Finance Minister, dated 7 February 1979, emphasis was laid on the policy of diversification in respect of foreign banks. To quote from the letter,

> in a meeting with the Deputy Prime Minister and Finance Minister it was confirmed that the RBI should continue to follow restrictive policy in allowing foreign banks to open branches in India and within that restrictive policy, aim should be to diversify the presence of the international community in India. The USA and UK banks will not be encouraged to enlarge their presence and we should prefer opening of new branches in India by banks from countries not already represented in India but where Indian banks have branches. This principle of reciprocity will be major consideration in dealing with such cases.[38]

This policy led to the opening of branches from countries which were hitherto unrepresented in India.

New Policy Measures for Foreign Banks

The banking policy was accompanied by liberalization in regards to opening representative offices of foreign banks. While restricting the branch expansion policy, the RBI took a generally liberal view in respect of the opening of representative offices of foreign banks that would act as liaison offices but not transact any banking business. The main consideration for giving permission for opening liaison offices was the international standing of the bank, its global affiliations and the benefits that would accrue to India through the opening of representative offices.

New measures were introduced in the foreign banking sector from 1988–9. A start-up capital of Rs.150 million was prescribed for new entrants. Lending to priority sectors was made obligatory and the banks were required to achieve a level of 10 percent of total lending by the end of March 1989; 12 percent by the end of March 1990; and 15 percent by the end of March 1992.[39] Twenty percent of the disclosed profit was to be retained in Indian books. Foreign banks were unhappy with the RBI's new policy, which required them to lend to the priority sector, was financially risky and to some extent unprofitable.[40]

Phase IV (1991–2005): From post-liberalization to globalization

This period witnessed far-reaching changes in the banking sector in India as a result of the economic reform process unleashed by the government coupled with the transformation of global banking. In India the banking system was liberalized in accordance with the recommendations of the first [Maidavolu] Narasimham Committee Report (1991).[41] With the liberalization of the banking sector, the country was flooded with foreign banks. There was a substantial increase in the number of foreign bank offices: from 145 in 1990 to 245 in 2005. The regulatory regime adopted by the RBI was non-discriminatory by global standards: foreign banks in India were given all the privileges given to domestic banks; a single class of banking licenses was provided to foreign banks; no restrictions were placed on their scope of operations; insurance deposit coverage was uniformly available at the same rates as domestic banks; the repatriation of profit was allowed; and similar prudential norms, capital adequacy and asset classifications were made applicable for both domestic and foreign banks. In 1991 India embarked on the process of financial reforms, which were necessitated by various internal and external factors. M. Singh, Finance Minister, in his address on 5 July 1991 said: 'The time has come to act now, if we have to ensure India is not marginalized in the comity of nations'.[42] He added that what was need most was strict fiscal discipline, the curbing of wasteful expenditure, and the need to free the economy from the shackles of unnecessary control. The country was moving from one disaster to another with regard to its balance of payments position; if the government had not acted fast, the country could have become bankrupt any day.

The First Narasimham Committee Report (1991)

The Narasimham Committee was appointed by the government in August 1991. It recommended far-reaching reforms in the Indian banking sector, which centred on transforming the banking system from a highly regulated to a more market-oriented system. It provided a road map for financial sector reforms. The following banking sector reforms were recommended: a reduction of 25 percent, phased in over five years, in the statutory liquidity ratio, synchronized with the planned contraction in the fiscal deficit; a progressive reduction in the cash reserve ratio; gradual de-regulation of interest rates; and all banks, including foreign banks, to attain capital adequacy of eight percent in a phased manner. Additionally, banks were to make substantial provisions for bad and doubtful debts; profitable and reputable banks were allowed to raise capital from the public; the establishment of new private sector banks was authorized, subject to the RBI norms; and the RBI was to be primarily responsible for the regulation of the banking system. New guidelines were issued for income-recognition, provisioning requirements, and asset classification; banks were to classify their assets into four broad groups: standard, sub-standard, doubtful and loss. The report emphasized that a proper system of income-recognition and provisioning was fundamental to the preservation of the strength and stability of the banking system. Accordingly, it recommended the adoption of the international practice of treating an asset as 'non-performing' when interest was overdue for at least two quarters.

The introduction of such norms was aimed at ensuring greater safety and soundness in the financial system, and imparting transparency and accountability in operations, thereby restoring credibility and confidence in the financial system as a whole. The capital adequacy standards of the Basel Accord were adopted to bring India's regulatory framework closer to international standards: to strengthen the loan recovery process, the Debt Recovery Tribunal was set up; and the banking ombudsman scheme was introduced in June 1995, for a quicker and inexpensive adjudication of customer complaints against deficiencies in banking services. By the end of 2000, almost all of the banks had achieved the prescribed capital to risk-weighted assets ratio (CRAR) of 9 percent.[43]

The banking reforms were essentially focused on three issues: the deregulation of the banking sector and relaxation of entry barriers to foreign and new private banks to foster greater competition; the introduction of accounting standards and income recognition and asset classification norms to bring greater transparency in bank accounts, along with prudential measures and provisioning norms; and capital adequacy for risks to which the banks were exposed.

The Second Narasimham Committee Report (1998)

The period 1992–7 saw the implementation of recommendations of the Narasimham Committee Report I, whereby the soundness of the Indian banking system was amply proven when India emerged unscathed from the major upheaval of the South East Asian financial crisis. The second Narasimham Committee Report was published in 1998[44]. These were second-generation reforms related to strengthening the banking system; up-grading technology and human resource development; and legislative measures to cover banking policy. Keeping in view the purview of our analysis, relevant recommendations affecting foreign banks were as follows: the risk to asset ratio was to increase from eight percent to ten percent in a phased manner; banks were to avoid lending to parties in financial difficulties in order to settle interest dues and to reduce the percentage of non-performing assets (NPAs): banks should reduce NPAs in a phased manner; and emphasis was laid on internal control and internal inspections and audit. Moves were also to be made towards the international practices of income recognition with the introduction of 90 days instead of the existing 180 days. Additionally, foreign banks could be allowed to set up subsidiaries or joint ventures in India and were to be treated on a par with private banks and be subject to same conditions in regard to branches and directed credit as other banks.

The committee's recommendations were directed towards operational flexibility, creating autonomy in the banking sector and improving the quality of portfolios so as to encourage healthy competition. The main objective of the financial sector reforms in India in the 1990s was to create an efficient, competitive and stable financial sector that could in turn contribute to stimulating economic growth.

Effective Supervision

Following the *Narasimham Committee Report on Financial Sector Reforms*, significant changes took place in the Indian banking system as well as in regulatory and supervisory approaches and strategies. The Board for Financial Supervision, which was constituted in 1994, changed the RBI's supervisory strategy from a system of periodic inspections to a system of continuous supervision and periodic inspections. The key elements of supervision were: the restructuring of the system of banking inspection: focus, process, reporting and follow up; off-site surveillance as a supplement to on-site inspection; an enhanced role for external auditors; and strengthened corporate governance and internal control and audit systems. This supervisory framework was largely in compliance with the principles of the Basel Committee on Core Principles for Effective Banking Supervision.

Changes to Disclosure Norms

With a view to bringing transparency in the banking system, banks were required to provide additional information in their balance sheets in respect of the maturity pattern of loans and advances; foreign currency assets and liabilities; and lending to sensitive sectors, as defined by the RBI. These norms became effective from 31 March 2000 and were applicable to Indian and foreign banks.

A Road Map for the Presence of Foreign Banks in India

After the process of the liberalization of the financial sector had begun in 1991, by 2005 the RBI had become confident that a robust banking system had been established, which was broadly in conformity with international standards. With the objective to further enhance its efficiency and stability to the best of global standards, the RBI released the *Road Map for Presence of Foreign Banks in India* in 2005.[45] It contained the following salient points: foreign banks wishing to establish a presence in India for the first time could choose to operate through a branch presence or a 100 percent wholly owned subsidiary; for new and existing foreign banks, it proposed to go beyond the existing commitment given to the World Trade Organization of permitting twelve branches in a year; foreign banks already operating in India would be allowed to convert existing branches into wholly owned subsidiaries while following criteria concerning the mode of presence the respective bank wished to pursue; and wholly owned subsidiaries would be treated on par with the existing branches of foreign banks in India for expansion purposes.

Initially, the entry of foreign banks would be permitted only in private sector banks that were identified by the RBI for restructuring. In such banks, foreign banks would be allowed to acquire a controlling stake in a phased manner. In considering an application made by a foreign bank for acquisition of a five percent or larger stake in a private bank, the RBI would take into consideration the history and reputation of the said foreign bank not only in India but globally, as well as the interests of stakeholders. The maximum limit allowed would be 74 percent. In the second phase that started in April 2009, limitations on the operations of wholly owned subsidiaries were to be removed and these would be treated on a par with domestic banks. In the second phase, after reviewing the extent of penetration of foreign investment in Indian banks, foreign banks could be permitted, subject to regulatory approval, to enter into mergers and acquisition transactions with any private bank in India. This was subject to a maximum ownership limit of 74 percent.

In 2004–5 no other issue had led to such public debate or acrimony than the one on foreign equity in Indian banks. The zeal of the advocates of liberalization and financial sector reforms, which would allow the free flow of foreign capital, was equally matched by the ideological antipathy of leftist parties to any such freedom. *The Banker* of London reported how the RBI ruling had 'dismayed bankers and investors'.[46] A few days after the issue of draft guidelines, Dr Yaga Venugopal Reddy, Governor of the RBI, in a lecture on 'India and the Global Economy' at Lal Bahadur Shastri National Academy of Administration, Mussorie, emphasised the appropriate timing for a significant entry of foreign banks in India: 'The Reserve Bank of India is currently examining various options for strengthening the financial sector, in general, and the banking sector, in particular, concurrent with the well calibrated de-regulation process already set in motion'.[47]

On the whole there was disenchantment in foreign financial circles over the new policy. Foreign banks perceived the Indian market as more attractive than China since it was endowed with established legal systems, a stock and securities market and other infrastructure. Many foreign banks had acquired stakes in Indian banks and were unhappy with the setback to their hopes. The rationale behind the RBI policy to adopt a gradual and cautious approach in allowing foreign banks to acquire stakes in private banks was whether foreign banks would meet the credit needs of domestic investors. There was a popular belief in India that the foreign banks were engaged in 'cherry picking' and leaving high-risk creditors and projects to the domestic banks so as to weaken them. Y. V. Reddy rightly said: 'A judgemental view needs to be taken whether and when a country has reached the "threshold" and the financial integration should be approached cautiously with a plausible road map by answering questions in country-specific context'.[48]

Operations of Foreign Banks: India Back on the International Stage

India became more and more of an attractive destination. The Indian market had always been an attractive and lucrative destination for foreign banks, but more so in the post-liberalization period. Several factors like growing demand, increased saving, a huge middle class (equal to the combined population of several European nations), high interest rates and consistent economic growth were the main drivers. Foreign banks were allowed to set up a presence in India through opening liaison offices. Generally foreign banks, in the first instance, set up a liaison office to get to know the economic environment of the country, explore business opportunities and to understand the systems and procedures governing the operations of banks. Liaison offices were not allowed to engage in the banking business or to trade directly or indirectly. In addition, they were prohibited from earning revenues in India and had to meet their expenses from the head office. The approval of the RBI was requested for establishing liaison offices. Liaison offices played a limited role in collecting information about possible opportunities in the sphere of banking and providing information about the parent bank and its products to Indian investors. From 1987 to 2005, 25 foreign banks opened their liaison offices in India and, interestingly, 68 percent of these offices were located in Mumbai. Germany opened five liaison offices, followed by Italy with four, and Russia with three, while Belgium and the USA each had two (see Table 7.3).

Table 7.3 - List of Foreign Banks having Liaison Offices in India as on 31 March 2005

Serial Number	Name of the Foreign bank	Country of Incorporation	Centre	Date of Opening
1	Commonwealth Bank	Australia	Bangalore	7 July 2005
2	Raiffeisen Zentral Bank Osterreich AG	Austria	Mumbai	1 November 1992
3	KBC Bank N.V	Belgium	Mumbai	6 October 1987
4	Emirates Bank International	Belgium	Mumbai	1 February 2003
5	Crédit industriel et commercial	France	Mumbai	16 June 2000
6	Natixis	France	New Delhi	1 April 1997
7	Bayerische Hypo-und Vereinsbank	Germany	Mumbai	4 January 1999
8	Fortis Bank	Germany	Mumbai	12 July 1995
9	DZ Bank Deutsche Zentral-Genossenchafts Bank	Germany	Mumbai	22 February 1996
10	Landesbank Baden-Wurttemberg	Germany	Mumbai	1 November 1999
11	Dresdner Bank	Germany	Mumbai	6 September 2002
12	Commerzbank	Italy	Mumbai	23 December 2002
13	Banca Intesa-Banca Commerciale	Italy	Mumbai	1 November 1988
14	San Paolo IMI Bank	Italy	Mumbai	20 January 1991
15	UniCredito Italiano	Italy	Mumbai	1 August 1998
16	Banca Populare Di Verona Enovora	Italy	Mumbai	18 June 2001
17	Everest Bank	Nepal	New Delhi	24 March 2004
18	Caixa Geral de Depositos	Portugal	Mumbai, Goa	8 November 1999
19	Vnesheconombank	Russia	New Delhi	1 March 1983
20	VTB India	Russia	New Delhi	May 2005
21	Banco de Sabadell	Spain	New Delhi	2 August 2004
22	Hatton National Bank	Sri Lanka	Chennai	1 January 1999
23	UBS	Switzerland	Mumbai	24 November 1994
24	Bank of New York	USA	Mumbai	27 October 1983
25	Wachovia Bank	USA	Mumbai	1 November 1996

Source: Statistical table of Reserve Bank of India

The areas of operation of foreign banks were extended; from the late nineteenth century to the middle of twentieth century, the operations of foreign banks were confined to financing foreign trade, lending and deposits, and dealings in foreign exchange but, after the liberalization of the economy, their area of operations extended to include foreign exchange trading, non-resident Indian banking accounts, investment banking, project financing, corporate finance, trade finance, derivatives, retail banking, credit cards and ATM's. Key players in these areas of operation were Citibank, Standard Chartered Bank, HSBC, Deutsche

Bank, BNP Paribas and ABN Amro, who had a network of 205 branches out of 258 foreign bank branches in the country.

The strong performance of the banking sector in the pre-liberalization and post-liberalization periods, as well as the future growth potential, succeeded in attracting many new entrants to start business in India. Historically, British and American banks always had a strong presence in India. But due to the RBI's policy of diversification, new players from Europe and Asia also started business in the country. As a result of this, competition in the banking sector became intense, which increased risk factors in operation.

An Evaluation of the Operations of Foreign Banks in India

The RBI and the government of India were initially very cautious in allowing foreign banks unrestricted permission to establish foreign banks in India, due to the fact that Indian banks were in the infant stage of growth and the unmatched competition would have destroyed them. The International Monetary Fund appreciated India's approach towards liberalization and the World Bank and emerging market economies were advised to follow it as a prototype. Until September 2006, 29 banks (see Table 7.4) with 258 branches accounted for 0.36 percent of the total branch network even as they had a share of 8.53 percent of banking assets.[49]

Table 7.4: List of the Foreign Banks Operating in India Country-Wide
(as at the end of September 2006)

Serial number	Name of the foreign bank	Country of incorporation	Number of branches
1	ABN AMRO Bank	Netherlands	24
2	Abu Dhabi Commercial Bank.	UAE	2
3	Arab Bangladesh Bank.	Bangladesh	1
4	American Express Bank.	USA	7
5	Antwerp Diamond Bank	Belgium	1
6	Bank of Indonesia	Indonesia	1
7	Bank of America	USA	5
8	Bank of Bahrain and Kuwait	Bahrain	2
9	Bank of Nova Scotia	Canada	5
10	Bank of Tokyo-Mitsubishi	Japan	3
11	BNP Paribas	France	8
12	Bank of Ceylon	Sri Lanka	1
13	Barclays Bank	UK	1
14	Calyon Bank	France	5
15	Citibank NA	USA	39
16	Shinhan Bank	South Korea	1
17	China Trust Commercial Bank	Taiwan	1
18	Deutsche Bank	Germany	8
19	DBS Bank.	Singapore	2
20	HSBC	Hong Kong	45

Serial number	Name of the foreign bank	Country of incorporation	Number of branches
21	JP Morgan Chase Bank	USA	1
22	Krug Thai Bank Public Company	Thailand	1
23	Mizuho Corporate Bank	Japan	2
24	Mashreq Bank	UAE	2
25	Oman International Bank	Sultanate of Oman	2
26	Standard Chartered Bank	UK	81
27	Sonali Bank	Bangladesh	2
28	Société générale	France	2
29	State Bank of Mauritius	Mauritius	3
		Total	258

The foreign banks helped Indian corporations and industries to raise foreign exchange and capital, especially when the country was passing through the foreign exchange crisis in the early 1990s. In addition, these banks not only brought financial resources but also a high degree of technical knowledge in operational activities. Foreign banks also played an important role in the Indian economy by financing the export and import trade. The profits of foreign banks in India jumped from Rs. 757billion in 1995–6 to Rs. 22,50billion after a decade, showing an impressive increase of 200 percent.[50] There was no doubt that Indian banks were facing stiff competition from foreign banks and their profits were adversely affected.

High operating costs of the Indian banking system had been a cause of concern for policy makers as it brought stickiness in lending rates through their spreads. Foreign banks in India brought along with them highly-computerized banking technology which placed them a cut above domestic banks in marketing banking products and services based on information communication technology. Initially, the customer-oriented approach and innovative products gave foreign banks a competitive edge over domestic banks. But with the development of information communication technology in India and its adoption by Indian banks, the technology gap was considerably narrowed down and domestic banks also attained higher levels of efficiency. With the passage of time and by adopting technological changes, the cost of operations was brought down, while increased competition in the market compelled all banks to align their cost structure close to the best practices in banking. Foreign banks came to India fully equipped with the latest technology and a new cocktail of financial services in favour of the introduction of new financial products in banking. They increased the diversity of customer and financial services. Domestic banks were compelled to shed their old style of working and to introduce quality services to the customer. The best practices followed by foreign banks in supervision, regulation and customer relations were also introduced by domestic banks.

The liberal policy for the entry of foreign banks in India was expected to raise the bar of efficiency, productivity and to introduce innovative practices in management and technology. The entry of foreign banks also led to intense competition in the banking sector in both credit and deposit markets. In the 1990s financial reforms and a liberalized policy towards foreign banks was conducive to their growth and paved the way for their expansion in India. The regulatory regime followed by the RBI in respect to foreign banks was non-discriminatory and liberal by global standards. Prudential norms applicable to foreign banks or capital adequacy, income recognition and asset classification were, by and large, the same as for the Indian banks. In fact, some Indian banks contend that a certain amount of positive discrimination existed in favour of foreign banks by way of low-priority sector lending compared to Indian banks.

Foreign banks operating in India were not keen on local incorporation unless the RBI treated them on a par with domestic banks in terms of branch expansion. Not a single foreign bank applied for local incorporation until 2005. Foreign banks were also not very keen to become wholly owned subsidiaries of overseas parents because they feared that the RBI would want them to list on local bourses. In addition, conversion into a subsidiary was not beneficial as it did not give them the advantage of opening more branches. This restriction had constrained their growth and was the biggest issue in their day-to-day operations.

On the other hand, domestic banks were critical of foreign banks for a variety of reasons. Whilst foreign banks brought financial resources and foreign exchange, this was accompanied by shocks from the international financial system. With the injection of huge financial resources, the money market witnessed radical changes. Domestic banks were at a disadvantage in competition with foreign banks as they possessed limited financial resources, expertise and technological exposure. There was some positive bias in favour of foreign banks as the priority sector lending of domestic banks was fixed at 40 percent, while for foreign banks it was 32 percent, including lending for foreign trade. Foreign banks were engaged in niche banking with a concentration in major towns with no exposure to rural and semi-urban areas, and were shy in lending to the agriculture sector, which they regarded as risky. They took the best credits and left the worst for domestic banks, making them more prone to risk-lending. Foreign banks encouraged lending in favourable economic conditions but in difficult times, they provided less.

This chapter had no intent at all to illustrate the ways in which British banks played an important role in India, or how those imperial banks interacted with the local native banks in the day-to-day business of the several market places; instead this chapter has focused on one key topic: the growing force of 'native' banks in face of 'imperial/colonial' banks. The initial suspicion, opposition and restrictive approach towards foreign banks has, to a large extent, subsided as, over the years, domestic banks have gained in experience and become technologically savvy. Domestic banks have also become strong and stable and have introduced innovative practices to remain in competition with foreign banks. This experience, interaction and competition has been mutually beneficial to foreign and domestic banks, resulting in assimilation and diffusion of sound banking practices and making the Indian banking system healthy, transparent, financially viable and integrated in the international financial system.

CONCLUSION

Hubert Bonin

The history of the deployment of non-Asian banks in the economic, trade and portuary centres of the various 'sub-regions' of Asia is already well-known – even if only via the exhaustive, multi-volume history of the *Hong Kong & Shanghai Bank* published by Frank King[1] (before Richard Roberts' publication on the occasion of HSBC's 150th anniversary, while yet another history of the Standard Chartered is in the works) and the other books and articles that have appeared on the *Yokohama Specie Bank,*[2] *Banque de l'Indochine, Deutsch-Asiatische Bank,*[3] *Citibank* and its predecessor. Perhaps the best way of concluding this book would be to derive some synthetic points which could serve as 'lessons' and as springboards of further, wider thought. The Introduction (pp. 1–19) has already dealt in detail with many of the ideas that have arisen from our collective research. This conclusion will focus on some complementary points.

Banks in the 'Asian Mediterranean'

The very first point is the question of the Asian markets' attractiveness for 'western' (French,[4] for example) and Japanese banks. One could very well ask how did these 'sub-regions' manage to insert themselves into the internal growth and territorial expansion strategies of the stakeholders in this 'region' which had turned into a banking battlefield within the globalization drive of the time. An essential, though obvious, motivation for every bank was to accompany and support its nation's enterprises when they set foot in foreign trading and production hubs and port-cities open to international trade, as was the case in China.[5] Bankers formed the links within the 'relational networks'[6] that were created at the Asian, American-Asian and Euro-Asian scales. Every major bank took upon itself the mission of honing the commercial (and sometimes industrial) competitiveness of its country's enterprises. I have myself published several articles on the role played by *Banque de l'Indochine*[7] in support of the French business community in various Chinese markets (Tianjin, Wuhan, Guangzhou) and Hong Kong[8] as it tried to pierce the British hegemony while fending off German, Japanese and American competition. A synthetic book is on the anvil.

We know that the Americans, with an eye on the West European and Russian push into China, did not fail to set up a banking tool for themselves in South China, around what ultimately turned into *City Bank*. It is clear that both Asia-specific as well as offshoots of European entities provided credit to their national 'mandate holders', discounted their bills and financed their stocks and cargo. They managed their FOREX operations and even provided credit to their Asian partners both upstream and downstream – for the purchase of local material and foodstuff or the sale of imported goods. They were thus like so many path-breakers, facilitating the entry of foreign capitalism in South East Asia and China. It is clear that it was a question of including Asia in the world of West-European, Japanese,[9] Russian and American capitalism.

This corresponds well to the famous phrase 'Asian Mediterranean' coined by geo-historian François Gipouloux,[10] as well as the earlier ideas of Fernand Braudel regarding the Euro-Africano-Asian Mediterranean region, from the Levant to Gibraltar, Seville/Cadix to Tangiers.[11] It was a question of taking advantage of Japan's entry into the 'Asian co-prosperity area', of reacting without delay to China's return to an 'open economy' and, especially, of giving some cohesion and solidarity both to South East Asian and South Chinese port-cities[12] and North Chinese and East Russian trading hubs. As Asia rejoined the maritime and merchant world-economy, banks inserted themselves in what we sometimes call 'the first globalization' which took shape at the turn of the twentieth century. Subsequently, we know that a series of events – civil war in China,[13] Japanese hegemony on its 'zone of Asian co-prosperity',[14] World War II, Communism, war in Indochina – contributed to the closure of a number of trading hubs and a reversal of Asian globalization. This resulted in a weakening of banking positions, except, of course, in Hong Kong and, later, Singapore, as well as the Japanese economic resurgence with its *keiretzu* from the mid-1950s.

Banking and Economic Imperialism

It is true that foreign banks contributed substantially to the so-called 'Western' economic imperialism,[15] but so did the Japanese, as can be seen in Clarence Davis' article and the pioneering analysis by John Laffey.[16] Their activities were definitely not 'neutral' though, as shall be shown presently: they also served a local clientele. They rounded off the relative advantages that their companies already enjoyed by providing them with an 'intangible capital' of banking and financial services, which allowed the latter to take full advantage of Asia's potential growth centres. They gave them a greater scope of action and 'firepower' in the battle between local and 'conquering' economies. It is clear that their action was part of an 'unequal exchange' between an already well-'banked' North and a South that was in the process of entering the 'modern' economy, that is to say, largely monetarized and open to informal monetary symbols (especially 'bank money') – especially as the banks active in Asia issued their own bills from several regions, or had been given the responsibility of issuing the central currency. And, at least in China, these banks formed part of this 'imperialist' economy structured within the framework of institutions and agreements of 'treaty ports' and 'unequal treaties'.[17]

The grand and imposing headquarters of these banks, whether on the Shanghai Bund,[18] the Hong Kong waterfront, the new business quarters along the *Straits* of Singapore and other Chinese trading cities, were all symbols of their emerging power, the power of money at the service of the colonizing powers in Asia. Edwin Green's histories of HSBC's branches,[19] BNP Paribas' ancestors in India[20] and of Citibank in China[21] show that they were made up of 'cohorts' of top and mid-level managers (especially in accounting, managing the 'books of account' and discounting). All of them (often along with their spouses or, sometimes, Asian partners) lived more or less isolated, within the confines of foreign quarters, especially in the concessions which had clubs, cultural hotspots, recreational and leisure facilities, etc. They were all subtle 'signs' of imperialism as practiced by the various business communities.[22]

Thus, key studies by Edward Saïd[23] and others[24] will take us to the heart of the 'imperialist Orient', whether this imperialism took a 'brutal' shape, with no thought regarding unequal relations, or whether it came in the guise of paternalism, with subtle forms of collaboration and association with the local elite[25] – before it came to be challenged, as in China.[26] Obviously, banks and bankers were 'objective allies' of this economic and financial imperialism. With mindsets that were at once united and competitive, they helped structure the penetration of foreign enterprises and money into the various 'sub-regions' of an Asia that was at last opening to capitalist globalization.

Towards a Spillover of Banking Expertise?

Does this mean that foreign bankers only helped to transform Asia into a hunting preserve for international imperialism? A number of chapters in this book have proven that it was not so. But for that, we need to have some 'positivism', that is to say, believe in the fact that there have emerged hubs of 'regional capitalism' around the 'local elite' in Asia. We know that the growth of such an entrepreneurial capitalism was a *fait accompli* in Japan during the Meiji era, due to a transfer of culture and competencies – symbolized by the sending of young students to Western universities and shown by the large paintings in Tokyo's National and Imperial Museum. But was this 'Japanese model' replicated in other colonized lands? We know that it did happen in some Chinese nationalist groups and of their relative incapacity to impose it on a Court stuck with old ideas. Karl Pomeranz has talked about the immense potential of Chinese economic cultures and their resilience.[27] A number of other authors have also noted the gradual formation of an Indian capitalism in keeping with the constitution of a modern merchant economy and industrialization towards the end of the twentieth century.

By and large, Western banks (and sometimes also the Japanese, where the *Yokohama Specie Bank* was present) supported the growth of local capitalists. In India, the two Chartered banks worked only with their British partners (and European counterparts) which made up the major part of their clientele. Gradually they began to enter the fledgling Indian entrepreneurial scene and to offer the support of their portfolio of banking activities to local enterprises, especially regarding foreign exchange, payment instruments, transfers and compensation and also, more and more, international (documentary credit, warrants) and even internal loans.

My own research shows that *Banque de l'Indochine* – just like HSBC, *Citibank, Russo-Chinese Bank*[28] and *Russo-Asiatic Bank* – provided credit to Chinese clients recommended by its compradors[29] in the major trading centres. Gradually, its branches began to work with Chinese wholesale merchants, importers and especially, exporters, like the silk merchants of Guangdong.[30] The entire issue revolves around Chinese capitalism's capacity of establishing itself as an autonomous economic power.[31] Without really getting into the debate on the stifling of local economies via the 'unequal treaties',[32] one must note that, according to French historian Marie-Claire Bergère,[33] there could not have been a local capitalism without a (somewhat incestuous) partnership with the central government (as is shown by the history of the Soong[34]) or the authorities in the major regions which formed somewhat self-centred 'cliques'.[35] On the other hand, Lucien Bianco had earlier believed in the formation of a local capitalism in certain regions and we can even see the shoots of entrepreneurship and capitalism in several communities that were undergoing marketization and 'modernization'.[36]

In fact, the two had gone hand-in-hand, as was the case in the textile industry.[37] It would be unwise to overlook the profound mutations that were taking place in the years 1920–30 in those regions which, more or less, were experiencing 'growth in an open economy' – in and around Guangzhu, Wuhan-Hankow, Tianjin and Shanghai (and the towns in its circle of influence) – despite all of the tensions generated by the recurrent civil war, the Japanese entry into Manchuria and Shanghai's textile market and systemic corruption. Hong Kong[38] remained an exception, but it also serves to prove just how much the Chinese bourgeoisie was open, adaptive and reactive to learning the ABCs of the modern banking economy. Certain sections of the economy and some regions were going through a process of 'Westernization' and the so-called 'imperialist' banks did not try to stifle it, though they did sometimes tighten their credit criteria in order to avoid the cyclic reversals or falling victim to the frauds perpetrated in a capitalism which was still in its infancy and little regulated.

Finally, it is obvious that the Western banking model was copied. Indian and Chinese histories clearly show the emergence and subsequent consolidation of local banks at the major financial centres. Banking imperialism did not stop this; on the contrary, we could say that these foreign banks welcomed the opportunity of being able to share the risks, as a banker's biggest fear is not having enough partners to share all the risks generated at a single market. Moreover, they, too, profited handsomely from the interbank operations generated by their local counterparts. The creation of a Chinese central bank in 1935 symbolized the formation of a national banking system which was still languishing in limbo when the Sino-Japanese war broke out. Only a counterfactual history can say whether China could have benefited from such a system in the years 1940–50 without the latter. It would have been a mixed system, with local bankers and foreign banks as in all developed countries or those in the process of development in a market economy – and such ideas have indeed arisen regarding pre-war Tianjin.[39]

Doing justice to all these themes would require many more chapters and this title was never intended to be some kind of exhaustive encyclopedia! Perhaps, like in India, the nationalization of banks[40] resulted in a mixed economy, combining local capitalism and 'national bourgeoisie' with 'government socialism', with both segments having large, international financial and banking networks thanks to the continued existence of establishments like HSBC and *Standard Chartered*.

NOTES

Bonin, 'Introduction: Issues Regarding Asian Imperial Banking'

1. Y. Cassis, *Capitals of Capital. A History of International Financial Centers, 1780–2005* (Cambridge: Cambridge University Press, 2006); and Y. Cassis and É. Bussière (eds), *London and Paris as International Financial Centres in the Twentieth Century* (Oxford: Oxford University Press, 2005).
2. See P. J. Cain and Anthony G. Hopkins, 'The Political Economy of British Expansion Overseas', *Economic History Review*, 33:4 (1980), pp. 463–90.
3. P. J. Cain and A. G. Hopkins, 'Gentlemanly Capitalism and British Expansion Overseas: New Imperialism, 1850–1945', *South African Journal of Economic History*, 7:1 (1992), pp. 182–215.
4. See S. Engerman, P. Hoffman, J.-L. Rosenthal and K. Sokoloff, *Financial Intermediaries in Economic Development* (Cambridge: Cambridge University Press, 2003).
5. R. Cameron and V. Bovykin (eds), *International Banking, 1870–1914* (Oxford: Oxford University Press, 1991).
6. See G. Jones (ed.), *Banks as Multinationals* (London: Routledge, 1990); G. Jones, *British Multinational Banking, 1830–1990* (Oxford: Clarendon Press, 1993); and R. Roberts, *Inside International Finance* (London: Orion Business Books, 1998).
7. Jones, *Banks as Multinationals*. See also G. Jones, *Multinational and International Banking* (Aldershot: Edward Elgar, 1991).
8. S. Mollan, 'International Correspondent Networks: Asian and British Banks in the Twentieth Century', in Shizuya Nishimura, Toshio Suzuki, & R. Michie (eds), *The Origins of International Banking in Asia: The Nineteenth and Twentieth Centuries* (Oxford: Oxford University Press, 2012), pp. 217–29; Shizuya Nishimura, 'British International Banks in Asia, 1870–1914: An Introductory Essay', *The Origins of International Banking in Asia*, pp. 55–85; and R. Michie, 'The City of London as a Centre for International Banking: The Asian Dimension in the Nineteenth and Twentieth Centuries', *The Origins of International Banking in Asia*, pp. 13–54.
9. See C. Davis, 'Financing Imperialism: British and American Bankers as Vectors of Imperial Expansion in China, 1908–1920', *Business History Review*, 56:2 (1982), pp. 236–64.
10. D. Merrett, 'Paradise Lost? British Banks in Australia', in Jones, *Banks as Multinationals*, pp. 62–84.
11. C. Clay, 'The Imperial Ottoman Bank in the Alter Nineteenth Century: A Multinational 'National' Bank?', in Jones, *Banks as Multinationals*, pp. 142–59.
12. Norio Tamaki, 'The Yokohama Specie Bank: A Multinational in the Japanese Interest, 1879–1931', in Jones, *Banks as Multinationals*, pp. 191–216; and Makoto Kasuya, 'The

Overseas Expansion of Japanese Banks, 1880–2006', in *The Origins of International Banking in Asia*, pp. 166–73.

13. Motoaki Akagawa, 'German Banks in East Asia: The Deutsche Bank (1870–1875) and the Deutsch-Asiatische Bank (1888–1913)', *Keio Business Review*, 45:1 (2009), pp. 1–20; and F. King, *The History of the Hong Kong and Shanghai Banking Corporation: Volume 1, The Hong Kong Bank in Late Imperial China, 1864–1902: On an Even Keel* (Cambridge: Cambridge University Press, 1987).

14. Mollan, 'International Correspondent Networks', pp. 217–29; C. Cook, 'The Hong Kong & Shanghai Banking Corporation on Lombard Street', in F. King, *Eastern Banking: Essays in the History of the Hong Kong & Shanghai Banking Corporation* (London: Athlone Press, 1983), pp. 193–203; and O. Checkland, Shizuya Nishimura & Norio Tamaki (eds), *Pacific Banking (1859–1959): East Meets West* (New York: St. Martin's Press, 1994).

15. P. Duus, R. H. Myers and R. M. Peattie (eds), *The Japanese Informal Empire in China, 1895–1937* (Princeton, NJ: Princeton University Press, 1989).

16. M. Meuleau, *Des pionniers en Extrême-Orient. La Banque de l'Indochine, 1875–1975* (Paris: Fayard, 1990).

17. S. Saul, 'Les Agences du Crédit lyonnais en Égypte : l'insertion d'une banque de dépôts dans une économie d'outre-mer (1875–1956)', in B. Desjardins, M. Lescure, R. Nougaret, A. Plessis and A. Straus (eds), *Le Crédit lyonnais, 1863–1986: Études historiques* (Geneva: Droz, 2002), pp. 521–48; and S. Saul, *La France et l'Égypte de 1882 à 1914: Intérêts économiques et implications Politiques* (Paris: Comité pour l'histoire économique et financière de la France, 1997).

18. H. Bonin, 'Le Comptoir national d'escompte de Paris, une banque impériale (1848–1940)', *Revue française d'histoire d'outre-mer*, 78:293 (1991), pp. 477–97.

19. G. de Lassus (ed.), *The History of BNP Paribas in India, 1860–2010* (Mumbai, BNP Paribas, 2010).

20. J. R. Winton, *Lloyds Bank, 1918–1969* (Oxford: Oxford University Press, 1982).

21. Barclays (ed.), *A Banking Centenary: Barclays Bank (Dominion, Colonial, Overseas), 1836–1936* (Plymouth: Brendon, 1938); and J. S. Crossley & J. Blanford, *The DCO Story: A History of Banking in Many Countries, 1925–1971* (London: Barclays Bank International, 1975).

22. D. Merrett, *ANZ Bank* (Sydney, Allen & Unwin, 1985).

23. S. Muirhead, *Crisis Banking in the East. The History of the Chartered Mercantile Bank of India, London and China, 1853–1893* (Aldershot: Ashgate, 1996).

24. E. Green & S. Kinsey, *The Paradise Bank: The Mercantile Bank of India, 1893–1984* (Aldershot: Ashgate, 1999).

25. See R. S. Sayers, *Banking in the British Commonwealth* (Oxford: Oxford University Press, 1952); W. T. Newlyn, *Money and Banking in British Colonial Africa* (Oxford: Oxford University Press, 1954); R. Fry, *Bankers in West Africa* (London: Hutchinson Benham, 1976); S. Jones (ed.), *Banking and Business in South Africa* (London: MacMillan, 1988); and W. Tessier Newlyn and D. Culloden Rowan, *Money and Banking in British Colonial Africa: A Study of the Monetary and Banking Systems of Eight British Territories* (Oxford: Clarendon Press, 1954).

26. G. Jones, 'British Overseas Banks as Free-Standing Companies, 1830–1996', in M. Wilkins & H. Schröter (eds), *The Free-Standing Company in the World Economy, 1830–1996* (Oxford: Oxford University Press, 1998).

27. See M. Venzin, *Building International Financial Services Firm: How Successful Firms Design and Execute Cross-Borders Strategies* (Oxford: Oxford University Press, 2009).

28. Crossley and Blandford, *The DCO Story*.

29. Ibid., p. 28.

30. G. Hatton, *Les enjeux financiers et économiques du protectorat marocain (1936–1954): Politique publique et investisseurs privés* (Paris: Publications de la SFHOM, 2009).

31. H. Bonin, 'L'Outre-mer, Marché pour la Banque Commerciale (1876–1985) ?', in J. Marseille (ed.), *La France & l'Outre-Mer. Les relations économiques & financières entre la France et la France d'outre-mer* (Paris: Comité pour l'histoire économique & financière de la France, 1998), pp. 437–83.

32. See P. Buckley and M. Casson, 'The Internalisation Theory of the Multinational Enterprise: A Review of the Progress of a Research Agenda After 30 Years', *Journal of International Business Studies*, 40 (2009), pp. 1563–80.

33. See Makoto Kasuya, 'The Activities of the Japanese Banks in Interwar Financial Centres: The Cases of the Yokohama Specie Bank's Offices in London and New York', *The Origins of International Banking in Asia*, pp. 196–216.

34. R. Allbert Dayer, *Finance and Empire: Sir Charles Addis, 1881–1935* (New York: Mac-Millan, 1988).

35. C. Schenk, *Hong Kong as an International Financial Centre: Emergence and Development* (London: Routledge, 2001).

36. See L. Davis and R. Gallman, *Evolving Financial Markets and International Capital Flows: Britain, the Americas and Australia, 1865–1914* (Cambridge: Cambridge University Press, 2001).

37. P. Bond, 'Debt, Uneven Development and Capitalist Crisis in South Africa: The First 200 Years', 'Repoliticizing Debt' conference paper (Kingston, Canada: Queen's University Development Studies, 20–31 May 2012).

38. Crossley and Blandford, *The DCO Story*, p. 184.

39. Bond, 'Debt, Uneven Development and Capitalist Crisis in South Africa', p. 5.

40. Crossley and Blandford, *The DCO Story*, pp. 9–17.

41. Ibid.

42. See C. Heckscher & P. Adler (eds), *The Firm as a Collaborative Community: Reconstructing Trust in the Knowledge Economy* (Stuttgart: Stern Verlag, 2007); M. Casson, *Studies in the Economics of Trust* (Aldershot: Brookfield: Elgar, 1995); and M. Casson, *Information and Organisation* (Oxford: Oxford University Press, 1997).

43. See H. Bonin, 'Le Lotus noir: le combat contre la fraude et la ruse dans les concessions françaises en Chine (années 1890–années 1940)', in M. Figeac-Monthus & C. Lasté-couères (eds), *Territoires de l'illicite: Ports et iles. de la fraude au contrôle (xvie–xxe siècles)* (Paris: Armand Colin, 2012), pp. 203–20.

44. See I. Huault, 'Embeddedness et Théorie de l'Entreprise: Autour des Travaux de Mark Granovetter', *Annales des Mines: Gérer et Comprendre*, (June) 1998, pp. 73–86; M. Casson, 'Entrepreneurial Networks: A Theoretical Perspective', in M. Moss, A. Slaven & C. E.Nunez (eds), *Entrepreneurial Networks and Business Culture* (Seville: Publicaciones de la Universidad de Sevilla, 1998), pp. 13–28; B. Edmonds, 'Capturing Social Embeddedness: A Constructivist Approach', *Adaptive Behavior*, 7 (1999), pp. 323–48; and G. Krippner, 'The Elusive Market: Embeddedness and the Paradigm of Economic Sociology', *Theory & Society*, 30:6 (2001), pp. 775–810.

45. C. Lloyd and R. Sutch (eds), *Settler Economies in World History* (London: Brill, 2013).

46. S. Jones, *The Great Imperial Banks in South Africa. A Study of the Business of Standard Bank and Barclays Bank, 1861–1961* (Pretoria, South Africa: UNISA Press, 1996); and S. Jones, 'The Apogee of the Imperial Banks in South Africa: Standard and Barclays, 1919–1939', *English Historical Review*, 103:209 (1988), pp. 892–916.

47. Crossley and Blandford, *The DCO Story*, p. 70.

48. Ibid., p. 71.

49. G. Verhoef, 'Afrikaner Nationalism in South African Banking: The Case of Volkskas and Trust Bank', in S. Jones (ed.), *Financial Enterprise in South Africa Since 1950* (Basingstoke: Macmillan, 1992); and A. C. M. Webb, *The Roots of the Tree: A Study in Early South African Banking: The Predecessors of First National Bank, 1838–1926* (Johannesburg: First National Bank of Southern Africa, 1992).

50. K. A. Monteith, 'Competition Between Barclays Bank (DCO) and the Canadian Banks in the West Indies, 1926–1945', *Financial History Review*, 7 (2000), pp. 67–87.

51. H. Bonin, 'Le Comptoir national d'escompte de Paris, une banque impériale (1848–1940)', *Revue française d'histoire d'outre-mer*, 293:78 (1991), pp. 477–97; and G. de Lassus, *The History of BNP Paribas in Australia and New Zealand, 1881–2011* (Paris: BNP Paribas, 2011).

52. E. Said, *Culture and Imperialism* (New York: Alfred Knopf, 1993); E. Said, *Culture et Impérialisme* (Paris: Fayard, 2000); V. Kennedy, *Edward Said: A Critical Introduction* (Cambridge: Polity Press, 2000); P. Williams, *Edward Said,* (London: Sage, 2001); and N. H. Aruri and M. A. Shuraydi, *Revising Culture, Reinventing Peace: The Influence of Edward W. Said* (New York: Olive Branch Press, 2001).

53. R. Robinson and J. Gallagher (with A. Delly), *Africa and the Victorians. The Official Mind of Imperialism* (London: Palgrave MacMillan, 1967).

54. See E. Ndekwu, *First Bank of Nigeria: A Century of Banking* (Ibadan, Nigeria: Spectrum Books, 1994), about the former BBWA.

55. C. Mackenzie, *Realms of Silver: One Hundred Years of Banking in the East (Chartered Bank of India, Australia & China)* (London: Routledge & Kegan Paul, 1954).

56. M. Hoogenboom, D. Bannink and W. Trommel, 'From Local to Global, and Back', *Business History*, 52:6 (October 2010), pp. 932–54.

57. H. Bonin, *CFAO (1887–2007): La réinvention permanente d'une entreprise de commerce outre-mer* (Paris: Publications de la SFHOM, 2008).

58. D. K. Fieldhouse, *Merchant Capital and Economic Decolonisation: The United Africa Company, 1929–1987* (Oxford: Clarendon Press, 1994); D. K. Fieldhouse, *Unilever Overseas* (London: Croom Helm, 1978); and C. Wilson, *The History of Unilever: A Study in Economic Growth and Social Change*, 2 vols (London: Cassell, 1954).

59. R. Blake, *Jardine Matheson: Traders of the Far East* (London: Weidenfeld & Nicholson, 1999); M. Keswick (ed.), *The Thistle and the Jade: A Celebration of 150 Years of Jardine Matheson & Cº* (London: Octopus Books, 1982); and S. Jones, *Two Centuries of Overseas Trading: The Origins and Growth of the Inchcape Group* (London: Macmillan, 1986).

60. Crossley and Blandford, *The DCO Story*, p. 203.

61. 'Report of Barclays DCO, 23 July 1962', in Crossley and Blandford, *The DCO Story*, p. 213.

1 Bonin, 'French Overseas Banking as an Imperial System: A Background for Asian Developments'

1. F. King, *The History of the Hongkong & Shanghai Banking Corporation*, 4 vols (Cambridge: Cambridge University Press, 1987–1991).

2. See J.-A. Henry & H.-A. Siepmann, *The First Hundred Years of the Standard Bank* (Oxford: Oxford University Press, 1963).

3. See: A. S. J. Baster, *The Imperial Banks* (New York: Arno Press, 1977 [1929]).

4. See N. Ferguson, M. Ackrill & L. Hannah, *Barclays. The Business of Banking, 1690–1996* (Cambridge: Cambridge University Press, 2001). Also see G. Jones, 'British Overseas Banks as Free-Standing Companies, 1830–1996', in M. Wilkins and H. Schröter (eds), *The Free-Standing Company in the World Economy, 1830–1996* (Oxford: Oxford University Press, 1998); and G. Tyson, *100 Years of Banking in Asia and African, 1863–1963* (London, National and Grindlays Bank, 1963).

5. R. Brion and J.-L. Moreau, *La Société Générale de Belgique, 1822–1997* (Anvers, Fonds Mercator, 1998).

6. D. K. Fieldhouse, *The Economics of Empire, 1830–1914* (Ithaca, NY: Cornell University Press, 1973); D. K. Fieldhouse, *The Theory of Capitalist Imperialism* (London: Longman, 1967); and D. K. Fieldhouse, '"Imperialism": An Historiographical Revision', *Economic History Review*, 14 (1961), pp. 187–209.

7. See R. Koerner and G. D. Schmidt, *Imperialism. The Story and Significance of a Political Word, 1940–1960* (Cambridge: Cambridge University Press, 1964); A. G. Hopkins, 'Imperial Business in Africa. Part I: Sources', *Journal of African History*, 57:1, (1976), pp. 29–48; and A. G. Hopkins, 'Imperial Business in Africa. Part II: Interpretations', *Journal of African History*, 57:2 (1976), pp. 267–90.

8. J.-F. Cady, *The Roots of French Imperialism in Eastern Asia* (Ithaca, NY: Cornell University Press, 1954); J. F. Laffey, 'Les racines de l'impérialisme français en Extrême-Orient: À propos des thèses de J.-F. Cady', *Revue d'histoire moderne et contemporaine*, 16 (April–June 1969), pp. 282–99 ; H. Brunschwig, *Mythes et réalités de l'impérialisme colonial Français, 1871–1914* (Paris: Armand Colin, 1960); J. Bouvier and R. Girault, *L'impérialisme Français d'avant 1914* (Paris: Mouton, 1976) ; J. Thobie, *La France impériale, 1880–1914* (Paris: Megrelis, 1982) ; W. Baumgart, *Imperialism: The Idea and Reality of British and French Colonial Expansion, 1880–1914* (Oxford: Oxford University Press, 1982); and J. Bouvier, R. Girault and J. Thobie, *L'impérialisme à la française, 1914–1960* (Paris: La Découverte, 1986).

9. See W. Hynes, *The Economics of Empire: Britain, Africa and the New Imperialism, 1870–1895* (London: Longmans, 1979); W. G. Clarence-Smith, 'Business Empires in Equatorial Africa', *African Economic History*, 12 (1983), pp. 3–11; S. Jones, 'Economic Interpretation of Nineteenth Century Imperialism', *South African Journal of Economic History*, 7:1 (March 1992), pp. 1–26; J. Gallagher & R. Robinson, 'The Imperialism of Free Trade', *South African Journal of Economic History,* 7:1 (March 1992), pp. 27–44; Fieldhouse, '"Imperialism": An Historical Revision', pp. 45–72; D. K. Fieldhouse, 'The Role of Economics in the Expansion of Empires, 1830–1914', *South African Journal of Economic History*, 7:1 (March 1992), pp. 107–123; and D. K. Fieldhouse, P. Burroughs and A. J. Stockwell (eds), *Managing the Business of Empire: Essays in Honour of David Fieldhouse* (London: Routledge, 1998).

10. See S. Schafer (ed.), *The Brokered World: Go-Betweens and Global Intelligence, 1770–1820* (Sagamore Beach, MA: Science History Publications, 2009).

11. C.-A. Julien, *Le Maroc face aux impérialismes, 1415–1956* (Paris: Éditions Jeune Afrique, 1978); P. Guillen, 'La finance française et le Maroc de 1902 à 1904', *Bulletin de la Société d'histoire du Maroc*, 2 (1969), pp. 37–42; M. Chappert, 'Le projet français de Banque d'État du Maroc (1889–1906)', *Revue française d'histoire d'outre-mer*, 299:62 (1975), pp. 567–91; J.-C. Allain, *Agadir 1911: une crise impérialiste en Europe pour la conquête du Maroc* (Paris: Publications de la Sorbonne, 1976); M. T. Tortella and G. Tortella, 'Second-Rate Imperialism: The Banque d'État du Maroc, Viewed from the Archives of the Bank of Spain', in J. Consiglio, J. C. Martinez Oliva and G. Tortella (eds), *Banking the Finance in the Mediterranean: A Historical Perspective*, (Burlington, VT: Ashgate, 2012), pp. 255–72; and A. Reynier, *La Banque d'État du Maroc et les banques d'émission coloniales* (Casablanca: Imprimerie de la presse marocaine, 1926).

12. S. Saul, *La Banque d'État du Maroc et la Monnaie sous le Protectorat* (Paris, Comité pour L'histoire economique et financière de la France, *La France et l'Outre-Mer*, 1998), pp. 389–427.

13. See M. Lazhar-Gharbi, 'La Tunisie et la Banque de l'Algérie, 1881–1903: divergence d'intérêts ou les paradoxes d'une relation', *Le Capital français, à la traîne: ébauche d'un réseau bancaire au Maghreb colonial (1847–1914)* (Tunis: Université de la Manouba, 2003), pp. 287–311; and Banque de l'Algérie et de la Tunisie, *Cinquante ans au service de la Tunisie* (Paris: Banque de l'Algérie et de la Tunisie, 1955).

14. P. Ernest-Picard, *La monnaie et le crédit en Algérie Depuis 1830* (Paris: Plon, 1930); and M. Lazhar-Gharbi, *Crédit et discrédit de la Banque d'Algérie* (Paris: L'Harmattan, 2005).

15. Y. Ekoué Amaïzo, *Naissance d'une banque de la Zone Franc, 1841–1901. La Banque du Sénégal* (Paris: L'Harmattan, 2001).

16. J. Alibert, *De la vie coloniale au défi international: Banque du Sénégal, BAO* [Banque de l'Afrique occidentale], *BIAO* [Banque internationale pour l'Afrique occidentale]: *130 ans de banque en Afrique* (Paris: Chotard, 1983).

17. M. Meuleau, *Des pionniers en Extrême-Orient: la Banque de l'Indochine, 1875–1975* (Paris: Fayard, 1990).

18. See A. Le Masson, *La Caisse centrale de la France d'outre-mer et le financement de la France d'Outre-Mer, 1944–1958*, PhD thesis, Paris-Nanterre University, 1996.

19. A. Buffon, *Monnaie et crédit en économie coloniale: Contribution à l'histoire économique de la Guadeloupe, 1635–1919* (Pointe-à-Pitre, Société d'histoire de la Guadeloupe, 1979); and D. Bruneel, *Des banques coloniales à l'IEDOM* (Pointe-à-Pitre: Société d'histoire de la Guadeloupe, 2011).

20. See P. Cottrell, 'Connections and New Opportunities: London as an International Financial Centre, 1914–1958', in Y. Cassis and É Bussière (eds), *London and Paris as International Financial Centres in the Twentieth Century* (Oxford: Oxford University Press, 2005), pp. 153–182; H. Bonin, 'The Challenged Competitiveness of the Paris Banking and Finance Markets, 1914–1958', in *London and Paris as International Financial Centres*, pp. 183–204; Y. Cassis, *Capitals of Capital. A History of International Financial Centers, 1780–2005* (Cambridge: Cambridge University Press, 2006); Y. Cassis, 'Les places de Londres et de Paris au début du XXe siècle: quelques réflexions comparatives', in O. R. Feiertag and I. Lespinet-Moret (eds), *L'économie faite homme. Hommage à Alain Plessis* (Genève: Droz, 2010), pp. 487–501; and H. Bonin, *La Société générale en Grande-Bretagne (1871–1996)* (Paris: La Collection historique de la société générale, 1996).

21. C. Malon, *Le Havre colonial de 1880 à 1960* (Le Havre: Publications des Universités de Rouen et du Havre-presses universitaires de Caen, 2005).

22. X. Daumalin, *Marseille et l'Ouest africain* (Marseille: Publications de la Chambre de commerce et d'industrie Marseille-Provence, 1992).

23. See A. Buffon, *Monnaie et crédit en économie Coloniale: Contribution à l'histoire économique de la Guadeloupe, 1635–1919* (Pointe-à-Pitre: Société d'histoire de la Guadeloupe, 1979).

24. See H. Bonin, *Banque et Bourgeoisies. La Société bordelaise de CIC (1880–2005)* (Brussels: Peter Lang, 2010), ch. 8; and L. Harding, 'Bordeaux et Hambourg: l'héritage colonial: expériences communes de deux cités portuaires', *Bordeaux porte océane, carrefour européen* (Bordeaux: Fédération historique du Sud-Ouest, 1997), pp. 55–66.

25. See H. Bonin, *French Banks and the Greek 'Niche Market' (Circa 1880–1950)* (Geneva: Droz, 2013).

26. H. Bonin, 'Le Comptoir national d'escompte de Paris, une banque Impériale (1848–1940)', *Revue française d'histoire d'outre-mer*, 293:78 (1991), pp. 477–97; and H. Bonin, 'The French Banks in the Pacific Area (1860–1945)', in O. Checkland, Shizuya Nishimura and Norio Tamaki (eds), *Pacific Banking (1859–1959): East Meets West* (London: Macmillan, 1994), pp. 61–74.

27. S. Saul, 'Les agences du Crédit lyonnais en Égypte : l'insertion d'une banque de dépôts dans une économie d'outre-mer (1875–1956)', in B. Desjardins, M. Lescure, R. Nougaret, A. Plessis and A. Straus (eds), *Le Crédit lyonnais, 1863–1986: Études historiques* (Geneva: Droz, 2002), pp. 521–48. Also see S. Saul, *La France et l'Égypte de 1882 à 1914: intérêts économiques et implications politiques* (Paris: Comité pour l'histoire économique et financière de la France, 1997).

28. See Meuleau, *Des Pionniers en Extrême-Orient.*

29. H. Bonin, 'L'Outre-Mer, marché pour la banque commerciale (1876–1985)?' in J. Marseille (ed.), *La France & l'outre-mer: Les relations économiques & financières entre la France & la France d'outre-mer)* (Paris: Comité pour l'histoire économique & financière de la France, 1998), pp. 437–83.

30. See Alibert, *De la Vie coloniale au défi international.*

31. Meuleau, *Des pionniers en Extrême-Orient*; Yasuo Gonjo, *Banque coloniale ou Banque d'affaires: la Banque de l'Indochine sous la IIIᵉ République* (Paris: Comité pour l'histoire économique & financière de la France, 1993).

32. H. Bonin, *Un outre-mer bancaire méditerranéen: Le Crédit foncier d'Algérie & de Tunisie (1880–1997)* (Paris: Publications de la Société Française d'histoire d'outre-mer, 2004); and H. Bonin, 'Une banque française maître d'oeuvre d'un outre-mer levantin: le Crédit foncier d'Algérie & de Tunisie, du Maghreb à la Méditerranée orientale (1919–1970)', *Outre-Mers: Revue d'histoire*, 342–3:91 (2004), pp. 239–72.

33. H. Bonin, 'La Compagnie algérienne, levier de la colonisation et prospère grâce à elle (1865–1939)', *Revue française d'histoire d'outre-mer*, 328–9 (2000), pp. 209–30; H. Bonin, 'Une histoire bancaire transméditerranéenne: la Compagnie algérienne, d'un ultime apogée au repli (1945–1970)', in D. Lefeuvre et al. (eds), *La Guerre d'Algérie au miroir des décolonisations françaises (En l'honneur de Charles-Robert Ageron)* (Paris: Société française d'histoire d'outre-mer, 2000), pp. 151–76 ; H. Bonin, 'La Compagnie Algérienne Levier de la Colonisation et Prospère Grâce à Elle (1865–1939)', *Revue Française d'Histoire d'Outre-Mer*, 328–9 (2000), pp. 209–30; and H. Bonin, 'Compagnie algérienne', 'Banque de l'Algérie', 'Crédit Foncier d'Algérie & de Tunisie', in J. Verdès-Leroux, *L'Algérie et la France: Dictionnaire coordonné par Jeannine Verdès-Leroux*, ed. by R. Laffont (Paris: R. Laffont, 2009). See also Saul, *La Banque d'État du Maroc et la Monnaie sous le Protectorat.*

34. H. Bonin, *CFAO (1887–2007): La réinvention permanente d'une entreprise de commerce outre-mer* (Paris: Publications de la Société française d'histoire d'outre-mer, 2008); H. Bonin, 'Les Banquiers', in J.-P. Rioux (ed.), *Dictionnaire de la France Coloniale* (Paris: Flammarion, 2007), pp. 563–8; and H. Bonin, 'Banques et outre-mer', in C. Liauzu, *Dictionnaire de la colonisation française* (Paris: Larousse, 2007).

35. A. Plessis, *Histoires de la Banque de France* (Paris: Albin Michel, 2002); and A. Plessis, 'The Banque de France and the Emergence of a National Financial Market in France During the Nineteenth Century', in P. Cottrell, E. Lange and U. Olsson (eds), *Centres and Peripheries in Banking. The Historical Developments of Financial Markets* (London: Ashgate & EABH, 2007), pp. 143–60.

36. See F. Gallice, 'Le Crédit lyonnais à Londres, 1870–1939', in B. Desjardins, M. Lescure, R. Nougaret, A. Plessis and A. Straus (eds), *Le Crédit lyonnais, 1863–1986: Études historiques* (Geneva: Droz, 2002), pp. 521–48 ; and H. Bonin, *La Société générale en Grande-Bretagne (1871–1996)* (Paris: La Collection historique de la Société générale, 1996).

37. H. Bonin, 'Des négociants français à l'assaut des places fortes commerciales britanniques: CFAO et SCOA en Afrique occidentale anglaise puis anglophone', in H. Bonin and M. Cahen (eds), *Négoce blanc en Afrique noire: le Commerce de longue distance en Afrique subsaharienne du XVIIIᵉ au XXᵉ siècles* (Paris: Publications de la Société française d'histoire d'outre-mer, 2001), pp. 147–69.

38. G. de Lassus (ed.), *The History of BNP Paribas in India, 1860–2010* (Mumbai: BNP Paribas India, 2010).

39. G. Jones (ed.), *The Multinational Traders*, 'Routledge International Studies in Business History' (London: Routledge, 1998).

40. See B. Marnot, *Les grands ports de commerce français et la mondialisation au XIXᵉ siècle (1815–1914)* (Paris: PUPS, 2011).

41. E. W. Edwards, 'The Origins of British Financial Co-operation with France in China, 1906–1961', *English Historical Review*, 86 (1971), pp. 285–317; E. W. Edwards, 'British Policy in China, 1913–1914: Rivalry with France in the Yangtze Valley', *Journal of Oriental Studies*, 40 (1977), pp. 20–36; and E. W. Edwards, *British Diplomacy and Finance in China, 1855–1914* (Oxford: Clarendon Press, 1987).

42. This scheme is inspired from the one presented by Meuleau, *Des pionniers en Extrême-Orient*, p. 159.

43. D. Barjot, D. Lefeuvre, A. Berthonnet and S. Cœuré (eds), *L'électrification outre-mer de la fin du XIXᵉ siècle aux premières décolonisations* (Paris: Publications de la Société française d'histoire d'outre-mer & Fondation EDF, 2002).

44. Terushi Hara, 'Les investissements ferroviaires en Algérie au XIXᵉ siècle', *Revue d'histoire économique et sociale*, 54:2 (1976), pp. 185–211.

45. 'Industrialisation et Grand Capital', in D. Lefeuvre, *Chère Algérie: La France et sa colonie, 1930–1962* (Paris: Publications de la Société française d'histoire d'outre-mer, 1997), pp. 327–9 ; J. Marseille, *Empire colonial et capitalisme français : histoire d'un divorce* (Paris: Albin Michel, 1984) ; and Bonin, 'Grands chantiers (BTP)', 'Centrales et réseaux électriques', 'Chemins de fer', 'Compagnies foncières de colonisation', 'Hydrocarbures (pétrole et gaz)', 'Mines', 'Plans de modernisation' in *L'Algérie et la France*.

46. J. Suret-Canale, 'Les banques d'affaires et l'outre-mer dans les années 1950–1980', in *La France et l'outre-mer: un siècle de relations monétaires et financières* (Paris: Comité Pour L'Histoire Economique et Financière de la France, 1998), pp. 485–95; Hubert Bonin, *La Banque de l'union parisienne (1874/1904–1974): De l'Europe aux outre-mers* (Paris:

Publications de la Société française d'histoire d'outre-mer, 2011) ; and É. Bussière, *Paribas, l'Europe et le Monde, 1872–1992* (Anvers: Fonds Mercator, 1992).

47. See R. Jablon, L. Quenouëlle-Corre and A. Straus, *Politique et finance à travers l'europe du xxᵉ siècle: entretiens avec Robert Jablon* (Brussels: Peter Lang, 2009).

48. H. Bonin, 'Banques coloniales', in J.-C. Daumas et al. (eds), *Dictionnaire historique des Patrons* (Paris: Flammarion, 2010), pp. 57–60; H. Bonin, 'Les réseaux bancaires parisiens et l'empire: comment mesurer la capacité d'influence des "banquiers impériaux"'? in H. Bonin, J.-F. Klein and C. Hodeir (eds), *L'Esprit économique impérial (1830–1970): groupes de pression & réseaux du patronat colonial en France & dans l'empire* (Paris: Publications de la Société Française d'histoire d'outre-mer, 2008), pp. 447–72; and H. Bonin, 'Les banquiers', in J.-P. Rioux (ed.), *Dictionnaire de la France coloniale* (Paris: Flammarion, 2007), pp. 563–8.

49. Fieldhouse, Burroughs and Stockwell, *Managing the Business of Empire*.

50. H. Bonin, 'The Complementarities Between Merchant Shipping and Ancillary Activities: The Case of Two French Firms, SCAC and SAGA (1880s–1990s)', *International Journal of Maritime History*, 23:1 (June 2011), pp. 95–114.

2 Kazuhiko Yago, 'Correspondent Banking Networks and Branch Activities in "Imperial Banking": The Russo-Chinese Bank in Shanghai in 1902'

1. G. Jones (ed.), *Banks as Multinationals* (London: Routledge, 1990), p. 6.

2. P. Buckley and M. Casson, 'The Internalisation Theory of the Multinational Enterprise: A Review of the Progress of a Research Agenda After 30 Years', *Journal of International Business Studies*, 40 (2009), pp. 1563–80.

3. See Kazuhiko Yago, 'Russo-Chinese Bank (1896–1910): An International Bank in Russia and Asia', in Shizuya Nishimura, Toshio Suzuki and R. Michie (eds), *The Origins of International Banking in Asia, the Nineteenth and Twentieth Centuries* (Oxford: Oxford University Press, 2012).

4. Following works are noteworthy on the history of the Bank: O. Crisp, 'The Russo-Chinese Bank: An Episode in Franco-Russian Relations', *The Slavonic and East European Review*, 52 (1974), pp. 197–212; R. Quested, *The Russo-Chinese Bank: A Multinational Financial Base of Tsarism in China* (Birmingham: Birmingham University Press, 1977); Nobutaka Shinonaga, *Huransu Teikokushugi to Chugoku, Daiichiji Taisen zen no Chugoku ni okeru Huransu no Gaikou, Kinnyuu, Shoukougyou* [French Imperialism in China: Diplomacy, Finance, Commerce and French Industries in China Before the First World War] (Tokyo: Shumpusha, 2008); and H. Bonin, 'Les Banquiers Français en Chine (1860–1950): Shanghai et Hong Kong, relais d'un impérialisme bancaire ou plates-formes d'outre-mers multiformes', in Musée Albert Kahn, *Le Paris de l'Orient, Présence Française à Shanghai (1849–1946)* (Boulogne, 2002).

5. See John MacMurray, *Treaties and Agreements With and Concerning China, 1894–1919* (New York: Oxford University Press, 1921), pp. 35–42; 74–91; 356–69, for the treaties and conventions regarding the Chinese loan.

6. As for the founding process of the bank, see Crisp, 'The Russo-Chinese Bank', pp. 197–201; and R. Girault, *Emprunts russes et investissements français en Russie, 1887–1914* (Paris: Comité pour L'histoire economique et financière de la France, 1999), pp. 305–8.

7. 'Besoins auxquels répondait la création de la banque', Banque russo-chinoise, Archives de BNP Paribas.

8. Обзоръ Внышней Торговли Россий6, СП6 [Summary of foreign trade in Russia] (St Petersburg, 1913), p. 38.

9. This paragraph depends on Quested, *The Russo-Chinese Bank,* pp. 6–20, unless otherwise noted.

10. Ryota Ishikawa, 'Kindai Higashi Azia no Roshia Tsuuka Ryuutsuu to Chosen' [Circulation of the Russian Money in Modern East Asia: The Case of Korea], *История Россий,* 78 (May 2006).

11. See Glyn, Mills & Company [Eric Gore Brown], *History of the House of Glyn, Mills & Company,* (London, 1933).

12. 'Rapport sur Pékin, Tientsin, janvier 1908', Banque russo-chinoise, Archives de BNP Paribas. This audit report has been addressed from the Tientsin branch to the Shanghai branch director Drossemeier.

13. 'Rapport sur Tientsin, Tientsin, le 10 Janvier 1908', Banque russo-chinoise, Archives de BNP Paribas. The Branch Manager, Murray-Campbell, of British nationality, had long been manager of Jiling branch; and Quested, *The Russo-Chinese Bank,* pp. 21–8.

14. 'Correspondance, Succursale de Hankow à la Banque russo-chinoise, St. Petersburg', Banque russo-chinoise, Archives de BNP Paribas.

15. Ibid.

16. 'Rapport sur Tientsin, Tientsin, le 10 Janvier 1908', Banque russo-chinoise, Archives de BNP Paribas.

17. 'Interpellation sur les agissements du directeur de la Chancellerie de crédit, Davydoff, Novoié Vriémia, 13–26 Février 1910', Banque russo-chinoise, Archives de BNP Paribas. This document is a French translation of an article published by the Russian press, translated and commented by CNEP, which was one of the most important shareholders of the Russo-Chinese Bank.

18. A study by Peter Gatrell gives an overall view of the industrial expansion in Russia during the period, contrasting the role played by 'civilian consumers' to that of the 'government purchase': P. Gatrell, 'Industrial Expansion in Tsarist Russia, 1908–14', *Economic History Review,* 35:1 (February 1982), pp. 99–110.

3 Horesh, 'Competing Imperial Banking: The Yokohama Specie Bank and HSBC in China – 1919 as a Watershed?'

1. L. Young, *Japan's Total Empire: Manchuria and the Culture of Wartime Imperialism* (Berkeley, CA: University of California Press, 1998); and Yasutomi Ayumu, *Manshūkoku no Kinyū* 「満洲国」の金融 / [Finance in 'Manchukuo'] (Tokyo: Sōbunsha, 1997). On Japanese monetary and banking history more generally, see also: Noda Masaho, *Nihon shōken shijō seiritsushi: Meijiki no tetsudō to kabushiki kaisha kin'yū* 日本証券市場成立史: 明治期の鉄道と株式会社金融 / [A History of Japanese Securities Markets] (Tokyo: Yuhikaku, 1980); Norio Tamaki, *Japanese Banking: A History, 1859–1959* (Cambridge: Cambridge University Press, 1995); Akinobu Kuroda, *Kahei Shisutemu no Sekaishi* 貨幣システムの世界史 [World History of Currency Systems] (Tokyo: Iwanami Shoten, 2003); Masayoshi Tsurumi, 'Kindai no Kahei Shinyō' [Early-Modern Currency and Credit] in Eiji Sakurai and Satoru Nakanishi (eds), *Ryūtsū Keizaishi* 流通経済史 / [Economic Histyory of Distribution] (Tokyo: Yamakawa, 2002), pp. 470–

513; Ishii Kanji, 'British-Japanese Rivalry in Trading and Banking', in J. E. Hunter and Sugiyama Shinya (eds), *The History of Anglo-Japanese Relations, 1600–2000*, 5 vols (Basingstoke: Macmillan, 2002), vol. 4, pp. 110–32.

2. China Proper (also Inner China) or Eighteen Provinces was a term used by Western writers on the Qing Dynasty to express a distinction between the core and frontier regions of China.

3. M. Metzler, *Lever of Empire: The International Gold Standard and the Crisis of Liberalism in Pre-war Japan* (Berkeley, CA: University of California Press, 2006); R. J. Smethurst, *From Foot Soldier to Finance Minister: Takahashi Korekiyo, Japan's Keynes* (Cambridge, MA: Harvard University Press, 2007); Tomoyuki Taira, 'Nihon Teikoku Shugi Seiritsuki, Chūgokuni Okeru Yokohama Shōkin Ginkō' [The Yokohama Specie Bank and the Beginning of Japanese Imperialism in China], *Tokyo Daigaku Keizaigaku Kenkyu* 東京大学経済学研究 / [The Tokyo University Journal of Economics], 25:11 (1982), pp. 67–81; and M. Schiltz, *Japan's Money Doctors and the Gold-Yen Block* (Cambridge, MA: Harvard University Press, 2011).

4. Yokohama Shōkin Ginkō (ed.), *Shōhyō no rekishi : bōeki tsuūka no ichi shiryō to shite*鈔票の歴史: 貿易通貨の一資料として [The History of our Banknotes: Information regarding Means of Exchange Variants] [Confidential In-house Survey Compiled at the YSB Dalian Branch in 1941 by Inspector Ogawa Seiitsu] (Yokohama-shi: Yokohama Shōkin Ginkō Chōsabu, 1941?). The author is indebted to Professor Michael Schiltz of the University of Tokyo for making scans of this archival material available to him.

5. M. Schiltz, 'An "Ideal" Bank of Issue: The Banque Nationale de Belgique as a Model for the Bank of Japan', *Financial History Review*, 13:2 (2006), pp. 179–96; and Metzler, *Lever of Empire*, p. 24.

6. Tōkyō Ginkō and Shinji Arai (eds), *Yokohama Shōkin Ginkō Zenshi* 横濱正金銀行全史 / [A Comprehensive History of the Yokohama Specie Bank], 6 vols (Tokyo: The Bank of Tokyo, 1980–4), vol. 2, pp. 32, 144; and *Meiji Taishō Zaisei Shi* 明治大正財政史 / [Financial History of the Meiji and Taisho Periods], 20 vols (Tokyo: Keizai Oraisha, 1955), vols 14–16. In 1947, the Supreme Command of the Allied Powers (SCAP) restructured the YSB into the Bank of Tokyo, which has more recently evolved into the Mitsubishi Tokyo Bank. After World War II, SCAP similarly re-structured other longstanding Japanese semi-official banks (*Tokushu ginkō* 特殊銀行) – which had been initially chartered on the German and French models-into purely privately-run banks. These banks had often incorporated with large private share subscription, but they won active Japanese government endorsement and proved pivotal to the country's military and industrial modernization.

7. Norio Tamaki, *Japanese Banking: A History*, pp. 17–18; and N. Horesh, *Shanghai's Bund and Beyond: British Banks, Banknote Issuance and Monetary Policy in China, 1842–1937* (New Haven, CT: Yale University Press, 2009).

8. McLean to Greig, 21 October 1875, School of Oriental and African Studies Archives (hereafter SOAS), McLean Papers, MS 380401, Box 3, Folder 13.

9. *North-China Herald* [hereafter, *NCH*], 1 July 1876, p. 13.

10. Tamaki Norio, *Japanese Banking*, pp. 69–73; and M. Schiltz, 'Money on the Road to Empire. Japan's Choice for Gold Monometallism', *Economic History Review* (Forthcoming).

11. Yokohama Shōkin Ginkō, *Shōhyō no Rekishi*, pp. 13–28.

12. Wu Chouzhong, 'Hengbin Zhengjin Yinhang Jiqi Zai Woguo Faxing de Chaopiao' [The Yokohama Specie Bank and Its Note Issuance in China], Zhongguo Qianbi, vol. 3, pp.

41–4; The People's Bank of China (ed.), *Ziben Zhuyi Guojia Zai Jiu Zhongguo Faxing he Liutong de Huobi* [Currencies of Imperialist Banks in Pre-war China] (Beijing, China: Wenwu, 1992), pp. 27–35; and A. Pick, *Standard Catalogue of World Paper Money* (Iola, WI: Krause Publications, 1990), vol. 1, pp. 285–8.

13. Tōkyō Ginkō and Arai Shinji (eds), *Yokohama Shōkin Ginkō Zenshi*, 6 vols (Tokyo: Tōkyō Ginkō, 1980–4), vol. 2, p. 144.

14. *NCH*, 23 May 1908, p. 479.

15. *NCH*, 21 Oct 1911, p. 153.

16. Tōkyō Ginkō and Arai Shinji, *Yokohama Shōkin Ginkō Zenshi*, vol. 6, pp. 399–401; for the YSB paid-up capital figures, see Nihon Ginkō Tōkeikyoku, *Hundred-Year Statistics of the Japanese Economy* (Tokyo: Nihon Ginkō Tōkeikyoku, 1966), pp. 166–7. The ¥ 100m cap subsequently remained intact until 1945.

17. Decennial Reports for 1919–21, Imperial Maritime Customs [hereafter IMC], SOAS Archive, p. 63.

18. Deng Chengfu, 'Riben Hengbin Zhengjin Yinhang dui Woguo de Jinrong Qinlue' [Japan's Yokohama Specie Bank and its Financial Invasion of China] (Beijing: *Beijing Liaowang*, 1995), vol. 6, pp. 27–64; Metzler, *Lever of Empire*, p. 65; Guo Yuqing, *Jindai Riben Yinhang Zai Hua Jinrong Huodong: Hengbin Zhengjin Yinhang, 1894–1919* [Pre-war Japanese Banks' Operations in China: The Yokohama Specie Bank, 1894–1919] (Beijing, China: Renmin Chubanshe, 2007), p. 117.

19. Decennial Reports for 1919–21, IMC, SOAS Archive, Appendix II, pp. 84–5

20. Ibid.

21. Norio Tamaki, *Japanese Banking*, pp. 111–68; Metzler, *Lever of Empire*, pp. 199–217; Schiltz, *Japan's Money Doctors and the Gold-Yen Bloc*.

22. Yokohama Shōkin Ginkō, *Shōhyō no Rekishi*, pp. 5–8.

23. Schiltz, *Japan's Money Doctors and the Gold-Yen Bloc*, ch. 4.

24. Tomoyuki Taira, 'Nihon Teikoku Shugi Seiritsuki, Chūgoku ni Okeru Yokohama Shōkin Ginkō' [YSB Operations in China during Japan's Early Imperial Expansion], in *Tōkyō Daigaku Keizaigaku Kenkyū*, 25:11 (1982), pp. 67–81. Tomoyuki Taira's view is supported by W. Wray, 'Japan's Big-Three Service Enterprises in China, 1896–1936', in P. Duus, R. H. Myers and R. M. Peattie (eds), *The Japanese Informal Empire in China, 1895–1937* (Princeton, NJ: Princeton University Press, 1989), pp. 31–64, 44–7.

25. Ishii Kanji, 'British-Japanese Rivalry in Trading and Banking'; D. K. Lieu, *Foreign Investments in China* (Nanjing, China: Chinese Government Bureau of Statistics, 1929), p. 86. An illuminating indication of the importance of local deposits is provided by D. K. Lieu: 'Deposits of Chinese and foreign customers, especially savings and long term deposits, are invested by [the foreign banks] in [China] or other countries ... although we are able to obtain their condensed balance sheets for all branches, it is impossible with a few exceptions to secure data concerning their China branches alone. As to the way they invest the deposits of their customers, detailed particulars for our purpose are also unavailable'.

26. Guo Yuqing, *Jindai Riben Yinhang Zai Hua Jinrong Huodong: Hengbin Zhengjin Yinhang, 1894–1919*, pp. 189, 191.

27. On the 'chop loan' and the 1910–12 financial crisis in Shanghai, see A. Lee McElderry, *Shanghai Old-Style Banks (Ch'ien-Chuang), 1800–1925: A Traditional Institution in a Changing Society* (Ann Arbor, MI: University of Michigan, 1976); and Shizuya Nishimura, 'The Foreign and Native Banks in China: Chop Loans in Shanghai and Hankow Before 1914', *Modern Asian Studies*, 39:1 (2005), pp. 109–32.

28. On the Ta Ching Bank, see Kong Xiangxia, *Daqing Yinhang Hangshi* [A History of the Ta Ching Bank] (Nanjing, China: Nanjing Daxue Chubanshe, 1991).

29. R. Quested, *The Russo-Chinese Bank: A Multinational Financial Base of Tsarism in China* (Birmingham: Birmingham University Press, 1977). On late-Qing attempts at stemming the spread of Russian banknotes in Manchuria, see, for example, S. A. Smith, *Like Cattle and Horses: Nationalism and Labor in Shanghai, 1895–1927* (Durham, NC: Duke University Press, 2002), p. 45.

30. F. Tamagna, *Banking and Finance in China* (New York: Institute of Pacific Relations, 1942), pp. 28–30; Ding Richu, *Shanghai Jindai Jingji Shi* (Shanghai, China: Shanghai Renmin Chubanshe, 1994), vol. 2, pp. 67–68, 101; and N. H. Pugach, *Same Bed, Different Dreams: A History of the Chinese American Bank of Commerce, 1919–1937* (Hong Kong, China: Hong Kong University Press, 1997).

31. S. Cochran, *Big Business in China: Sino-Foreign Rivalry in the Cigarette Industry, 1890–1930* (Cambridge, MA: Harvard University Press, 1980).

32. Hirofumi Takatsuna, *Kokusai Tōshi Shanhai no Naka no Nihonjin* [Japanese Expatriates in Cosmopolitan Shanghai] (Tokyo, Japan: Kenbun, 2009); Guo Yuqing, *Jindai Riben Yinhang Zai Hua Jinrong Huodong: Hengbin Zhengjin Yinhang, 1894–1919*; and C. F. Remer, *A Study of Chinese Boycotts, With Special Reference to Their Economic Effectiveness* (Baltimore, MD: Johns Hopkins University Press, 1933).

33. Kikuchi Takaharu, *Chūgoku Minzoku Undo no Kihon Kozo* [The Basic Structure of Chinese Nationalist Movements] (Tokyo, Japan: Daian, 1996), p. 182.

34. *Sant ō Shuppei to Hai Nikka Undō* [The Shandong Expedition and Anti-Japanese Boycott] (Shanghai, China: Shanghai Nihon Shōgyo Kaigisho, 1927).

35. *Tsūshō Kōhō*通商 公報 (16 June 1919) and *Tsūshō Kōhō*通商 公報 (17 July 1919).

36. Intelligence Report, 20 November 1919, Japan Centre for Asian Historical Records, reel n°1–0517, folio 0273. On the longer-term Japanese mercantile anxiety that the May Fourth boycott unleashed, see also Junji Banno, 'Japanese Industrialists and Merchants and the Anti-Japanese Boycotts in China, 1919–1928', *The Japanese Informal Empire in China*, pp. 314–17. However, Junji Banno does not discuss the impact of boycotts specifically on banking.

37. E. S. K. Fung, *The Diplomacy of Imperial Retreat: Britain's South China Policy, 1924–1931* (Hong Kong, China: Oxford University Press, 1991), p. 44.

38. Rinbara Fumiko, *Sō Sokkyū to Tenshin no Kokka Teishō Undō* [Song Zejiu and the Origins of the Tianjin Movement for the Promotion of Chinese Goods] (Kyoto: Dōhōsha, 1983), p. 47. F. Rinbara's case-study illustrates well the failure to address boycotts of quasi-foreign banknotes as one of the most significant characteristics of anti-foreign agitation in 1919–27. Rinbara cursorily describes how students in Tianjin had tried to force merchants to encash Japanese-issued notes in 1919 but, like other scholars, does not analyse the consequences for Japanese banks in the city. Notably, the first boycott against quasi-foreign banknotes in Tianjin had actually targeted the French-run *Banque industrielle de Chine* as early as 1916. See B. Sheehan, *Trust in Troubled Times: Money, Banks and State-Society Relations in Republican Tianjin* (Cambridge, MA: Harvard University Press, 2003), p. 82.

39. See *Wusi Yundong Zai Shanghai Shiliao Xuanji* [Select Historical Materials on the May Fourth Movement in Shanghai] (Shanghai, China: Shanghai Renmin Chubanshe, 1961), pp. 11, 215.

40. Ren Jianshu, *Xiandai Shanghai da Shiji* [A Chronicle of Modern Shanghai] (Shanghai, China: Shanghai Cishu Chubanshe, 1996), pp. 11–16; and *Wusi Yundong zai Shanghai*

Shiliao Xuanji, pp. 212–13, 689–92. On Taiwan's colonial economy, see S. P. S. Ho, *Development of Taiwan 1860–1970* (New Haven, CT: Yale University Press, 1978), ch. 3.

41. A. S. J. Baster, *The International Banks* (New York: Arno Press, 1977 [1935]); and C. B. Davis, 'Financing Imperialism: British and American Bankers as Vectors of Imperial Expansion in China, 1908–1920', *Business History Review*, 56:2 (1982), pp. 236–64.

42. Imperial Japanese Consulate to Shanghai (ed.), *Shanhai Jijō* [The Situation in Shanghai] (Tokyo, Japan: Gaimushō Tsūshōkyoku, 1924), p. 131; and D. J. Orchard, 'China's Use of the Boycott as a Political Weapon', *The Annals of the American Academy of Political and Social Science. China*, 152 (1930), pp. 252–4. See Pan Liangui, *Shanghai Huobi Shi* [The History of Shanghai's Currencies] (Shanghai, China: Shanghai Renmin Chubanshe, 2004), p. 130.

43. Horesh, *Shanghai's Bund and Beyond*, ch. 4.

44. The boycott of Japanese-issued notes re-awakened in 1923 in response to Japan's refusal to waive its territorial claims in Northeast China. See *NCH*, 14 April 1923, p. 81.

45. See, for example, an article by a member of the Shanghai branch of the Royal Asiatic Society, A. Sowerby, in *NCH*, 8 August 1925, p. 1925; and Orchard, 'China's Use of the Boycott as a Political Weapon', p. 256.

46. *Shen Bao* 申報 (27 November 1919), p. 6; *Shen Bao* 申報 (28 November 1919), p. 10.

47. Tōkyō Ginkō and Arai Shinji, *Yokohama Shōkin Ginkō Zenshi*, vol. 2, pp. 360, 385. The YSB may have tried to increase its Hankou circulation in the early 1920s in order to offset the fall in demand in Shanghai.

48. Tōkyō Ginkō and Arai Shinji, *Yokohama Shōkin Ginkō Zenshi*, vol. 1, p. 336.

49. On Yuan Shikai's interventionism, see Linsun Cheng, *Banking in Modern China: Entrepreneurs, Professional Managers, and the Development of Chinese Banks, 1897–1937* (London: Cambridge University Press, 2003), pp. 37–57.

50. On the dynamics of subsequent boycotts in 1923–1932, see W. Wray, 'Japan's Big-Three Service Enterprises in China, 1896–1936', *The Japanese Informal Empire in China*, pp. 31–64; and K. Gerth, *China Made: Consumer Culture and the Creation of the Nation* (Cambridge, MA: Harvard University Press, 2003).

51. Many of the YSB's records were transferred to Washington DC during the American occupation of Japan. These include, among other valuable items, the YSB in-house monetary surveys but apparently little by way of internal branch correspondence.

52. Share price data compiled from *Meiji Taishō Kokusei Sōran* [An Overview of Meiji and Taisho-era Official Statistics] (Tokyo, Japan: Tōyō Keizai Shimposha, 1975), p. 315.

53. P. Boomgaard and I. Brown, 'An Introduction', *The Economies of Southeast Asia in the 1930s Depression* (London: Routledge, 1989), pp. 1–19.

54. *NCH*, 24 May 1919, pp. 507, 598.

55. *NCH*, 7 February 1920, p. 374.

56. *NCH*, 4 January 1919, p. 30. Monday's run on Bank of Taiwan was thought to have resulted in 'less than $25.000 of its notes' and about half the amount in YSB silver dollar notes cashed.

57. N. Horesh, *Shanghai's Bund and Beyond*, ch. 4.

4 Tomoko Shiroyama, 'Native Banking vs Imperial Banking in Early Twentieth Century China: The Formation of the Joint Reserve Board in Shanghai to Foster Credit and Credibility'

1. Bank of Japan, http://www.boj.or.jp/index.html, [accessed 6 July 2011].
2. People's Bank of China, http://www.pbc.gov.cn/publish/english/952/index.html, [accessed 6 July 2011].
3. For example, by 1907, two government banks, one commercial bank, and one provincial government bank had been granted the right to issue notes. By 1927, in addition to the two government banks, no fewer than 28 commercial and 11 provincial banks were printing money. As for the foreign banks' note issuance, see N. Horesh, *Shanghai's Bund and Beyond: British Banks, Banknote Issuance, and Monetary Policy in China, 1842–1937* (New Haven, CT: Yale University Press, 2009).
4. F. Tamagna, *Banking and Finance in China* (New York: Institute of Pacific Relations Publications Office, 1942), pp. 17–21.
5. Yang Yinpu, *Zhongguojinronglun* [Remarks on Chinese Banking] (Shanghai, China: Liming Shuju, 1936), p. 257.
6. P. Chu, 'The Various Methods of Bank Clearing in Shanghai', *Finance and Commerce*, 26:8 (21 August 1935), p. 198.
7. Ibid., p. 199.
8. Tamagna, *Banking and Finance in China*, pp. 25–7.
9. Chu, 'The Various Methods of Bank Clearing in Shanghai', pp. 200–1.
10. Ibid., p. 201.
11. Hong Jiaguan and Zhang Jifeng, *Jindai Shanghai Jinrongshichang* [Modern Shanghai Financial Markets] (Shanghai, China: Shanghai Renmin Chubanshe, 1989), pp. 58–9.
12. Liu Dajun, *Shanghai Gongyehuayanjiu* [A study of Industrialisation in Shanghai] (Shanghai, Shangwuyinshuguan, 1937), pp. 70–1.
13. 'Minami Manshū Tetsudō Kabushiki Kaisha Chōsabu, Shanghai ni Okeru Fudōsan kankō Chōsa shiryō sono ichi', *Shanghai Niokerufudōsankankōchōsashiryōsono* [Materials on Real Estate Practices and Customs about Real Estates in Shanghai], Wagatsuma Collection, Institute of Higher Asian Studies, University of Tokyo), vol. 1, pp. 11, 46.
14. R. Feetham, *Report of the Hon Mr. Justice Feetham to the Shanghai Municipal Council* (Shanghai, China: North China Daily News, 1931), p. 317.
15. 'Minami Manshū Tetsudō Kabushiki Kaisha Shangai jimusho Chōsashitsu', pp. 10vv11.
16. Richard Feetham, *Report of the Hon Mr. Justice Feetham*, *op.cit.*, pp. 108–9.
17. 'Minami Manshū Tetsudō Kabushiki Kaisha Chōsabu, *Chūshitoshi Fudōsan Kankōchōsashiryō* [Research Materials about Customs of Real Estates in the Cities in Eastern China], Wagatsuma Collection, Institute of Higher Asian Studies, University of Tokyo, vol. 2.
18. Yukio Imura, *Shina no Kin' yū to Tsūka* [Chinese Banking and Currency] (Shanghai, Shanghai Shuppankyōkai, 1924), p. 195. The relationship between local financial institutions and foreign banks from the late nineteenth century to the mid-twentieth century is an essential, but little researched, topic in modern Chinese economic history. Essays about indigenous credit suppliers in Asia, Africa, and Latin America, and their relations with Western banks, in G. Austin and Kaoru Sugihara (eds), *Local Suppliers of Credit in the Third World, 1750–1960* (New York: St. Martin's Press, 1993), p. 1, provide important cases for comparison. Austin and Sugihara argue that, depending on the context

within which it is supplied, credit operates variously as an instrument of exploitation and impoverishment, as a condition of survival, or as a means of mutual prosperity for lender and borrower.

19. Hong Kong and Shanghai Banking Corporation Archives, Shanghai Ledgers 203.
20. Tamagna, *Banking and Finance in China*, pp. 70–1. For a review of issues concerning personal ties versus law in business dealings in China, see 'Introduction', in Tahirih V. Lee (ed.), *Chinese Law: Social, Political, Historical and Economic Perspectives. Volume 3: Contract, Guanxi, and Dispute Resolution in China* (New York: Garland Publishing, 1997), pp. XIII–XIX.
21. Fukusaburō Hisashige, 'Bukkayorimita Shinakeizai no Ichimen' (The Chinese Economy Seen from its Price Trends), *Shinakenkyū* 36, March 1935, pp. 105–112.
22. Shanghai Municipal Archives, S177-1-73.
23. Shanghai Municipal Archives, S177-2-7-8.
24. Tamagna, *Banking and Finance in China*, pp. 177–9.
25. J. Gallagher and R. Robinson, 'The Imperialism of Free Trade', *The Economic History Review*, 6:1 (1953), pp. 1–15.
26. Kaoru Sugihara, 'British Imperialism, the City of London and Global Industrialization', in Shigeru Akita (ed.), *Gentlemanly Capitalism, Imperialism and Global History* (Hampshire: Palgrave Macmillan, 2002).
27. Wei-ying Lin, *The New Monetary System of China: A Personal Interpretation* (Chicago, IL: University of Chicago Press, 1936), p. 85.

5 Man-han Siu, 'British Banks and the Chinese Indigenous Economy: The Business of the Shanghai Branch of the Chartered Bank of India, Australia and China (1913–37)'

1. For example, P. J. Cain and A. G. Hopkins, *British Imperialism: Crisis and Deconstruction, 1914–1990* (London: Longman Group, 1993); and R. Allbert Dayer, *Finance and Empire: Sir Charles Addis, 1861–1945* (London: Macmillan Press, 1988).
2. F. Tamagna, *Banking and Finance in China* (New York: Institute of Pacific Relations Publications Office, 1942), pp. 197–8,
3. Linsun Cheng, *Banking in Modern China: Entrepreneurs, Professional Managers, and the Development of Chinese Banks, 1897–1937* (London: Cambridge University Press, 2003), pp. 70–8.
4. G. Jones, *British Multinational Banking, 1830–1990* (Oxford: Oxford University Press, 1993), pp. 186–60.
5. F. H. H. King, *The History of the Hong Kong and Shanghai Banking Corporation*, 4 vols (Cambridge: Cambridge University Press, 1987–91), vols 2 and 3.
6. C. Mackenzie, *Realms of Silver: One Hundred Years of Banking in the East* (London: Routledge & Kegan Paul, 1954).
7. The bank was named as the Bank of the Board of Households (*Hubu Yinhang*) in 1905 and its name was changed to Great Qing Government Bank (*Daqing Yinhang*) in 1908. In 1912, the bank was re-established as Bank of China.
8. Mackenzie, *Realms of Silver*, pp. 161–2.
9. The categorization of depositors has been undertaken by the writer of this text. Chinese depositors can be identified from the characteristics of their names. Chinese names

typically consist of three syllables, with each syllable having a particular tone and being written as a single Chinese character.

10. 'Rate of interest. We have allowed interest at the rate of 2% p.a. on the minimum monthly balances of local dollar accounts; on balances in excess of $100,00, no interest is allowed except by special arrangement. Interest on Savings Accounts is allowed at the rate of 3% per annum on minimum monthly balances. Our present rates for Fixed Deposits are: 12 months 4% p.a., 9 months 4% p.a., 6 months 3% p.a., 3 months 2.5%, which are the rates conceded by other foreign Banks: Half-Yearly Letter from Shanghai Branch to London Head Office, 2 February 1937, SASSEI, CB146. On the other hand, the Chinese Government Banks gave 4% p.a. on current accounts and 7% p.a. on twelve-month deposits; Letter From Shanghai Branch to London Head Office, 23 April 1937, SASSEI, CB228).

11. Diary Entry of 10 May 1931, in Shanghaishi [Shanghai Municipal Archives] (ed.), *Chen Guangpu Rizi* [Diary of Chen Guangpu] (Shanghai: Shanghai shudian chubanshe, 2002), p. 169.

12. Tamagna, *Banking and Finance in China*, p. 228.

13. King, *The History of the Hong Kong and Shanghai Banking Corporation*, vol. 2, pp. 494–6; 579–80.

14. The Board's income consisted of a Conservancy Surtax of three percent on the Shanghai Maritime Customs dues, one and a half per mille on duty free goods and 0.045 percent on treasure, on importation only, and the proceeds from the sale of foreshore lands. R. Feetham, *Report of the Hon. Mr. Justice Feetham, C.M.G. to the Shanghai Municipal Council*, 4 vols (Shanghai, China: North China Daily News, 1931–2), vol. 1, pp. 256–60.

15. Ibid., pp. 299–300.

16. W. F. Spalding, *Foreign Exchange and Foreign Bills in Theory and in Practice* (London: Pitman, 1915), pp. 168–70.

17. Half-Yearly letter From Shanghai Manager to London Head Office, 2 February 1937, SASSEI, CB146.

18. Ibid.

19. Ibid.

20. The categorization of buyers and sellers of forward exchange has been undertaken by the writer of this text. The categorization is based on the following three points: (1) Foreign banks were banks that were members of the Shanghai Foreign Exchange Bankers' Association; (2) Chinese banks were banks that were members of Shanghai Bankers' Association; (3) Chinese firms and individuals could be identified from the characteristics of their names.

21. During World War I, Chinese began to transact through the Shanghai Gold Stock Exchange, a commodity Exchange organized by Chinese. The gold transaction involved the buying and selling of foreign currencies for settlement. At least before 1926, the most involved currency was Japanese yen because yen was not on the gold standard and fluctuated against US Dollars perpetually. The significance of the Shanghai Gold Stock Exchange was emphasized in E. Kann, *The Currencies of China: An Investigation of Silver and Gold Transactions Affecting China with a Section on Copper*, 2nd edn (Shanghai, China: Kelly & Walsh, 1927), pp. 339–55.

22. He Pin, 'Shixi jindai Shanghai zhongwai yingquanye sanfang de hudongguanxi: Yishangahi zhongwai yingqianye lianghehui zhi choujian we izhongxin (1921–1929)' [An Analysis of the Interrelationship Between the Three Chinese and Foreign Banking Organizations: Focusing on the Establishment of the Association of Shanghai Banks], in Wu Jingping and Ma Changlin (eds), *Shanghai jinrong de xiangdaihua yu guojihua* [The

Modernization and Internationalization of Shanghai Finance] (Shanghai: Shangai guji chubanse, 2003), pp. 209–35.

23. Fixed loans in this article included items under heading of fixed loans, fixed loans against imports and leased property in the balance sheets.

24. The categorization of borrowers of fixed loan has been undertaken by this author. Chinese borrowers could be identified from the characteristics of their names as mentioned before.

25. Kikuike Tosio, '1930 Nendai Kinyūkiki to Shinshin bōseki kōshi' (Shenxin Textile Company and the Financial Crisis in the 1930s)' in *Syanhai: Jyūsōsuru nettowaku* [Shangai: Multilayered Networks] (Shanghai: Jyūsōsuru Nettowaku, Kyukōsyōinn, 2000).

26. Recorded in the balance sheet of the Shanghai Branch of Chartered Bank, December 1933.

27. Of $32 million of debt owned by the Rong family enterprises by 1931, the influential Chinese banks, Shanghai Commercial and Savings Bank and the Bank of China, owned 5.4 million and 4.3 million respectively (Linsun Cheng, *Banking in Modern China*, pp. 87–9)

28. The loan given was split into two accounts. One of the accounts was the loan given to the Foh Sing and Mow Sing Flour Mills (under the name of Wong Yue Ching in the new contract). Another account was the loan given to Sung Sing Cotton Spinning & Weaving Co. (Letter from Shanghai Branch to London Head Office, 11 February 1936, SASSEI, CB182).

29. Kikuike Tosio, '1930 Nendai Kinyūkikito Shinshin bōseki kōshi', pp. 166–71.

30. A Letter from Zhang Jiaao to Bei Zui, Song Hangzhang, Feng Gengguang and Li Ming, 16 September 1929 in 'Zhang Jiaao zhi Bei Zui deng ren shuxinxuan' [Selected letters from Chang Kia-Ngau to BeiZuyi and Others], *Danganyushixue* [Archives and History], 6 (December 1997). Archibald Rose served as a director of Chartered Bank from 1925 to 1953. He took the place of Sir John Newell Jordan, a famous British diplomat in China, after his death. Rose was also a diplomat in China and retired in 1921. Mackenzie, *Realms of Silver*, pp. 272–3.

31. The British policy towards China was discussed in detail in J. Osterhammel, 'China', in W. R. Louis and J. M. Brown (eds), *The Oxford History of the British Empire, Volume 4: The Twentieth Century* (Oxford: Oxford University Press, 1999).

32. I would like to thank Dr Duncan Campbell-Smith, the commissioned author of the business history of the Chartered Bank, forthcoming, for giving me this information.

33. J. Osterhammel, 'Imperialism in Transition: British Business and the Chinese Authorities, 1931–37', *The China Quarterly*, 98 (1984). Osterhammel mainly focused on companies with operations outside Shanghai.

34. W. H. Evans Thomas, *Vanished China: Far Eastern Banking Memories* (London: Unwin Brothers, 1952), pp. 161–2.

35. Ibid., pp. 156–7.

36. Ibid., p. 162.

37. Half-yearly Letter From the Shanghai Branch to the London Head Office, 23 April 1937, SASSEI, CB228.

38. Shanghai Branch to the London Head Office, 26 February 1937, SASSEI, CB151.

39. W. Kirby, *Germany and Republican China* (Stanford, CA: Stanford University Press, 1984), pp. 102–44.

40. Shanghai Branch to the London Head Office, 26 February 1937, SASSEI, CB151.

41. Ibid.

42. Shanghai Branch to the London Head Office, 23 April 1937, SASSEI, CB151.
43. This information was also offered courtesy of Dr Duncan Campbell-Smith.

6 Salomatina, 'Russian and Soviet Imperial Banking in Asia in the 1890s–1920s'

1. Kazuhiko Yago, 'The Anatomy and Pathology of Empire: Three Balance Sheets of Russian and Soviet Banks', in K. Matsuzato (ed.), *Comparative Imperiology* (Sapporo: Slavic Research Center, Hokkaido University, 2010), pp. 61–77.
2. A. Blum, *Istorija Kreditnyh Uchrezhdenij i Sovremennoe Sostojanie Kreditnoj Sistemy v SSSR* (Moscow: Gozfinizdat USSR, 1929). The English study on this subject: A. Arnold, *Banks, Credit, and Money in Soviet Russia* (New York: Columbia University Press, 1937).
3. State Corporation, 'Bank for Development and Foreign Economic Affairs', (*Vnesheconombank* or VEB).
4. A. P. Zabaznov, J. P. Golicyn and A. G. Sarkisjanc, *VEB: Vneshekonombank: 75–letiju Vneshekonombanka Posvjawaetsja*] (Moscow: Typo graphic design, 1999).
5. N. I. Krotov, *Moskovskii Narodnyi Bank: Sto Let Istorii* (Moscow: Mezhdunarodnye otnosheniia, 2011), pp. 93–122.
6. The Discount and Loan Bank of Persia: B. V. Anan'ich, *Rossijskoe Samoderzhavie i Vyvoz Kapitala. 1895–1914gg.* [The Russian Autocracy and the Export of Capital, 1895–1914] (Leningrad, 1975); and S. G. Beljaev, *P. L. Bark i Finansovaja Politika Rossii. 1914–1917 gg.* [P. L. Bark and the Financial Policy of Russia, 1914–1917] (Sankt-Petersburg, Russia: Izd-vo SPbGU, 2002), pp. 467–95. The Russo-Chinese Bank: B. A. Romanov, *Rossija v Man'chzhurii (1892–1906)* [Russia in Manchuria (1892–1906)] (Leningrad, Russia: Leningradskii Vostochnyi institut, 1928); O. Crisp, 'The Russo-Chinese Bank: An Episode in Franco-Russian Relation', *The Slavonic and East European Review*, 52:127 (April 1974), pp. 197–212; R. K. I. Quested, *The Russo-Chinese Bank: A Multinational Financial Base of Tsarism in China* (Birmingham: Birmingham University Press, 1977); V. S. Mjasnikov, 'Russko-Kitajskij Bank i Ego Rol v Istorii Mezhdunarodnyh Otnoshenij v Vostochnoj Azii', *Vostokovedenie i Mirovaja Kul'tura* (Moscow: Pamiatniki ist. mysli, 1998), pp. 234–71; I. V. Lukojanov, 'Russko-Kitajskij Bank (1895–1904 gg.)', *Nestor: Ezhekvartal'nyj Zhurnal Istorii i Kul'tury Rossii i Vostochnoj Evropy* [Quarterly Journal of the History and Culture of Russia and Eastern Europe] 2 (2000), pp. 177–202; and Choj Dokkju, *Rossija v Koree: 1892–1905 gg.* [Russia in Korea: 1892–1905] (Sankt-Petersburg, Russia: Zero, 1996), pp. 59–66. The Mongolian bank: Beljaev, *P. L. Bark i Finansovaja Politika Rossii* [P. L. Bark and the Financial Policy of Russia], pp. 496–546.
7. Kazuhiko Yago, 'The Russo-Chinese Bank (1896–1910): An International Bank in Russia and Asia', in Shizuya Nishimura, Norio Suzuki and R. C. Michie (eds), *The Origins of International Banking in Asia: The Nineteenth and Twentieth Centuries* (Oxford: Oxford University Press, 2012), pp. 145–165.
8. Anan'ich, *Rossijskoe Samoderzhavie i Vyvoz Kapitala*, pp. 55–67, 185–7.
9. Ji Zhaojin, *A History of Modern Shanghai Banking: The Rise and Decline of China's Finance Capitalism* (Armonk, NY: M. E. Sharpe, 2003), pp. 70–2.
10. Now the Tuva Republic is a subject of the Russian Federation.
11. Anan'ich, *Rossijskoe Samoderzhavie i Vyvoz Kapitala*, p. 16; and Russian State Archive of the Economy (hereafter RSAE), fond 7590, opis 3, delo 25, list 34–5.

12. Anan'ich, *Rossijskoe Samoderzhavie i Vyvoz Kapitala*, pp. 187–95.
13. Beljaev, P. L. *Bark i Finansovaja Politika Rossii*, pp. 535–8, 542–3.
14. *Svodnyi Balans Aktsionernykh Bankov Kommercheskogo Kredita, Deistvuiushchikh v Rossii (v 1000-kh rubl.) na 1 Ianvaria 1906 g.* [The Consolidated Balance Sheet of Joint-Stock Commercial Banks Operating in Russia (in Thousands of Rubles) on 1 January 1906] (Sankt-Peterburg, Russia: Kom. s'ezdov predstavitelei akts. kom. bankov, 1906), p. 3.
15. *Otchet po Operatsiiam Russko-Kitaiskogo Banka za 1905 g.* [Report on Operations of the Russo-Chinese Bank in 1905] (Sankt-Peterburg, Russia, 1906).
16. Yago, 'The Russo-Chinese Bank', p. 161.
17. Ibid., pp. 162–3.
18. See R. Cameron and V. I. Bovykin (eds), *International Banking, 1870–1914* (New York: Oxford University Press, 1991), pp. 150–6, 265–76, 464–6; and Ji Zhaojin, *A History of Modern Shanghai Banking*, pp. 70–2.
19. V. V. Lavrov (ed.), *Akcionerno-Paevye Predprijatija Rossii po Oficial'nym Dannym* [The Russian Joint-Stock Companies according to Official Data] (Moscow: M. Lavrov, 1913), pp. 474–5; and A. Golubev (ed.), *Russkie Banki: Sprav. i Stat. Svedenija o Vseh Dejstvujuwih v Rossii Gos., Chast. i Obwestv. Kredit. Uchrezhdenijah. God 4 (1908)* [Russian Banks: Information and Statistics on all State, Private and Cooperative Credit Institutions, Operating in Russia. The Fourth Year (1908)], (Sankt-Peterburg, Russia: Kom. s'ezdov predstavitelei akts. kom. bankov, 1908,) p. 31.
20. *Otchet po Operatsiiam Russko-Kitaiskogo Banka za 1905 g.* [Report on Operations of the Russo-Chinese Bank in 1905], (Sankt-Peterburg, 1906); 'Balans na 1 Ianvaria 1906 g' [Balance Sheet on 1 January 1906]; S. Salomatina, 'The Statements of the Russo-Chinese Bank, 1897–1910', at www.hist.msu.ru/Dynamics/data/ 12_017.xls [accessed 28 October 2014].
21. 'Kopiia Obzora o Razvitii Torgovli Rossii s Persiei s Otdalennykh Vremen (s VI veka po 1919 g.), 1924 g'[A Copy of Review on the Development of Trade between Russia and Persia since Remote Times (from the 6th century to 1919), 1924], RSAE, fond 7590, opis 3, delo 25, list 40–2.
22. Ibid., list 40.
23. Ibid., list 40–1.
24. Anan'ich, *Rossijskoe Samoderzhavie i Vyvoz Kapitala*, pp. 55–67.
25. Ibid., pp. 200–201; and Beljaev, P. L. *Bark i Finansovaja Politika Rossii*, pp. 470–1.
26. Anan'ich, *Rossijskoe Samoderzhavie i Vyvoz Kapitala*, p. 54.
27. Ji Zhaojin, *A History of Modern Shanghai Banking*, p. 72.
28. Anan'ich, *Rossijskoe Samoderzhavie i Vyvoz Kapitala*, pp. 185–95.
29. Ibid., pp. 508–9.
30. 'Otchet Russko-Kitaiskogo Banka za 1907 g.' [Report of the Russo-Chinese Bank for 1907], in *Vestnik Finansov, Promyshlennosti i Torgovli. Otchety Obiazannykh Publichnoi Otchetnost'iu Predpriiatii* [The Bulletin of Finance, Industry and Trade. Reports of Companies, Obliged by Public Reporting], 33 (1908), p. 1115; and Salomatina, 'The Statements of the Russo-Chinese Bank', n. 2, 21.
31. 'Zakliuchenie Revizionnoi Komissii po Balansam Otdelenii na 1ˢᵗ ianv. 1907 i 1908 g' [The Resolution of the Audit Committee on Balance Sheets of Branches on 1 January 1907 and 1908], Russian State Historical Archive (hereafter RSHA), fond 632, opis 1, delo 158.
32. The State Bank of the USSR from 1922.

33. About Olof Aschberg see: A. C. Sutton, *Wall Street and the Bolshevik Revolution* (New Rochelle, NY: Arlington House, 1974); Zabaznov, Golicyn and Sarkisjanc, *Vneshekonombank*, p. 19; and Ulf Abel and Vera Moore, *Icons: Catalogue of the Collection by Ulf Abel with Vera Moore* (Stockholm, Sweden: National Museum, 2002). See also: 'National Museum, Icons', at www.nationalmuseum.se/sv/English-startpage/Collections/Painting/Icons [accessed 28 October 2014].

34. Zabaznov, Golicyn and Sarkisjanc, *Vneshekonombank*, pp. 15–27, 33.

35. Ibid., p. 41.

36. RSAE, fond 7590, opis 3, delo 11, list 149ob.

37. Zabaznov, Golicyn and Sarkisjanc, *Vneshekonombank*, pp. 33–35.

38. Ibid., pp. 57–9, 63.

39. Ibid., p. 55.

40. Ibid., pp. 63–6.

41. Ibid., pp. 37, 59, 69, 71.

42. Ibid., p. 63.

43. Ibid., pp. 33, 57–9, 63.

44. Ibid., pp. 33, 63.

45. Ibid., pp. 49, 57.

46. Ibid., pp. 43–7.

47. RSAE, fond. 7590, opis 3, delo 77, list 8–11, 18, 21, 36, 38, 46, 52, 64, 66, 79, 81, 92, 94, 117, 119, 123, 124.

48. Ibid.

49. Ibid., delo 9, list 12–4; delo 77, list 8–11, 79, 81.

50. Ibid., delo 90, list 18.

51. D. R. Watson, 'The Rise and Fall of the Russo-Asiatic Bank: Problems of a Russian Enterprise with French Shareholders, 1910–1926', *European History Quarterly*, 23 (1993), pp. 39–49.

52. Ibid., p. 46.

53. N. E. Ablova, *KVZhD i Rossiiskaia Emigratsiia v Kitae: Mezhdunar. i Polit. Aspekty Istorii (Pervaia Polovina XX v.)* [Chinese Eastern Railway (CEP) and Russian Emigration in China: International and Political Aspects of the History (the First Half of the 20th Century)] (Moscow: Rus. panorama, 2005), p. 91.

54. Watson, 'The Rise and Fall of the Russo-Asiatic Bank', p. 46.

55. RSAE, fond 7590, opis 3, delo 140, list 12–12ob.

56. Watson, 'The Rise and Fall of the Russo-Asiatic Bank', pp. 44–6.

57. See Ablova, *KVZhD i Rossiiskaia Emigratsiia v Kitae*, p. 85–120.

58. Ibid., pp. 85–120

59. Ibid., pp. 120–5.

60. Ibid., p. 125.

61. Ibid., p. 127.

62. RSAE, fond 7590, opis 3, delo 140, list 12–12ob.

63. Ji Zhaojin, *A History of Modern Shanghai Banking*, p. 72.

64. About Far Eastern bank in Khabarovsk: RSAE, fond 7590, opis 3, delo 140, list 47–47ob; A. E. Zav',ialov (ed.), '*Finansovo-Kreditnyi Slovar'* [Financial and Credit Dictionary], 3 vols (Moscow: Finansy i Statistika, 1994), vol. 1, p. 329; *Putevoditel' po Fondam Gosudarstvennogo Arkhiva Khabarovskogo Kraia i Ego Filiala v Gorode Nikolaevske-na-Amure* [Guide to the State Archives of Khabarovsk Krai and its Branch in Nikolaevsk-on-Amur], 2 vols, (Khabarovsk: RIOTIP, 2006), vol. 1, pp. 109–10; and 'Dal'nevostochnyi

Kommunal'nyi Bank (1922–1939)' at http://guides.rusarchives.ru/browse/guidebook. html?bid=215&sid=735195 [accessed 28 October 2014].

65. RSAE, fond 7590, opis 3, delo 140, list 47.
66. Ibid., delo 191. The file ('delo') devoted to lending to the fishing industry, documents of 1925–1928.
67. Ibid., delo 140, list 47.
68. Ibid., list 47–47ob.
69. *Rossiiskii Gosudarstvennyi Arkhiv Ekonomiki. Putevoditel* [Russian State Archive of the Economy. A Research Guide] (Moscow: Blagovest, 1994), p. 5, in Zabaznov, Golicyn and Sarkisjanc, *Vneshekonombank*, pp. 37, 69.
70. Zabaznov, Golicyn and Sarkisjanc, *Vneshekonombank*, pp. 69–70.
71. See N. L. Mamaeva, *Komintern i Gomin'dan, 1919–1929* [Comintern and Kuomintang, 1919–1929] (Moscow: ROSSPEN, 1999), pp. 344–7.
72. Go Khen'iui and M. L. Titarenko (eds), *VKP(b), Komintern i Natsional'no-Revoliutsion-noe Dvizhenie v Kitae: Dokumenty* [The Comintern and the National and Revolutionary Movement in China: Documents], 5 vols (Moscow: Dokumenty, 1994–2007).
73. Ibid., vol. 1: 1920–1925, pp. 209–11, 226, 238–9, 723.
74. Extract from 'Protocol N°94 (Special N°72) of the Meeting of the Politburo TsK VKP (b), 7 April 1927', Go Khen'iui and Titarenko, *VKP(b)*, vol. 2, part 2: 1926–1927, p. 662. Copies of the extract were sent to Aron Scheinman, the Chairman of the State Bank of the USSR, and M. I. Frumkin, the Deputy of People's Commissars (Ministers) of Foreign Trade and Finance of the USSR.
75. See V. N. Khaustov, 'Nekotorye Problemy Deiatel'nosti Organov Gosbezopasnosti v 1920–1930-e Gody' [Some Aspects of the State Security Agencies' Activities in the 1920s to 1930s], in *Istoricheskie Chteniia na Lubianke. 1999 God. Otechestvennye Spetss-luzhby v 1920–1930-kh Godakh* [The Historical Conferences at the Lubyanka. 1999. Russian Special Services in the 1920s to 1930s] (Moscow: Velikii Novgorod, 2000), pp. 3–7; and V. N. Usov, *Sovetskaia Razvedka v Kitae: 20-e Gody XX Veka* [Soviet Intelligence in China in the 1920s] (Moscow: OLMA-Press, 2002). The relations between the Comintern and the Soviet intelligence service can be retraced in the volumes of the archival documents, Go Khen'iui and Titarenko, *VKP(b)*, using references to the Head of the Foreign Department of OGPU, Mikhail Trilisser (Moskvin), and the Head of Fourth Directorate of the Red Army Staff, Ian Berzin.
76. Usov, *Sovetskaia Razvedka v Kitae*.
77. P. P. Balakshin, *Final v Kitae: Vozniknovenie, Razvitie i Ischeznovenie Beloi Emigratsii na Dal'nem Vostoke* [Finale in China: Origin, Evolution and Disappearance of White Emigration in the Far East], 2 vols (San Francisco, CA: PUBLISHER, 1958, volume 1, p. 141, cited from: Usov, *Sovetskaia Razvedka v Kitae*, p. 131.
78. Krotov, *Moskovskii Narodnyi Bank: Sto Let Istorii*, pp. 113–22.
79. S. K. Roshchin, *Politicheskaia Istoriia Mongolii (1921–1940)* [Political History of Mongolia (1921–1940)] (Moscow: IV RAN, 1999), p. 52, 307–8; N. P. Moskalenko, *Etnopoliticheskaia Istoriia Tuvy v XX Veke* [Ethnic and Political History of Tuva in the Twentieth Century] (Moscow: Nauka, 2004), pp. 95–8; and Baabar, *Istoriia Mongolii: Ot Mirovogo Gospodstva do Sovetskogo Satellite* [History of Mongolia: From World Domination to the Soviet Satellite] (Kazan, Russia: Tatarskoe Knizhnoe Izd-Vo, 2010), pp. 263, 267.
80. Beljaev, *P. L. Bark i Finansovaja Politika Rossii*, p. 544.

81. RSAE, fond 7590, opis 3, delo 140, list 66 ; Zabaznov, Golicyn and Sarkisjanc, *Vneshek-onombank*, p. 59; and Baabar, *Istoriia Mongolii*, p. 246.
82. RSAE, fond 7590, opis 3, delo 140, list 66.
83. On 2 November 1927 Mongolbank had offices in Altan-Bulak, San Beise, Kobdo, Ulias-sutai, Tszain-Shabi, as well as temporary offices in Tsetsen-Khan and Yugodzyr (RSAE, fond 7590, opis 3, delo 140, list 178).
84. RSAE, fond 7590, opis 3, delo 92, list 16, 18–19, 41–2.
85. Ibid., list 18, 20.
86. RSAE, fond 7590, opis 3, delo 92, list 33; Moskalenko, *Etnopoliticheskaia Istoriia Tuvy v XX veke*, pp. 120–1; 'Iz Istorii Bankovskogo Dela v Respublike Tyva' [Some Facts of the Banking History in the Republic of Tuva], *Vestnik Banka Rossii* [The Bulletin of the Bank of Russia], 46:1137 (2009), pp. 35–7, at www.cbr.ru/publ/Vestnik/ves090805046.zip [accessed 28 October 2014].
87. Zabaznov, Golicyn and Sarkisjanc, *Vneshekonombank*, pp. 37, 69.
88. 'Doklad Pravleniia k Sobraniiu Aktsionerov 31 Marta 1916 g' [The Address of the Board to the Shareholders' Meeting of 31 March 1916], *Otchet Russkogo Dlia Vneshnei Torgovli Banka za 1915 g.* [The Report of the Russian Bank for Foreign Trade of 1915], (Petro-grad, Russia, 1916).
89. V. I. Bovykin, 'Uchetno-Ssudnyi Bank Persii' [The Discount and Loan Bank of Persia], in *Ekonomicheskaia Istoriia Rossii s Drevneishikh Vremen do 1917 g.: Entsiklopediia* [Eco-nomic History of Russia from Ancient Times to 1917: Encyclopedia], 2 vols (Moscow: ROSSPEN, 2009), vol. 2, pp. 1019–20.
90. See Beljaev, *P. L. Bark i Finansovaja Politika Rossii*, pp. 495–572.
91. A. E. Zav'ialov (ed.), *Finansovo-Kreditnyi slovar'* [Financial and Credit Dictionary], 3 vols (Moscow, Russia: Finansy i Statistika, 1994), vol. 3, p. 81; and Zabaznov, Golicyn and Sarkisjanc, *Vneshekonombank,* pp. 37, 59.
92. Thirteen branches, based on 1924–1928, the archives of which are kept in the RSAE: Babol, Bazaar (Tehran office), Barfrush, Bandar-Gyaz, Isfahan, Qazvin, Mashhad, Pahl-avi, Anzali, Rasht, Sabzevar, Tabriz, Hamadan, Shiraz. William Chase, Jeffrey Burds, S. V. Prasolova, A. K. Sokolov and E. A. Tiurina (eds), *Rossiiski Gosudarstvennyi Arkhiv Ekonomiki. Putevoditel* [Russian State Archive of the Economy. A Research Guide] (Moscow: Blagovest, 1994), p. 5. The difference with the Discount and Loan Bank of Persia: Ruspersbank had Baboland Shiraz branches, the Discount and Loan Bank of Persia had the agencies in Birjand, Kashan, and Urmia (*Akcionerno-Paevye Predprijatija Rossii*, p. 479).
93. RSAE, fond 7590, opis 3, delo 98, list 7, 23.
94. Ibid., list 2, 7, 24.
95. Ibid., list 15.
96. Ibid., list 2.
97. Ibid., list 15.
98. Ibid., list 60ob.
99. Ibid.
100. Ibid., list 8, 9, 48.
101. Ibid., list 8, 21.
102. Ibid., list 11.
103. Ibid., list 58–60ob.
104. Ibid., list 56–9.
105. Zabaznov, Golicyn and Sarkisjanc, *Vneshekonombank*, op. cit., p. 69.

106. RSAE, fond 7590, opis 3, delo 77, list 29–30.
107. *'Finansovo-Kreditnyi Slovar'* [Financial and Credit Dictionary], 3 vols (Moscow: Finansy i Statistika, 1994), vol. 3, p. 159.
108. Blum, *Istorija Kreditnyh Uchrezhdenij...*, op.cit., pp. 205–206.

7 Ashok Kapoor, 'Challenging Imperial Banking in India: From the Legacy of Empire to Nationalistic Rules'

1.   Y. Cassis, *Capitals of Capital: A History of International Financial Centers, 1780–2005* (Cambridge: Cambridge University Press, 2006).
2.   Reserve Bank of India, *Report of the Central Board of Directors on the Working of the Reserve Bank of India for the Year Ended June 30, 2005 Submitted to the Central Government in Terms of Section 53(2) of the Reserve Bank of India Act, 1934* (Mumbai: Reserve Bank of India, 2005).
3.   Accession Number 139336, Reserve Bank of India Archives, p. 8.
4.   Ibid., p. 12.
5.   Ibid., p. 5.
6.   Ibid., p. 6.
7.   Indian Central Banking Enquiry Committee, 1981.
8.   Ibid.
9.   See Simha, *History of the Reserve Bank of India, Volume 1*; G. Balachandran, *History of the Reserve Bank of India, Volume 2: 1951–1967* (Bombay: RBI, 1998); and A. Vasudevan et al., *History of the Reserve Bank of India, Volume 3: 1967–1981* (Bombay: RBI, 2005). See also State Bank of India, *The Evolution of the State Bank of India*, 3 vols (London: SAGE Publications, 2003), vol. 3: *The Era of the Imperial Bank of India, 1921–1955*.
10. RBI Act 1934, Stipulated Cash Reserve of the Scheduled Bank to be kept with the Bank
11. Proceedings of the Central Board of Directors of Reserve Bank of India, Reserve Bank of India Archives, Accession n°14701-40860.
12. Banking Regulating Act, 1949 was passed as Banking Companies Act & became effective on 16 March 1949
13. Simha, *History of the Reserve Bank of India,* vol. 1, pp. 66–7.
14. Banking Companies Act, 1949.
15. RBI Act 1934.
16. Indian Companies Act 1956.
17. Proceedings of the Central Board of Directors 1941.
18. Ibid.
19. Proceedings of the Central Board of Directors, 1942.
20. Ibid.
21. *The Eastern Economist*, 12 January 1945.
22. Simha, *History of the Reserve Bank of India*, vol. 1, p. 738.
23. August 1943.
24. The act was first attempt to regulate Banking in India and came into effect of 16 March 1949.
25. 18 February 1949.
26. Balachandran, *History of the Reserve Bank of India*, vol. 2, p. 422.
27. Deposit Insurance Corporation, *Directors' Report and Balance Sheet and Accounts for the Year Ended 31st December 1962* (Bombay: Reserve Bank of India, 1962).

28. RBI Archives, Accession Number F33575, pp. 28a-c.
29. See N. Chandra Joshi, *Indian Banking* (New Delhi: Ashish Publishing House, 1978); and T. A. Vaswani, *Indian Banking System: A Critical Study of the Central and Commercial Banking Sectors* (Bombay: Lalvani Publishing House, 1968).
30. Vasudevan, *History of the Reserve Bank of India*, vol. 3, p. 54.
31. Balachandran, *History of the Reserve Bank of India*, vol. 2, p. 166.
32. Ibid., p. 54.
33. *RBI History (1967–1981)*, volume III, p. 833.
34. Ibid.
35. Vasudevan, *History of the Reserve Bank of India*, vol. 3, p. 59.
36. Ibid., pp. 836–7.
37. Ibid., p. 844.
38. Ibid., p. 1953
39. RBI, *History of the Reserve Bank of India, Volume 4: 1981–1997* (Bombay: Academic Foundation, 2013), part 1, pp. 335–6.
40. See V. Desai, *Indian Banking: Nature and Problems* (Bombay: Himalaya Publishing House, 1987).
41. The Committee on Financial System (Chairman – M. Narasimham), 1991.
42. Speech of the Finance Minister in Parliament.
43. RBI, *Annual Report of the Central Board on the Working of the Reserve Bank of India during the year ended the 30th June 2001* (Mumbai: Reserve Bank of India, 2001).
44. The Committee of Banking Sector Reforms (Chairman – M. Narasimham), 1998.
45. Press Release of RBI, 28 February 2005.
46. The Hindu, 4 April 2005.
47. Yaga Venugopal Reddy, "Perspective on Central Banking", Governor Lecture, 2010.
48. Ibid.
49. RBI, 'Report of Trend & Progress of Banking in India', 2007–8.
50. Ibid.

Hubert Bonin, 'Conclusion'

1. F. King, 'Does the Corporation's History Matter? Hongkong Bank/HSBC Holdings: A Case', in A. Godley and O. M. Westall (eds), *Business History and Business Culture* (Manchester: Manchester University Press), 1996, pp. 116–37; F. King, *The History of the Hong Kong and Shanghai Banking Corporation: Volume 1, The Hong Kong Bank in Late Imperial China, 1864–1902: On an Even Keel* (Cambridge: Cambridge University Press, 1987); F. King, *The History of the Hong Kong and Shanghai Banking Corporation: Volume 2, The Hong Kong Bank in the Period of Imperialism and War, 1895–1918: Wayfoong, the Focus on Wealth* (Cambridge: Cambridge University Press, 1988); and F. King, *The History of the Hong Kong and Shanghai Banking Corporation: Volume 3, The Hong Kong Bank Between the Wars and the Bank Interned, 1919–1945: Return from Grandeur* (Cambridge: Cambridge University Press, 1988).
2. P. Duus, R. H. Myers, and R. M. Peattie (eds), *The Japanese Informal Empire in China, 1895–1937* (Princeton, NJ: Princeton University Press, 1989); Norio Tamaki, 'The Yokohama Specie Bank. A Multinational in the Japanese Interests, 1879–1935', in G. Jones (ed.), *Banking as Multinationals* (London: Routledge, 1990); Kanji Ishii, 'Japan', in R. Cameron and V. Bovykin (eds), *International Banking, 1870–1914* (Oxford: Oxford University Press, 1991); and Kanji Ishii, 'Japanese Foreign Trade and the Yokohama Spe-

cie Bank, 1880–1913', in O. Checkland, Shizuya Nishimura, and Norio Tamaki (eds) *Pacific Banking, 1859–1959. East Meets West* (London: MacMillan: St. Martin's Press, 1994), pp. 1–23.

3. Motoaki Akagawa, 'German Banks in East Asia: The Deutsche Bank (1870–1875) and the Deutsch-Asiatische Bank (1889–1913)', *Keio Business Review*, 45:1 (2009), pp. 1–20; M. Müller-Jabusch, *Fünfzig Jahre Deutsch-Asiatische Bank, 1890–1939* (Berlin: Deutsche Bank, 1940); and B. Becker, 'German Business in Hong Kong Before 1914', *Journal of the Royal Asiatic Society Hong Kong Branch*, 44 (2004), pp. 91–113.

4. H. Bonin, 'The French Banks in the Pacific area (1860–1945)', in O. Checkland, Shizuya Nishimura and Norio Tamaki (eds), *Pacific Banking (1859–1959: East Meets West* (London: Macmillan: St. Martin's Press, 1994), pp. 61–74; H. Bonin, 'Les banquiers français en Chine (1860–1950): Shanghai et Hong Kong, relais d'un impérialisme bancaire ou plates-formes d'outre-mers multiformes', in L. Césari and D. Varaschin (eds), *Les relations franco-chinoises au vingtième siècle et leurs antécédents* (Arras, France: Artois Presses Université, 2003), pp. 157–71.

5. G. Cyril Allen and A. Donnithorne, *Western Enterprise in Far Eastern Development: China and Japan* (London: Georges Allen & Unwin, 1954); and Chi-Ming Hou, *Foreign Investment and Economic Development in China, 1840–1937* (Cambridge, MA: Harvard University Press, 1965).

6. G. S. Hamilton (ed.), *Business Networks and Economic Development in East and Southeast Asia* (Hong Kong: University of Hong Kong Press, 1991).

7. M. Meuleau, *Des pionniers en extrême-orient: histoire de la banque de l'indochine (1875–1975)* (Paris: Fayard, 1990); and Yasuo Gonjo, *The History of the Banque de l'Indochine (1875–1939): French Imperialism in the Far East* (Tokyo: Tokyo University Press, 1985).

8. H. Bonin, 'French Banking in Hong Kong: From the 1860s to the 1950s', in Shizuya Nishimura, Toshio Suzuki and R. Michie (eds), *The Origins of International Banking in Asia: The Nineteenth and Twentieth Centuries* (Oxford: Oxford University Press, 2012), pp. 124–44.

9. Ishii Kanji, 'British-Japanese Rivalry in Trading and Banking', in J. E. Hunter and Sugiyama Shinya (eds), 5 vols, *The History of Anglo-Japanese Relations, 1600–2000*, vol. 4 (Basingstoke: Macmillan, 2002), pp. 110–32.

10. F. Gipouloux, *La Méditerranée asiatique. Villes portuaires et réseaux marchands en Chine, Japon et en Asie du Sud-Est, XVIe–XXIe siècles* (Paris: CNRS Éditions, 2009); F. Gipouloux, *The Asian Mediterranean: Port Cities and Trading Networks in China, Japan, and Southeast Asia, 13th–21st Century* (Cheltenham: Elgar, 2011); and F. Gipouloux, *Gateways to Globalisation: Asia's International Trading and Finance Centres* (Cheltenham: Elgar, 2011).

11. F. Braudel, *La Méditerranée et le monde méditerranéen à l'époque de Philippe II* (Paris: Armand Colin, 1949).

12. F. Broeze, K. McPherson, and P. Reeves, 'Studying the Asian Port City', in F. Broeze (ed.), *Brides of the Sea: Port Cities of Asia from the Sixteenth to the Twentieth Centuries* (Kensington, Australia: University of South Wales Press, 1989).

13. H. Tertrais, 'Une révolution sous influence: la République chinoise face au consortium bancaire', *Matériaux pour l'histoire de notre temps*, 109–10 (2013), pp. 25–31.

14. E. Hotta, *Pan Asianism and Japan's War, 1931–1945* (New York: Palgrave-Macmillan, 2008); and Shigeru Akita & N. White (eds), *The International Order of Asia in the 1930s and 1950s* (Burlington, VT: Ashgate, 2009).

15. J. F. Cady, *The Roots of French Imperialism in Eastern Asia* (Ithaca, NY: Cornell University Press, 1954); J. Laffey, *French Imperialism and the Lyon Mission to China*, (Ithaca, NY: Cornell University Press, 1966); and J. Laffey, 'Les racines de l'impérialisme français en Extrême-Orient: À propos des thèses de J.-F. Cady', *Revue d'histoire moderne et contemporaine* (April–June 1969). Also see N. Tixier, 'La Chine dans la stratégie impériale: le rôle du Quai d'Orsay et de ses agents', in H. Bonin, C. Hodeir, and J.-F. Klein (eds), *L'esprit économique impérial (1830–1970). Groupes de pression & réseaux du patronat colonial en France & dans l'empire* (Paris: Publications de la SFHOM, 2008), pp. 65–84; or J. E. Schrecker, *Imperialism and Chinese Nationalism: Germany in Shantung*, (Cambridge, MA: Harvard University Press, 1971).

16. C. Davis, 'Financing Imperialism: British and American Bankers as Vectors of Imperial Expansion in China, 1908–1920', *Business History Review*, 56:2 (1982), pp. 236–64.

17. J. King Fairbank 'The Creation of the Treaty System', in D. C. Twitchett and J. King Fairbank (eds), 15 vols, *The Cambridge History of China*, vol. 10 (Cambridge: Cambridge University Press, 1970), pp. 213–63; and A. Feuerwerker, *The Foreign Establishment in China in the Early Twentieth Century* (Ann Arbor, MI: Center for Chinese Studies, University of Michigan, 1976).

18. M.-C. Bergère, 'The Geography of Finance in a Semi-Colonial Metropolis: The Shanghai *Bund* (1842–1943)', in H. A. Diedricks and D. Reeder (eds), *Cities of Finance* (Amsterdam, Netherlands: Koninklijke Nederlandse Akademie van Wetenschappen, 1996), pp. 303–17.

19. E. Green, 'The Migration of British Bank Personnel to the Pacific Region, 1850–1914', in O. Checkland, Shizuya Nishimura & Norio Tamaki (eds), *Pacific Banking (1859–1959): East Meets West* (London, Macmillan: St. Martin's Press, 1994), pp. 75–99. Also see F. King, 'The Transmission of Corporate Cultures: International Officers in the HSBC Group', in A. J. H. Latham and H. Kawakatsu (eds), *Asia Pacific Dynamism 1550–2000* (London: Routledge, 2000), pp. 245–64.

20. G. de Lassus (ed.), *The History of BNP Paribas in India, 1860–2010* (BNP Paribas India, 2010).

21. H. van B. Cleveland and T. F. Huertas, *Citibank 1812–1970* (Cambridge, MA: Harvard University Press, 1985); Citicorp, *Citicorp in China: A Colorful, Very Personal History Since 1902* (New York: Citicorp, Citibank, 1989); P. Starr, *Citibank: A Century in Asia* (Singapore: Didier Millet and Citicorp, 2002); and Ayumu Sugawara, 'American International Banking in China Before World War II: Beijing, Tianjin and Guangdong Branches of International Banking Corporation', *Tohoku Management & Accounting Research Group*, 78 (2007), pp. 1–19.

22. R. Bickers, *Britain in China: Community, Culture, and Colonialism, 1900–1949* (Manchester: Manchester University Press, 1999); R. Bickers and C. Henriot (eds), *New Frontiers: Imperialism's New Communities in East Asia, 1842–1953* (Manchester: Manchester University Press, 2000); and R. Mak, 'Nineteenth-Century German Community', in C. Yik-Yi Chu (ed.), *Foreign Communities in Hong Kong, 1840s–1950s* (New York: Palgrave Macmillan, 2005), pp. 61–83.

23. E. W. Said, *Orientalism*, (New York: Random House, 1991); I. Warraq, *Defending the West: A Critique of Edward Said's Orientalism* (Amherst, NY: Prometheus Books, 2007).

24. Among numerous ones: J. A. Hobson, *Imperialism. A Study* (Ann Arbor, MI: University of Michigan Press, 1965); D. K. Fieldhouse, *The Theory of Capitalist Imperialism* (London: Longman, 1967); H. Gollwitzer, *L'Impérialisme de 1880 à 1918* (Paris: Flammarion, 1970); W. R. Louis, R. E. Robinson, and J. Gallagher (eds), *Imperialism:*

The Robinson and Gallagher Controversy (New York: New View Points, 1976); and J. Osterhammel, *Britischer Imperialismus im Fernen Osten Strukturen der Durchringung und Einheimischer Widerstand auf dem Chinesischen Markt, 1932–1937* (Bochum, Germany: Studenverlag Brockmeyer, 1982).

25. L. E. Davis, R. A. Huttenback and S. Gray Davis, *Mammon and the Pursuit of Empire : The Political Economy of British Imperialism, 1860–1912* (Cambridge: Cambridge University Press, 1986) ; P. J. Cain and A. G. Hopkins, 'Gentlemanly Capitalism and British Overseas Expansion. II. The New Imperialism, 1850–1945', *Economic History Review,* 11 (February 1987); P. J. Cain and A. G. Hopkins, *British Imperialism, 1688–2000,* 2nd edn (New York: Macmillan, 2001) ; Shigeru Akita (ed.), *Gentlemanly Capitalism, Imperialism and Global History* (London : Palgrave Macmillan, 2002) ; and R. Dumett (ed.), *Gentlemanly Capitalism and British Imperialism: The New Debate on Empire,* (New York: Longman, 1999).

26. D. Clayton, *Imperialism Revisited. Political and Economic Relations Between Britain and China, 1950–1954* (London: Macmillan, 1997).

27. K. Pomeranz, *The Great Divergence: China, Europe, and the Making of the Modern World Economy* (Princeton, NJ: Princeton University Press, 2000).

28. R. Quested, *The Russo-Chinese Bank: A Multinational Financial Base of Tsarism in China* (Birmingham: Birmingham Slavonic Monographs, 1977).

29. Yen-P'ing Hao, *The Comprador in Nineteenth Century China: Bridge between East and West* (Cambridge, MA: Harvard University Press, 1970); C. Smith, '*Compradore* of the Hong Kong Bank', in F. King (ed.), *Eastern Banking* (London: Athlone, 1983); and Kai Yiu Chan, 'A Turning Point in China's Comprador System: KMA's Changing Marketing Structure in the Lower Yangzi Region, 1919–1925', *Business History,* 43:2 (April 2001), pp. 51–72.

30. M. Boisot and J. Child, 'From Fiefs to Clans and Network Capitalism: Explaining China's Emerging Economic Order', *Administrative Science Quarterly,* 41 (December 1996), pp. 600–28; M. Bastid, 'Le développement des filatures de soie modernes dans la province du Guangdong avant 1894', *Policy and Economy of China: The Late Professor Yuji Muramatsu Commemoration Volume,* (1975), pp. 175–178; Lillian Li, *China's Silk Trade: Traditional Industry in the Modern World, 1842–1937* (Cambridge, MA: Harvard University Press, 1981); Ho Pui-Yin, 'Les marchands du delta de la Rivière des Perles et de Chaozhou au Guangdu', in Y. Chevrier, A. Roux, and Xiahong Xiao-Planes (eds), *Citadins et citoyens dans la Chine du XXᵉ siècle (Essais d'histoire sociale), En hommage à Marie-Claire Bergère* (Paris, Éditions de la Maison des sciences de l'homme, 2010), pp. 207–26.

31. W. K. K. Chan, *Merchants, Mandarins, and Modern Enterprise in Late Ch'ing China* (Cambridge, MA: East Asian Research Center, Harvard University, 1977). To extend the arguments until recent times: Françoise Lemoine, 'Y a-t-il un Capitalisme Chinois?', *Cahiers Français,* 349 (March–April 2009), pp. 51–5.

32. R. Murphey, *The Treaty Ports and China's Modernization: What Went Wrong?*, Michigan Papers in Chinese Studies, 7 (Ann Arbor, MI: University of Michigan, 1970) ; M.-C. Bergère, 'The Consequences of the Post First Wold War Depression for the China Treaty-Port Economy, 1921–1923', in I. Brown (ed.), *The Economy of Africa and Asia During the Interwar Depression* (London: Routledge, 1989, pp. 221–52; J. King Fairbank 'The Creation of the Treaty System', in D. C. Twitchett and J. King Fairbank (dir.), *The Cambridge History of China,* 15 vols (Cambridge: Cambridge University Press, 1970), vol. 10., pp. 213–63.

33. M.-C. Bergère, 'The Chinese Bourgeoisie', in D. C. Twitchett and J. King Fairbank (dir.), *The Cambridge History of China*, 15 vols (Cambridge: Cambridge University Press, 1983), vol. 12; M.-C. Bergère, *L'Âge d'or de la bourgeoisie chinoise, 1911–1937* (Paris: Flammarion, 1986); M.-C. Bergère, *The Golden Age of the Chinese Bourgeoisie* (Cambridge: Cambridge University Press, 1989); and M.-C. Bergère, *Capitalismes et Capitalistes en Chine, des Origines à Nos Jours* (Paris: Perrin, 2007).

34. S. Seagrave, *The Soong Dynasty* (New York: Harper & Row, 1985).

35. B. Sheehan, 'Myth and Reality in Chinese Financial Cliques in 1936', *Enterprise & Society*, 6:3 (September 2005), pp. 452–91.

36. A. McElderry, 'Confucian Capitalism? Corporate Values in Republican Banking', *Modern China*, 12:3 (July 1986), pp. 401–16; G. Hofstede and M. H. Bond, 'The Confucius Connections: From Cultural Roots to Economic Roots', *Organisational Dynamics*, 16:1 (1988), pp. 4–11; and Yen-P'ing Hao, *The Commercial Revolution in Nineteenth-Century China: The Rise of Sino-Western Mercantile Capitalism* (Berkeley, CA: University of California Press, 1986).

37. R. Bush, *The Politics of Cotton Textiles in Kuomintang China, 1927–1937* (New York: Garland Publishing, 1982); M.-C. Bergère, *Capitalisme national et impérialisme. La crise des filatures chinoises en 1923* (Paris: École des hautes études en sciences sociales, 1980); E. Köll, *From Cotton Mill to Business Empire: The Emergence of Regional Enterprises in Modern China* (Cambridge, MA: Harvard University Press, 2003).

38. J. Carroll, *Edge of Empires: Chinese Elites and British Colonials in Hong Kong* (Cambridge, MA: Harvard University Press, 2005).

39. B. Sheehan, *Trust in Troubled Times. Money, Banks and State-Society Relations in Republican Tianjin* (Cambridge, MA: Harvard University Press, 2003).

40. See Chapter Seven.

INDEX

Printed and bound by CPI Group (UK) Ltd, Croydon, CR0 4YY

08/05/2025

01864355-0003